The Feminine Dimension *of the* Divine

I0022097

The FEMININE DIMENSION *of the* DIVINE

Revised Edition

JOAN CHAMBERLAIN ENGELSMAN

Chiron Publications • Wilmette, Illinois

Second Printing, 1995

© 1987, 1994 by Chiron Publications. All rights reserved. No part of this publication may be reproduced, stored in a retrieval system, or transmitted, in any form by any means, electronic, mechanical, photocopying, recording, or otherwise, without the prior written permission of the publisher, Chiron Publications, 400 Linden Avenue, Wilmette, Illinois 60091.

First edition published in 1979 by The Westminster Press. Revised edition with new introduction in 1994 by Chiron Publications. Reproduced by permission of The Westminster Press.

Library of Congress Catalog Card Number: 94–22539

Printed in the United States of America.
Cover design by D.J. Hyde.

Grateful acknowledgment is made to the following:

Bobbs-Merrill Company, for citations from *Hellenistic Religions: The Age of Syncretism*, ed. Frederick C. Grant, © 1953 by Liberal Arts Press. Used by permission of Bobbs-Merrill Company.

Doubleday & Company, Inc., for citations from *Proverbs. Ecclesiastes* (The Anchor Bible), trans. and ed. by R. B. Y. Scott. © 1965 by Doubleday & Company, Inc.

Oxford University Press, for citations from *The Apocrypha and Psuedepigrapha of the Old Testament in English*, ed. R. H. Charles. © 1913; and from *The Odes of Solomon*, ed. and trans. James H. Charlesworth, 1973.

Thames and Hudson, Ltd., London, and Harry N. Abrams, Inc., New York, for excerpts from Eberhard Otto, *Egyptian Art and the Cults of Osiris and Amon*, 1968.

Scripture quotations from the Revised Standard Version of the Bible are © 1946, 1952, 1971, 1973 by the Division of Christian Education of the National Council of the Churches of Christ in the U.S.A., and are used by permission.

Library of Congress Cataloging-in-Publication Data:
Engelsman, Joan Chamberlain, 1932–
The feminine dimension of the divine / Joan Chamberlain Engelsman.— Rev. ed.
p. cm.
Includes bibliographical references and index.
ISBN 0–933029–91–8 : $14.95
1. Femininity of God. 2. God — History of doctrines. 3. Goddesses. I. Title.
BT102.E52 1994
231′.4—dc20 94–22539
CIP

ISBN 0–933029–91–8

For Ralph

Companion on "the road less traveled"

Contents

Acknowledgments

Like most scholars, I am indebted to both books and people for information, guidance, support, and inspiration. The books that have influenced me most are included in the Selected Bibliography. Here I want to mention the human resources that I feel have been most significant.

First, and foremost, has been my family—my parents, my husband, and our two children, Marc and Dan. In addition, I have been gifted with remarkable grandparents, aunts, great aunts and uncles, and numerous cousins. I have learned from all of them the wonder and complexity of human nature and human relationships, as well as the ambiguities and dualities which are part of human life and history.

The second major influence on my work has come from my women friends. From Northfield School for Girls and Sweet Briar College through my participation on over a dozen community and church boards, I have known and worked with women all my life. I have found them to be not only intelligent, able administrators and money managers, but also clearheaded, precise, creative, resourceful, patient, persistent, courageous, assertive, dedicated, generous, sensitive, and dependable. In fact, I have known so *many* women who possessed these qualities in good measure that

I cannot believe they are exceptions to, or unrepresentative of, the female sex in general. Thus long before "consciousness-raising," they exposed me to the full variety of positive attributes possessed by women. Recently four groups of women have been particularly important to me: thus I would like to thank specifically each member of the Auburn group, the Princeton group, and *Les Femmes*, as well as my colleagues at the Women's Resource Center at the Theological School of Drew University. Surely, like Persephone, I have been in the company of goddesses.

Finally I want to acknowledge those teachers and scholars who made significant contributions to my intellectual growth. Dr. Gerhard Masur, formerly professor of history at Sweet Briar College; Drs. Carl Michalson, Will Herberg, and Bard Thompson at Drew University; Dr. David Bakan, York University, Canada, Aquinas Visiting Lecturer at Drew in 1970–1971; and Dr. Lawrence D. McIntosh, former theological librarian at Drew University and now principal librarian, Torrens University, Adelaide, Australia. These men helped introduce me to the historical and intellectual tradition in which we all stand; and each went to some pains to teach me *how* to think rather than *what* to think. For that I shall always be grateful.

Certain persons have directly contributed to the successful completion of this study. Dean Bard Thompson, Fr. Gabriel Coless, O.S.B., and Dr. Herbert Huffmon gave generously of their time and expertise. I would also like to acknowledge the patience and resourcefulness of the professional staff at Drew University library; the encouragement from my friends in the graduate school; Dr. Marianne Torza for her assistance with some of the German material; Joseph Canose, M.L.S., for checking my bibliography and notes; Helen LePage Chamberlain, who helped edit the manuscript; and Paul Grosjean, my careful and intelligent typist.

Introduction to the Revised Edition

The Feminine Dimension of the Divine was originally written during the years 1975–1976. It was a time of debate and controversy surrounding issues of women's ordination, then unresolved for various denominations such as Episcopalian, as well as the use of sexist language in most Christian liturgies. Not surprisingly, this was also a time of research and preparation as women scholars, struggling with standard biblical and theological interpretations, began to formulate ideas which ultimately challenged traditional images of God and women's role in the church, both now and in the past.

An example of the questions underlying the debate asked not only how Christians can access the feminine dimension of the divine, but whether there IS a female face of God. Although the Eastern and Orthodox traditions have always honored the image of Sophia, allowing her to play a role in their understanding of Christianity, philosophical and systematic theologians from the European and American Protestant traditions turn their attention to the second part of the question, insisting that orthodoxy demands an absence of the feminine. For this reason, both Sophia and the Virgin Mary were excised from their piety, and a heavily patriarchal interpretation of Christianity, focusing almost entirely on the Father-Son relationship, became normative.

The Feminine Dimension of the Divine was originally written to address the latter position. Biblical scholars had recently rediscovered a Wisdom trajectory carrying through from Jewish to Christian scriptures. Contemporary students of the intertestamental and early patristic periods had also produced more complete and dynamic translations of classic texts which revealed a complex theological struggle among various Christian groups, including the gnostic sects. One of the most important elements of this work was a new awareness of Sophia; what remained underappreciated was the feminine nature of Wisdom and the impediment that fact represented.

Simultaneously, this ferment in biblical and post-biblical studies was echoed in psychological circles, particularly those influenced by the work of C. G. Jung. His studies revealed a number of feminine archetypes, particularly those of the great mother and the anima, a representative of the female side of the male psyche. The yearning he felt for some divine representation of these archetypal figures focused primarily on the Virgin Mary, an image rejected by his father's church and made unavailable to Jung by the Swiss Protestant tradition in which he was raised.

The theological and psychological work of these two groups come together in *The Feminine Dimension of the Divine*. Using the psychological insights of Freud, as well as Jung, I specifically raised the sexual question and concluded that the feminine characterization of Wisdom may have been the principal reason for her suppression in Christian tradition. What I was unable to determine in 1975 was if, or how, any female image of the divine would or could be integrated into mainstream Christianity.

A tense symbolic interregnum was still in evidence when I wrote the preface for the 1987 edition. Although fed by my work and that of others for more than a decade, the brewing storm I sensed in the offing had not occurred. The image of Sophia, or the Wisdom of God, which had wreaked such havoc in early Christian theology seemed to have little impact on the contemporary church. Several books had appeared, such as the excellent one by Elizabeth Schussler-Fiorenza, *In Memory of Her*. There were also published lectures such as the one I gave in Chicago in 1985, "Beyond the Anima: The Female Self in the Image of God" (in *Jung's Challenge to Contemporary Religion*.) In addition, intense scrutiny had been given to the works of women mystics and to the role of women in the church. Nevertheless, the yearning for access to some feminine dimension of the divine seemed to have moved outside the church to goddess groups or into the psychospiritual arena as represented by the work of Jean Shinoda Bolen and Clarissa Pinkola Estes.

This apparent lack of interest was suddenly shattered by the voices of 2,000 women gathered in Minneapolis for a conference in November 1993 celebrating the midpoint of the World Council of Churches decade of the woman. Entitled "RE-imagining," the Wisdom of God was directly addressed and the blessings of Sophia were invited for speakers and participants alike. For three days, the assembly struggled to hear the words and stories of a diverse group of women from different racial, ethnic, sexual, national, and denominational backgrounds. Only the arts (music, dance, and drawing) and the invocations of Sophia seemed to weave the group together.

In the firestorm that followed this conference, it has become clear that questions inspired by the presence of Sophia in the early church have not been settled. Now, as then, there are charges of heresy and threats to expel those who do not denounce the proceedings in Minneapolis. Today, as in the past, there are zealots on both sides who believe Sophia is a Goddess removed from Jewish-Christian tradition. For conservatives, particularly those from mainline Protestant churches, she has more in common with the figure of the Foreign Woman (Proverbs 1–9) than with the aspect of divine wisdom portrayed in the same verses. For many academic feminists, who have little or no contact with local congregations, Sophia appears to represent a welcome break from mainstream Christianity. Strengthened by gnostic interpretations, she is a point of connection to, if not another name for, Kuan Yin, Kali, Isis, and the spirits of body and nature esteemed in many Indian and tribal cultures.

Clearly, what has developed in the fifteen years since *The Feminine Dimension of the Divine* was originally published is a growing desire on the part of many women and men for access to the feminine divine. If, as scripture insists, God created male and female in the image of God, then how should we appropriately describe the sexualized aspects of the divine? Because many contemporary Christians are willing to explore the writings of authors outside their own denomination and their own era, it becomes possible to recognize that this current debate has many mothers and fathers.

Today many Christians are searching through the whole treasure chest of faith in what appears to be a genuine search for deeper and more meaningful spirituality. Stanley Hauerwas, as Kierkegaard before him, articulates the difficulties of being Christian in a "Christian" society. Where Christianity has become enmeshed in the social fabric, how can it come as good news to anyone? For some, the answer is to be "born again" and reattach to a conventional church. For others, a rejuvenated faith becomes a personal quest, which seeks to negotiate its way between the Scylla of patriarchal Christianity and the Charybdis of nontraditional faiths. For many Christians, reluctance to jettison ties to the church universal must be balanced against their desire for a more dynamic faith which includes, among other things, a feminine dimension of the divine.

Not only has there been an outpouring of books and articles, but the energy and excitement generated by this search seems to indicate that the female face of God may be the aspect of the divine turning toward us today. The republication of Christian classics, the rediscovery of women writers and mystics, and a returning interest in spiritual direction and discipline should probably be considered as parts of this new development. So also is the entire concept of re-imagining the divine, explored at the conference in Minneapolis as well as at countless smaller retreats and gatherings around the country.

The image of Sophia has much to offer those yearning for a deeper spirituality. Although never regarded as a Goddess within the Jewish or Christian traditions, Sophia is recognized as a hypostasis of God, a personified attribute of the divine. As such, she commands our attention and invites us to seek her, promising good things to those who love her. The extent of her independence and her outspoken ways may jar the ears of those reared to a patriarchal standard, but for women and men yearning for a female face of the divine, Sophia can provide access to an underdeveloped image of God. These metaphors are scriptural—many mystics and theologians have developed them—but in the mainstream of Western Christianity they lie abandoned and unused. The reactions to the "RE-imagining" conference in Minneapolis indicates that the traditional focus on the Father-Son relationship is still a stumbling block.

A major source of this developing interest in Sophia is the renewed emphasis on scripture. Linguistic and historic studies, augmented by contributions from sociology and anthropology, have led to new translations and commentaries. The important contributions of Phyllis Trible (*God and the Rhetoric of Sexuality*; *Texts of Terror*) and Elizabeth Fiorenza accompany those of Raymond Brown (*The Birth of the Messiah*; *The Death of the Messiah*; *Commentary on John*), Joseph Fitzmyer (*Commentary on Luke*), and others who are changing our awareness of the Judeo-Christian milieu. Today, it is hard to miss the subtle shift away from a reliance on theological and philosophical speculation to a more personal engagement with the original texts.

Among other factors driving this transformation are the myriad challenges facing traditional Christianity. Trailing along with feminine images of God come an interest in healing, overcoming the mind-body split, exercising more responsibility toward the earth and environment, increasing use of sacramental liturgies, and a variety of other issues either unknown or not widely popular in the nineteenth and twentieth centuries. There is also a certain sensuality and concern for stewardship of this world which sets these new spiritual concerns at odds with the more traditional emphases on atonement and a triumphant church.

In a time of rapid social change and disorientation, it is not surprising that many people turn inward and concern themselves with personal salvation. This was true in the Hellenistic world, and it is an important factor in today's spirituality. Although the varieties and elements of individual religious experience differ from age to age, an emphasis on divine immanence and personal knowledge of the deity is an important component of the contemporary quest. The work of Nelle Morton (*The Journey Is Home*) and the authors of *The Feminine Face of God* are among contemporary writers who speak of their own encounters with the divine, surprisingly, but not uniquely, in female form.

Today, this religious search frequently coincides with, and underscores, a search for self-understanding, maturity, or individuation. In whatever guise, it represents a quest for meaning in a world out of control, and for this reason alone, it seems to me that insights gathered from psychology are appropriate for use in exploring the puzzles of spiritual life. Theologians from Augustine to Kierkegaard constantly draw on their observations of human life, but this commonplace ingredient gradually fell into disuse, and psychology became its own discipline. Now, once again, the insights of Jung, Freud, Winnicott, and others present themselves as viable tools for opening up aspects of scripture and theology that have been hidden; they can expose some of the deeper meanings of religious texts.

This conviction underlies the methodology used in *The Feminine Dimension of the Divine.* Twenty years ago, I believed I had stumbled onto something quite unusual or outre, as I described it in the preface to the first edition. At the time, cooperation between these two disciplines was not common, but it seemed apparent to me that psychological insights could help revitalize the imagery of scripture and clarify its overall message. This new resource was not intended to replace others, to be exclusionary, but to allow the insights of psychology to augment the contributions of literary criticism, archeology, history, and tradition, taking its place as an additional element in biblical interpretation.

Today, affinities between psychology and spirituality are more widely recognized, and as scholars continue to explore the common boundaries between them, precedents have been discovered in traditions as divergent as mysticism and midrash, a venerable Jewish form of commentary which directs light on the interior meaning of difficult texts. Important to both is an understanding of symbolism and a penetrating focus on the work of the divine in every human life. Once again, dreams, visions, poetry, and personal story have become valued ways to discern the nature and presence of the Holy.

This renewed interest in an individual's response to the divine underlies both the burgeoning field of spiritual direction and meditation, as indicated by the popularity of books such as *Care of the Soul* (Thomas Moore) and the work of Marjory Zoet Bankson, and the way psychologists and social workers are beginning to understand and appreciate the spiritual needs of their clients. Some of the images which emerge from these various efforts will be at odds with conventional Christian practice, and psychological insights can be useful in separating the wheat from the chaff, the rational from the psychotic.

In *The Feminine Dimension of the Divine*, psychological and theological questions are largely isolated from most practical issues facing the church and individual Christians. I am now more aware how removing theology from everyday life tends to dehumanize it; thus, were I to write this book today, I would bring praxis and theory into much closer alignment. My experience working at women's centers and with clergy and victims of domestic violence has underscored how closely the psychological, theological, and practical intertwine and impact each other.

Given these realities, my more recent lecture, "Shadows on the Rock: Women, Violence, and the Church," given for a 1991 conference on the shadow archetype (available on audiotape from the C. G. Jung Institute of Chicago) probably represents a better way of doing theology than more abstract works of mine and others. Theological questions do not become important until they are asked in the context of real life, where questions surrounding evil, suffering, atonement, forgiveness, hope, love, and justice take on an immediate urgency and relevance. Then the ability to connect the immanent with the transcendent in both the human and the divine becomes a vital concern.

Psychological insights can be a significant part of this more practical theology as long as psychology itself does not become remote and focused on the transcendent level of images, ideas, and archetypes. In this new congenial environment, scholars of psychology and religion need to be aware that while the former may be used as a reality check on theology, there is a countervailing movement which threatens to drag psychology into the realm of the abstract. Results of this intellectualizing tendency can already be seen in the works of some psychologists and philosophers, particularly among those who find the archetypal images of C. G. Jung all too ethereal and beyond material existence. It is also necessary to recognize that the patriarchal and stereotypical elements of all psychological theory, especially Freudian, must be acknowledged and corrected before the enduring insights of this discipline should be employed to help open up a closed tradition.

Despite these caveats, psychology can make major contributions to current religious debates and bring greater insight into a church besieged by many issues reflecting an obsession with the feminine and a desire to exclude it and the experience of women from the mainstream. These sexually related issues include not only ordination (still a vital question in the Roman Catholic church) and language in liturgy, but questions surrounding reproduction, abortion, and gay and lesbian rights in church and society. Clearly, these challenging matters are deeply connected and influenced by the current search for female images of the divine. Denying this connection and splitting the issues apart in any significant way will falsify what is happening in the church as well as what is important in the human psyche.

Today, many people are yearning for ways to experience

their lives as connected to, and in relationship with, the divine. When a young, theologically conservative woman expresses to me how important it is for her to find a resonance of her self in a feminine dimension of the divine, it is possible to appreciate the scope of longing prevalent among all types of Christians. Her desire reflects only one part of a theological and psychological quest impelling people to reexamine a tradition they may have abandoned or never seriously considered. Even current reinvestigation of the Virgin Mary demonstrates how the meek, obedient mother image promoted during the past two centuries is giving way to a dynamic understanding of her role in Christian tradition, which can make Mary much more relevant to those who had sloughed her off as a tool of a patriarchal church.

These new developments do not occur in a vacuum, and counter movements are inevitable. No wonder the spiritual temper of the times often appears more analogous to a descent into chaos than a move into a bright new age. When the tension between both sides of these "feminine" issues is great, it can feel as though traditional Christianity and its values are being torn asunder. The resurgence of patriarchal fundamentalism, which is dominated by nostalgia for the past, the violence of "pro-life" advocates, the challenge raised by abused women and children, problems of sexuality and sexually transmitted disease, the hatred and fear of homosexual persons, as well as the desire for *and* resistance to feminine images of the divine, have become signs of these turbulent times.

Challenges to the traditional, one-dimensional images and focus of the church match the desire for wholeness and balance in one's personal life. Recovering female images of the divine is part of this contemporary endeavor. It is part of our pain, and part of our deliverance, that we should live in interesting times where these issues are being discussed with an urgency not seen since the Reformation. Obviously, there are no quick answers or solutions to these questions, but rather than signaling the end of Christianity, the effort to retrieve a feminine dimension of the divine may help save it, and help ensure the survival of the church after the eclipse of patriarchy. Not only do a multitude of divine images reflect actual scriptural usage, but perhaps these new developments will also enable us see beyond our one-sided tradition to a less pretentious Christianity which can bring a more balanced, healing message to our diverse world.

Eastertide 1994
Madison, New Jersey

CHAPTER 1

The Archetype

> One of the necessary preliminary tasks is to train the "eye for the archetypal."[1]

A major contribution to theological speculation in this century has been made by noted psychotherapists of Europe. Outstanding among them are Sigmund Freud and Carl Gustav Jung. A major contribution is Jung's concept of archetypes which is of particular importance in discovering the feminine dimension of the divine. Jung's psychology is predicated on the distinction between consciousness and unconsciousness and on his discovery that the unconscious is both personal and collective. Consciousness is the domain of the ego, which mediates between the inner world and the outer world. The material not perceived by the ego constitutes the unconscious.

This unconscious is composed of two layers. The first layer is the personal. It contains lost memories, painful ideas that are repressed (i.e., forgotten on purpose), sense perceptions not strong enough to reach consciousness, and contents that are not yet ripe for consciousness.[2] Although the personal unconscious is particular to each individual, Jung believes it would be "a fatal mistake to regard the human psyche as a purely personal affair and to explain it exclusively from a personal point of view."[3] This is because he believes in a second psychic system which is of a "collective, universal, and impersonal nature identical in all individuals. This collective unconscious does not develop individually but is inherited."[4] Thus every individual has a dual unconscious; part of it is personal and private, and part is collective and common to all. Jung's controversial thesis is amplified by the discovery of archetypes which derive from the collective unconscious, the place "where the primordial images common to humanity lie sleeping."[5]

Jung has observed the human penchant for repeating certain themes or motifs in myths, folklore, dreams, and symbols.[6] These motifs are the archetypes and presumably emerge from patterns of the human mind that are transmitted by tradition as well as by heredity.[7] This latter point is indispensable, since Jung notes that complicated archetypal images can be produced in dreams and fantasies even though they are not represented in the dreamer's culture. In other words,

> the archetypes of the collective unconscious . . . appear among all peoples at all times in identical or analogous manner and can arise just as spontaneously—i.e., without any conscious knowledge—from the unconscious of modern man.[8]

Jung does not endorse the inheritance of ideas, only the inheritance of the "formal possibility of producing the same or similar ideas over and over again."[9] He calls this possibility the archetype.

There are two classes of archetypes. Those in the first class can be personified. They include the shadow, the wise old man, the animus, the anima, the mother, the maid, and the child.[10] For example, Jung sees Demeter and Persephone as mythological archetypal examples of the mother and the maid. The child archetype is often portrayed as a hero figure; the anima, the feminine side of man's nature, may appear as Athena. These figures are merely illustrative of the possible personifications of this class of archetype; the variety of personifications is endless, although the number of archetypes is not.

The second class is archetypes of transformation. These

archetypes are not personified but represent a situation, place, or means which symbolize a kind of transformation.[11] Journeys, death, or rebirth belong to this class of archetype, and of this kind Jung believes "there are as many archetypes as there are typical situations in life."[12] The significance of both classes of archetypes is that they are true and genuine symbols that cannot be exhaustively interpreted either as signs or as allegories. They are ambiguous, full of half-glimpsed meanings, and in the last resort inexhaustible.[13]

In addition to being inexhaustible, the archetypes are dynamic and autonomous, existing today as they did in the past. Without this acknowledgment there is a tendency to see the archetypes as merely "archaic elements and primitive ideas"[14] in modern man. Such a notion denies the archetypes their eternal and compelling nature. This living dimension makes them difficult to grasp, but it is what makes them relevant to contemporary discussion. Finally, Jung believes that the archetypes are thrown up from the collective unconscious as things are brought up from the depths of the sea and thrown upon the beach. As such, the archetypes are "an urgent question of psychic hygiene," and even without proof of their existence "we would have to invent them forthwith in order to keep our highest and most important values from disappearing into the unconscious."[15]

The similarity between Jung's statement about the need to invent the archetypes if they did not exist and Voltaire's statement that if God did not exist we would have to invent him is probably not a coincidence. Jung believes that the "unparalleled impoverishment of symbolism" which exists today has enabled us "to rediscover the gods as psychic factors, that is, as archetypes of the unconscious."[16] However controversial this statement may be, there is no doubt that Jung attributes a numinous and compelling quality to the archetypes that has hitherto been attributed only to God. The archetypes are eternal images to which people should succumb. "They are meant to attract, to convince, to fascinate, to overpower. They are created out of the primal stuff of revelation and reflect the ever-unique experience of divinity." Thus they give human beings a "premonition of the divine" at the same time that they protect persons from an unmediated encounter with the Holy.[17]

If numinosity is one characteristic of the archetypes, a second is their givenness. This is not intended to be a comment on the number of archetypes, although Jung does imply they are somewhat limited. Rather, it is a caution against rationalizing or intellectualizing them. "Consciousness cannot 'make' a symbol or 'choose' to experience an archetype."[18] Because Jung is aware of the archetypes as the conscious part of an unconscious iceberg, he believes that "man must remain conscious of the world of the archetypes, because in it he is still a part of Nature and is connected with his own roots." Reason alone only illuminates what is already known and spreads darkness over what "would be most needful for us to know and become conscious of." Therefore, Jung says any culture that cuts people off "from the primordial images of life . . . is a prison."[19] Thus the quality of givenness describes the fact that the archetypes are there in the collective unconscious, they emerge without conscious effort, and they resist rational manipulation.

The third characteristic of the archetypes is their symbolic nature. It is through the symbol that the archetypes become visible and the unconscious is brought to consciousness. Jung and Neumann recognize that certain symbols tend to coalesce around each specific archetype and so form an archetype's symbolic group. These symbols are like the archetype itself: "they take hold of the human personality as a whole, arouse it and fascinate it, and attract consciousness which strives to interpret them."[20] Since they contain conscious and unconscious elements, only some of these elements can be assimilated easily; the rest remain irrational or become conscious only after long development. This is why the great symbols, such as the cross, the trinity, or the mandala, seem to demand interpretation, and why the resulting interpretations always seem so inadequate.

A fourth quality common to all archetypes is ambivalence. A person with a discriminating intellect will naturally try to establish a single meaning for each archetype "and thus miss the essential point; for what we can above all establish as the one thing consistent with their nature is their *manifold meaning,* their almost limitless wealth of reference, which makes any unilateral formulation impossible."[21] Neumann attributes this manifold meaning to the fact that the primordial archetypes combine opposites, that is, positive and negative attributes. This contradiction in motifs and symbols makes the archetypes a paradox. Consciousness splinters the unity of the archetype by seeing its various aspects as separate and unrelated entities. For instance, the great mother archetype becomes the basis for both the good and the bad goddess. An even higher consciousness is needed to perceive the oneness that underlies the duality.

Since these four major characteristics—numinosity, givenness, symbolism, and ambivalence—are together the hallmark of the archetypes, it is not surprising that Jung connects them with the divine. He elaborates this point in his discussion of Christian dogma which he believes once channeled the archetypes into "a well-controlled stream . . . of creed and ritual." In even more ancient days the same effect was produced by the Mysteries. Now, however, as a result of the "iconoclasm of the Reformation" and the progressive loss of church authority, modern human beings face an "alarming poverty of symbols."[22] The appearance of archetypes as Jung knows them is both the result and the remedy of this situation. The absence of powerful communal rituals and creeds forces the archetypes to emerge from each individual's unconscious to provide contact with the highest and most important values, that is, with God.

One of the most important ramifications of Jung's theory is the recognition that some of the archetypes are feminine; therefore, the mother, the maid, and the anima represent a dimension of the divine. Erich Neumann concurs when he says that the symbolic expression of the psychic phenomenon known as the great mother archetype "is to be found in the figures of the great goddesses represented in the myths and artistic creations of mankind."[23] The sequence, therefore, begins with a premonition of the divine which appears as an archetype in the collective unconscious. This archetype then emerges into consciousness, where it finds expression as a great goddess. Thus, in fact, the goddess is an appropriate aspect of the divine for all people, in all places, and at all times and not merely in pagan or primitive cultures.

CHAPTER 2

The Feminine Archetypes

> In all ages and in all places men have conceived of a Great Mother. . . . These Great Mothers whose worship has dominated the religious thoughts of peoples far removed from each other in time, space and culture, have an essential similarity which cannot but amaze us.[1]

There are three archetypes that can be personified as feminine figures: the mother, the maid, and the anima. Jung devoted a large share of his corpus to discussing these archetypes in their various manifestations in mythology, Chinese philosophy, alchemy, astrology, and Christianity. Erich Neumann extended Jung's work through his own books *The Great Mother* and *Amor and Psyche.* The third major contributor to the study of the feminine archetypes is Mary Esther Harding. Although these three psychotherapists laid the groundwork, they completed their investigations before the recent upsurge of feminism and critical feminist scholarship. It is also appropriate to note that both Jung and Neumann were men and approached the feminine archetypes accordingly. This perspective is probably the basis for (1) their fascination with the anima, the feminine side of the male psyche, and (2) their tendency to blur the distinctions between the mother and the maid or maid and anima. Jung, at least, shows an awareness of the problem and indicates that analysis of these archetypes by women should produce new and different insights.[2] For instance, *mater* and maid may assume new importance as mother and daughter and have different and separate significance for women. Jung acknowledges this potential in his discussion of the Demeter-Kore myth by saying that that myth "exists on the plane of mother-daughter experience, which is alien to man and shuts him out."[3] But until women comment on these archetypes from their own experience, the work of Jung, Neumann, and Harding must form the basis for any interpretation of the feminine archetypes.[4] For the sake of clarity, the three feminine archetypes will be analyzed together as part of a super archetype, the great mother.

The Great Mother

The great mother archetype has a dual nature and manifests herself in four different ways. In one nature she appears as *mater,* both bad and good; in her other nature she is manifested as *anima,* both bad and good. As *mater* she is the one who conceives a child, supports it in her womb, and finally brings it forth into the world at birth. After birth she is the nurturing and caring mother. As a result, the child perceives her as the all-enveloping source of life. This is the aspect of the great mother that Neumann calls the elemental mother. The relationship between mother and child is strong, and, in a way, each needs the other. The child needs the mother to live; and the mother needs the child as an expression of herself. It is not surprising, then, that the aspect of the great mother known as *mater* has both a positive and a negative pole.

In her positive guise, *mater* frequently appears as the sorrowing mother who, deprived of her child, moves heaven and earth to be restored to it. The ultimate reunion of the two is a cause of universal rejoicing. One of the most familiar myths of the sorrowing mother is that of Demeter, who gives birth to Persephone, who is later abducted and separated from her mother. Demeter mourns her daughter and searches for her and after many adventures is reunited with her. This myth had such a powerful hold on the imagination of the Greeks that it became the basis for the Eleusinian mysteries. For similar reasons, the Egyptians developed the Isiac mysteries surrounding Isis, Osiris, and Horus. The early church incorporated similar expressions of the great mother into its understanding of the church as mother of Christians and in its descriptions of Mary.

As the great mother is connected with birth and nurturing, she is also connected with death and devouring. Such is the negative pole of *mater* as she is personified, say, by the Gorgon, or Medea. It is never the great mother who dies; it is the child. She can appear terrifying and pitiless. She is Demeter in her rage, Isis in her capriciousness, and Lilith in her destructiveness. The primary symbol of the elemental mother is the vessel. It represents her own body, and depending on whether the personification is positive or negative, can appear as cave or coffin, grail or caldron.

The second characteristic of the great mother is her transformative mode. This is the figure that Jung and Neumann call the *anima.* They believe she is characteristically the feminine part of a man's psyche and she represents a higher or later consciousness than *mater.* The *anima* has a more youthful image, which makes her quite analogous to the archetype of the maid. In this guise, the great mother presides over bodily and material transformations. The root of this image is the bodily transformations that occur within women during menstruation, pregnancy, and lactation. By extension, women are also connected with the transformation of material things from one state to another. Turning wheat into bread, grapes into wine, and flax into cloth are examples of their power. These transformations are regarded as mysteries and they are the result of hidden or magical powers possessed only by women.

As with the *mater,* the transformative *anima* is both positive and negative. Her positive side is represented by Sophia, goddess of wisdom, who leads man to higher things. A late, but clear example of the positive *anima* is Beatrice in Dante's

Divine Comedy; and this theme appears repeatedly in the concept of the Eternal Feminine who leads men to God. The *anima* is personified as Hokhmah in the Jewish tradition and as Athena in the Greek. But she is also Isis and Mary in certain of their aspects.

Again, there is a negative dimension to this image. The bad *anima* appears as the temptress, the young witch or foreign woman who leads men astray. Intoxication, madness, and shipwreck await the unwary man who consorts with her. The primary symbol for the *anima* seems to be the moon which is constantly changing, waning and waxing, dying or disappearing, yet always being reborn. As the guide in the night or the bringer of lunacy, the moon is a potent feminine symbol.

Jung and Neumann are particularly interested in the positive *anima,* or the transforming aspects of the great mother.[5] However, they are aware of the negative dimension of this archetype, and also recognize the presence of the elemental mother, or *mater,* in the transforming mother. Therefore, Sophia, or personified wisdom, is always rooted in the loving, nurturing mother, and as such she represents the antithesis of "pure" speculation or theoretical knowledge.

In summary, the great mother archetype contains both *mater* and *anima* and both have positive and negative guises. *Mater* represents the maternal qualities of the archetype, while the *anima* (and/or maid) represents her transformative powers.

There are various representations of the great mother archetype. Jung begins by noting the influence of real women: first, the personal mother, grandmother, stepmother, and mother-in-law; secondly, any woman with whom a relationship exists. However, Jung does not impute to them the power or the ambivalence of the great mother. He attributes to the personal mother only a limited aetiological significance. That is to say all those influences which the literature describes as being exerted on the children do not come from the mother herself, but rather from the archetype projected upon her, which gives her a mythological background and invests her with authority and numinosity.[6]

Next in importance are the mothers in a figurative sense, such as the goddesses, "especially the Mother of God, the Virgin, and Sophia." Others in this category appear as "things representing the goal of our longing for redemption, such as Paradise, the Kingdom of God, or the Heavenly Jerusalem." Still other mother symbols that arouse our feelings of devotion or awe are "Church, university, city or country, heaven, earth, the woods, the sea or any still waters, matter even, the underworld and the moon." In addition, the archetype is often associated with things or places that represent fertility and fruitfulness, such as a cornucopia, garden, or plowed field, as well as with vessels like a cave, well, baptismal font, or "vessel-shaped flowers like the rose or lotus." Even Jung's favorite symbol, the mandala, can be a form of the great mother.[7]

"All these symbols can have a positive, favourable meaning or a negative, evil meaning." The evil symbols include the witch, the dragon, "or any devouring and entwining animal," while the ambivalent aspects of the archetype are portrayed as the goddesses of fate. All of these symbols, and countless more, convey the qualities associated with the great mother such as

maternal solicitude and sympathy; the magic authority of the female; the wisdom and spiritual exaltation that transcend reason; any helpful instinct or impulse; all that is benign, all that cherishes and sustains, that fosters growth and fertility. The place of magic transformation and rebirth, together with the underworld and its inhabitants, are presided over by the mother. On the negative side the mother archetype may connote anything secret, hidden, dark; the abyss, the world of the dead, anything that devours, seduces, and poisons, that is terrifying and inescapable.[8]

Erich Neumann greatly amplifies the work of Jung in his two books on the feminine, especially in *The Great Mother.* It is he who distinguishes so clearly between *mater* and *anima.* The elemental *mater* is the more familiar and is characterized by Neumann as that part of the feminine which

> tends to hold fast to everything that springs from it and to surround it like an eternal substance. Everything born of it belongs to it and remains subject to it, and even if the individual becomes independent, the Archetypal Feminine relativizes this independence into a nonessential variant of her own perpetual being.[9]

The concept of the *anima,* however, is more complicated. Jung invented the term to apply to the soul image of the male, "his own inner femininity and soulfulness, an element in his own psyche" which he experiences in the female, or as a female. Neumann perceives the *anima* dynamically as "the mover, the instigator of change, whose fascination drives, lures and encourages the male to all the adventures of the soul and spirit of action and creation in the inner and the outward world." Here again, as with the *mater,* a man's perception of his *anima* is based on both his personal experiences with women and, to even a larger extent, on the archetypal experience of the feminine. Thus, the *anima* is "not a mere manifestation of male projections upon a woman."[10]

The separation of the negative and positive dimensions of *mater* and *anima* are a late development. According to Neumann, the earliest expressions of the archetype held them together.[11] The unity of diverse qualities is characteristic of the archetype and can be found even in late manifestations because any one aspect of the great mother, taken to its extreme, bends back around and turns into its opposite. This view of Neumann's is reflected in a complex circular diagram which is a major contribution of his book. Nevertheless, he also divides *mater* and *anima* into positive and negative. The negative *mater* and *anima* are portrayed as witches, distinguished only by age. Their mysteries are those of death and drunkenness (dead drunk) and Neumann sees such similarities between them "that it seems less important to differentiate them."[12] The positive *mater* is represented by maternal deities such as Isis and Demeter and the vegetation mysteries over which they preside bring rebirth and immortality. The positive *anima* is expressed by the virgin goddesses such as Mary and Sophia and their mysteries are inspirational and bring wisdom and vision.[13]

The two basic symbols connected with the great mother archetype are based on the biological functions of a woman. For the *mater* the central symbol is the vessel which corresponds to her body. This symbol represents, for both men and women, the first and most basic experience of the feminine. "Woman as body-vessel is the natural expression of the human experience of woman bearing the child 'within' her and of man entering 'into' her in the sexual act."[14] The most important symbol for the *anima* is the moon because of the connections between its cycle and the menstrual cycle in women. The transformative mysteries of the *anima* are blood mysteries and involve not only menses, the onset of bleeding, but pregnancy, the cessation of bleeding, and the creation of a child from the unexpelled blood, and lactation, during which time the woman supposedly makes milk from the unexpelled blood. According to Neumann, the blood transformation mysteries lead a woman "to experience her own creativity and produce a numinous impression on man."[15]

These principles of transformation are identifiable with the feminine because her body is the source of incarnation, birth, and rebirth. Therefore, "whenever we encounter the symbol of rebirth we have to do with a matriarchal transformation mystery, and *this is true even when its symbolism or interpretation bears a patriarchal disguise.*"[16]

> Transformation is possible only when what is to be transformed enters wholly into the Feminine principle; that is to say, dies in returning to the Mother Vessel, whether this be earth, water, underworld, urn, coffin, cave, mountain, ship, or magic caldron.[17]

Here the original body images of the woman are expanded to include nature and material symbolism as well. This connection with nature, matter, and body prevents the feminine from losing contact with the material or natural element and therefore "grounds" it. This is an important and consistent feature of the archetype. As Neumann says, the *anima* image of the great mother never appears as pure spirit, because it sees itself as "historically generated, as a creature, . . . and does not negate its bond with Earth Mother."[18] Matriarchal transformation is "never a free-floating, rootless, 'upper' process" such as the Apollinarian-solar-patriarchal spirit the abstract male intellect typically imagines.[19]

This transformative quality is not restricted to persons, but extends to the material world, where it forms the basis for human culture, which Neumann describes as "transformed nature."[20] "The preparation of food and drink, the fashioning of garments, vessels, the house" and other natural things are part of the primordial mysteries of the feminine which "stand at the beginning of human culture." Originally transformations of this kind are not the result of a " 'technical' process, as our secularized consciousness sees it, but a mystery."[21] Robert Briffault expresses the same view in an earlier study entitled *The Mothers,* where he attributes to women the origins of both culture and religion.

This highly structured view of the great mother archetype can be amplified by a more detailed analysis of the symbols connected with *mater* and *anima.* The symbolism of the great moon goddesses, for instance, is typical of the extended symbol group and falls into three general categories: trees, animals, and representations of the moon in all or various phases.

The general category "tree" contains such related symbols as cones, wooden pillars, pillars of stone and trees capped by a crescent moon. This moon tree is covered with fruit or lights or ribbons and resembles the traditional Maypole or the Christmas tree, which may be a Christianized remnant of a moon goddess cult. Cutting down the tree is often an important element in the ritual of the goddess, where it usually forms a part of the reenactment of the death or passion of the god connected with her worship. The tree can also be stylized into a cross, an ankh, or a flower such as a rose, lotus, or fleur-de-lis. Soma, the drink of immortality, comes from the fruit of this moon tree, as does the drink which conveys secret knowledge and inspiration which was so highly prized and so jealously guarded by the gods. Although "in the garden of Eden the fruit of knowledge and the fruit of immortality grew on separate trees . . . [usually] both these gifts are thought of as the fruit of the one tree which grows in the 'central place of the earth.' "[22] The connection between the moon goddess and the tree is dramatized when the goddess is worshiped in a natural grove such as the groves sacred to Asherah which drew the ire of the Biblical prophets.

The second symbolic group connected with the goddess is animals. "The farther back we go in our search for origins and meaning of the Moon Goddess the nearer do we come to the animal concept. . . . First the moon deity was an animal, then the spirit of the god is an animal. Later the god or goddess is attended by animals."[23] These animals help symbolize the negative and positive aspects of the archetype. Thus, in her fierce aspect she can be portrayed as a bear, lion, panther, serpent, or fish. She sits astride a lion, or in a chariot pulled by lions; or she has snakes as, or in, her hair. The dragon is another negative personification of her, as is the whale. The cow or bull, the goat and the dog show her benign features. Generally, small animals or birds represent her positive side; they are her *familiars* and a sign of her epiphany.[24]

The third symbolic group arises from the actual identification of the goddess with the moon itself. A direct result of this identification is the representation of the goddess as a triune figure in which one figure represents the waxing moon, one the full moon, and one the waning moon. Sometimes this is expressed by a three-headed feminine figure, sometimes by grouping three separate goddesses together. The three-headed hound of Hecate is another illustration of the triune figure. There are also numerous groups of goddesses that come in threes, or multiples of three, such as the Fates, the Muses, and the Erinyes. The dynamic, cyclic quality of the goddess is often portrayed by a cosmic wheel which makes music as it spins. This connection of the goddess with the muse and music is also represented by the sistrum, or rattle, which she often carries. The sistrum is made of four things which stand for earth, air, fire, and water.[25] The goddess shakes them up—sometimes making noise, sometimes music. Thus she is the goddess of disturbances and of creative activity in both the inner and the outer world.

The connection between moon and goddess is almost universal.[26] Although in some cases the moon was originally personified as male rather than female, the moon god is usually displaced by a goddess or ultimately limited to a minor role as her son. Thus the goddess is called virgin because she is not under the control of a husband, father, or other male relative. She may have a lover, or lovers, but she does not form part of a syzygy, nor is she paired with a god as Hera is with Zeus. She rules alone. Although she is a virgin, that is, one-in-herself, she is not a "virgin intacta." She frequently bears a son by spontaneous conception. Considered as a group, or class of goddesses, the stories of their lives are remarkably similar: "their sons die and rise again; they are mothers of all life on earth; givers of fertility; and also, they are destroyers of the world, especially by flood."[27]

Because the goddess is related to the moon she is also connected with water and light. Obviously the flood represents her negative aspect; but oceans, springs, fountains, rain, and dew reveal her positive qualities. In this guise she is the goddess of healing and magic, and the presence of water is an important part of her ritual. Because she is connected with weather she can also appear as clouds or wind. Her association with light is self-explanatory. Torches, candles, and sudden appearances of bright light are also manifestations of the goddess; and an "eternal" flame, constantly attended, is often part of her ritual.

Conclusion

This analysis of the great mother shows that the archetype contains *mater* and *anima* (and *maid*) and that each has positive and negative dimensions. Both the good and the bad *mater* represent the elemental mother, while the good and the bad *anima* represent a more youthful figure which is thought to be the feminine side of the male psyche. The archetype of the *maid,* which is usually described by male analysts as part of the *anima,* is also a youthful figure; but, as a universal archetype, that is, not restricted to the male psyche, she probably has more in common with the child and/or hero archetype. Therefore, she may be considered a daughter, sister, or hera and, as such, have a special importance for women.[28] For instance, Persephone, or the Kore, may represent the *anima* for a man, but she is also the archetypal *maid.* Although the attributes may be the same, interpretation and emphasis will differ. The presence of several archetypes in one figure may pose some difficulties in interpretation, but it is not uncommon to find them together: for instance, the Virgin Mary is both *mater* and *anima* and, as the daughter of Saint Ann, also the *maid.*

Jungians would probably argue that all goddesses with their associated symbols and attributes are cultural representations of these archetypes. Nevertheless, *mater, anima,* and *maid* still appear today in the individual dreams and fantasies of modern persons. Generally speaking, then, these archetypes can be ymbolized by real women, or goddesses, places like paradise, or by things like the church. These symbolic places or things may originally represent a woman's biological nature, but they rapidly expand beyond that limitation to include most of nature from the heavens to the underworld, the earth and sea, plants and animals. This inclusive spectrum of symbols may account for the hostility of the male spirit for all nature symbols.[29] Archetypal feminine symbols also include cultural products that either imitate a woman's figure—vessels, fountains, enclosed spaces such as cities—or are symbolic of her work—the staff, spinning wheel, winnowing fan. Thus the archetypal feminine can be expressed by an enormous variety of things. She can also be expressed by processes, such as transformation. These symbols derive from her ability to bear and nurse children, but they, too, are extended to include material and psychic manifestations. Since the transformation is done internally, it is regarded as hidden or mysterious; these two attributes are an important component of feminine symbolism. Because women possess this knowledge, they are regarded as wise: they do not command speculative or abstract wisdom, but are wise in the ways of the world. They understand the nature of things and people: their wisdom is always rooted in the practical, the everyday, the earth.

This analysis of the various modes and symbols of the archetypal feminine will provide the basis for describing the feminine dimension of the divine and for recognizing its presence in human history. Because they are part of the archetypal structure of the collective unconscious, *mater, anima,* and *maid* will always seek expression, whether or not such expression is sanctioned by consciousness.

CHAPTER 3

The Repression of the Feminine

> The evolution from mother to father archetype is absolutely essential for both sexes. . . . The terms set by these patriarchal powers always involve a "slaying," a repression and suppression of the matriarchal world of the unconscious.[1]

A major deterrent to the free expression of the archetypal feminine is repression. Originally discovered and defined by Freud, repression is now widely recognized by most psychotherapists as a term that describes an important aspect of human development. Basically it can be characterized as the tendency to "forget," or screen from memory, unpleasant experiences and subsequently to avoid situations and persons that recall those unpleasant memories. Such forgetting is not a conscious decision for which the individual would take responsibility, but a thoughtless reaction. At the very least, repression tends to truncate the growth of the individual involved. Frequently, it can cause neurosis, as when a basic instinct of a child is repressed, or when the repressed experiences were so unpleasant as to be traumatic.

Repression might be an acceptable method of dealing with trauma if it worked effectively; however, the instinctual needs of a person cannot be ignored indefinitely. That which was repressed seeks to return to consciousness. Because the normal outlets are closed, the repressed returns in disguised and distorted forms which are totally cut off from conscious control. Sometimes that which has been repressed merely appears in slips of the tongue or in dreams; sometimes it is more intrusive and results in idiosyncratic behavior; sometimes it is able to exert such a powerful hold over the total personality that it results in neurosis or psychosis.

Individuals are not alone subject to this process; whole cultures or peoples can become involved in repression. It seems to be the price we pay for civilization. At the time of its institution, repression may have been the best possible alternative to promote both personal and societal growth. Because the repressed inevitably returns, however, that solution should not be regarded as permanent. Eventually, the person or the culture is forced to examine the past, returning the repressed to consciousness so that a new integration is possible. This process may be distasteful and disturbing, but the alternative, perpetuating the repression, can be disastrous. A person or a society may be driven toward destruction by forces it does not understand and cannot control.

The phenomenon of repression was first articulated by Freud. When an instinctual demand arises calling for satisfaction, the ego may refuse to comply "either because it is paralyzed by the magnitude of the demand or because it recognizes it as a danger." The ego defends itself against this danger through the process of repression, that is, by "inhibiting" the initial impulse and by "forgetting" the original cause of that impulse. The process, however, continues. The basic instinct still "retains its forces, or collects them again, or it is reawakened by some new precipitating cause." When this happens the instinct renews its demand, and, although the usual outlet leading to satisfaction remains sealed by the "scar of repression," the instinct will erupt at a weak spot and "come to light as a symptom, without the acquiescence of the ego, but also without its understanding."[2] Although the repressed is composed of what is forgotten and inaccessible to consciousness, certain of its aspects may evade this process, remaining accessible to memory and occasionally emerging into consciousness.

Even so, these fragments are isolated, like foreign bodies out of connection with the rest, and they cannot retard the drive of the repressed which "retains its upward urge." Eventually, the repressed enters consciousness; however, it does not do it "smoothly and unaltered; it must always put up with distortions which testify to the influence of the resistance" which is not entirely overcome.[3]

Jung differs slightly from Freud because he separates suppression and repression. Suppression "amounts to a conscious moral choice"; it is a deliberate disposal of antisocial tendencies, the "statistical criminal" in the human psychic structure. The elements that are repressed, however, are "usually of a somewhat doubtful character. They are not so much anti-social as unconventional and socially awkward." These tendencies are repressed because of cowardice or because of reasons of respectability. Thus, "repression is a rather immoral 'penchant' for getting rid of disagreeable decisions," and the neurosis that results "is always a substitute for legitimate suffering."[4] Nevertheless, repression and/or suppression are components of every human psyche. "No human individual is spared . . . traumatic experiences; none escapes the repressions to which they give rise."[5]

In general, what is valid for the individual is judged to be valid for society as a whole. This assumption is based on an opinion shared by most psychotherapists that the development of a culture mirrors the development of the child, specifically the male child.[6] For them, in other words, phylogeny recapitulates ontogeny. This point of view is reflected in their discussions of the repression of the feminine in religion. They concur with Brenner that "the eventual triumph of the paternal deities over the maternal deities must present some parallels to the individual boy's achievement of his personal masculine identity."[7] Repression of the earlier stages, anxieties, and defenses against those anxieties are as much a part of the cultural process as they are a part of the process in an individual.

The repression of the feminine in religion is discussed by psychotherapists of all schools. Comments focus around either the murder of the mother or her banishment, while the competition between father and son takes center stage.

Erich Neumann's remarks on the murder of the mother include a description of its cause, its manifestations in Western religion, and the resulting sense of guilt which accompanies such a drastic act. In unusually strong language he says that "patriarchal culture is founded on matricide and that its basic sacrifice is the slain mother."[8] Furthermore, he believes that

> patriarchal development of consciousness has an indisputable inner need to "murder the mother," that is, as far as possible to negate, exclude, devalue, and repress the "maternal-feminine" world which represents the unconscious.

There are numerous symptoms of this murder, such as the "widespread lack of a mother goddess in patriarchal culture and the exclusion of women from cult and ritual." Because the great mother is so closely bound to nature, the world, and the body, these things are also "branded as heretical and are abhorred, together with the unconscious and the feminine."

In patriarchal culture, the stress is on the father archetype, on "spirit" and consciousness. This type of culture sets forth the view that the feminine is secondary and woman emerges from the man. In these cultures, Neumann says, the undeniable fact that all persons are born of women is explained as a "pollution brought about by . . . original sin and the blame for this evil is shifted to the maternal feminine." Furthermore, "the feeling of inherited 'original sin' and of the insufficiency of life in a sinful, natural world is an essential element of what we have called the 'patriarchal guilt feeling.'" This guilt feeling is expressed positively by a feeling of dependence on an "extrahuman act of grace" or on a gnostic system which proves the true reality of the spirit. Neumann also notes that negatively this guilt can be seen in all compulsive acts that seek to overcome one's own "evil nature." In addition,

> it is symptomatic of this condition that, along with the profound sense of guilt, not only neurotics but modern men as a whole share the feeling of being lost and abandoned, lonely and exposed.

Finally, Neumann indicates that the tension between mother and father archetypes may necessitate a division into consciousness and unconsciousness, but such a psychic split "can be disastrous if it leads to a splitting apart of the systems and the absolute rule of the father archetype."

Freud and members of his school approach patriarchal religion differently; they emphasize the conflict between father and son, and, although they do not believe in the murder of the mother, they do relegate her to the background. Freud assumed that religion originally began as the result of a primordial crime in which the sons murdered and ate their father. This event was followed by a sense of guilt and a longing for the deceased father. These feelings led to monotheism which replaced the primal father with a single male god who would tolerate no other gods beside him. Thus, the Jews responded to Yahweh with "admiration, awe and thankfulness for having found grace in his eyes. . . . The conviction of his [God's] irresistibility, the submission to his will, could not have been more unquestioning in the helpless and intimidated son of the father of the horde."[9]

According to Freud, however, devotion to the Great Father expressed in Judaism was not the final development of father-religion. It did not allow for any expression of the hostility "which had once driven the sons into killing their admired and dreaded father." On the contrary, the only feelings that were allowed to emerge were "a sense of guilt on account of that hostility, [and] a bad conscience for having sinned against God and for not ceasing to sin." This set the scene for the theology of Paul which Freud believed changed father-religion by introducing a scapegoat and declaring that Christ freed human beings from guilt by sacrificing his life to absolve them. "In this formula the killing of God was of course not mentioned, but a crime that had to be atoned by the sacrifice of a victim could only have been murder."[10] The "liberating sense of redemption" which resulted from this theology enabled Christianity to "overthrow every obstacle" and become the dominant religion of the Western world. Finally, Freudian analysis explains why patriarchal religion is so fearful of and hostile toward the mother—lust for her was the cause of the primordial murder. Thus "patriarchal religions may very well reflect defenses of the ego, both individually and collectively, against the barely suppressed but infinitely greater fear of the mother-goddesses and the actual maternal figures they presuppose."[11]

Freud's psychoanalytic theories on the origin and development of patriarchal religion are widely accepted by most of his followers. However, their appraisal of and attitude toward the role of the feminine in religion differ markedly. For instance, Ernest Jones comments on how "for centuries the Jews, with their pronounced and patriarchal Monotheistic tendencies, strove, with varying success, to abolish Mother-worship, and it is doubtless because of its Jewish component that it plays only a veiled part in Christianity."[12] Jones observes that the Christian trinity does not resemble other Eastern trinities which consist of Father, Mother, and Son. Rather, it replaces Mother with an "ambiguously nebulous character,"[13] the Spirit. "This subordination of the primal Mother . . . would seem to accord well with the . . . tendency in the Christian myth to exalt the Father at the expense of the Mother."[14] Jones also maintains that religion offsets the wish for Father-murder and Mother-incest by means of "a sublimated homosexuality."[15] Thus men win the love and approval of a male God by adopting a feminine attitude toward him: "Peace of mind is purchased by means of a change in heart in the direction of a change of sex."[16]

An entirely different appraisal of the role of the Mother in religion is expressed by Erich Fromm in his impassioned work *The Dogma of Christ.* In his opinion it is the Father-God who is transformed into "the mother full of grace who nourishes the child, shelters it in her womb, and thus provides pardon." Consequently,

> Catholicism signified the disguised return to the religion of the Great Mother who had been defeated by Yahweh. Only Protestantism turned back to the father-god . . . [and permitted] an active attitude on the part of the masses in contrast to the passively infantile attitude of the Middle Ages.[17]

Freud also recognizes the presence of the Mother in the Christian religion, but he sees her as an additional personage rather than as a substitute for the father-god. Christianity, he says, is not "strictly monotheist, . . . it re-established the great mother-goddess and found room to introduce many of the divine figures of polytheism"[18] who, only lightly veiled, were put back into religion although in subordinate positions.

Although Fromm and Freud find the presence of the mother-goddess in Christianity quite overt, Erik Erikson recognizes her only as a hidden presence. He believes Western religion grows out of and perpetuates "an extreme emphasis on the interplay of initiative and guilt" and thus has an exclusive emphasis on the divine Father-Son. Even in this scheme, however, he notes that the mother appears as a shadowy figure, a counterplayer. "Father religions have mother churches."[19]

The variety of these opinions on the appearance of the feminine in the Judeo-Christian tradition is a testament to the kind of distortions that accompany the return of the repressed. Whether the male believer becomes a woman, i.e., a homosexual, or the father-god becomes a mother-god, or the goddess rules openly beside the god, or merely functions behind the scenes, the mother-goddess is there. Even in Judaism "the evidence of the Aggadah indicates how incessantly she who was repressed returned, not only in the worst fears of the rabbis but also in their deepest yearnings."[20] Thus, "no matter how violently patriarchal religions attempt to uproot traces of matriarchal religions, the results are at best only partially successful."[21]

There are several ramifications of the repression of the feminine in religion and the return of the mother-goddess in disguised and distorted forms.[22] First is the question of the feminine and evil. "The question, 'where is evil?' is not, of course, the same as the question, 'where is the feminine?' Yet in actual psychological practice, especially with male patients, the two questions are often inseparable."[23] This circumstance may result from the phenomenon described by David Bakan. "When separations are made and parts denied, diabolical qualities are attributed to the denied parts, rather than to the separation itself."[24] There is little doubt that diabolical qualities have been attributed to the feminine in the Judeo-Christian tradition. On the human level women are frequently described as witches; at the very least they are burdened with the curse of Eve. They are regarded as seductive; they lead men into a life of sin and alienation from God Father. Since they are sexually powerful, and morally weak, they are regarded with fear and horror. Even on the divine level, theologians often focus on the violent and threatening expressions of the great mother-goddesses, such as Cybele, rather than on her more benign representations, such as Isis and Demeter. This comparison of the bad goddess with the good god helps perpetuate the original negative view of the feminine.

A second problem that appears as a result of the repression of the goddess is the inadequacy of the image of God. This is particularly true in Protestantism which must bear the "odium of being nothing but a *man's religion* which allows no metaphysical representation of woman."[25] This creates an impoverishment which can take many forms. Primarily, the missing feminine can create "a serious psychological problem" for modern man because it stresses the divisive nature of patriarchal religion and presents no divine feminine symbols to complete, compliment, and inspire human wholeness. As Victor White observes:

> Where the god is male and father only, and . . . is associated with law, order, civilization, *logos* and super-ego, religion—and the pattern of life which it encourages—tends to become a matter of these only, to the neglect of nature, instinct, . . . feeling, *eros,* and what Freud called the 'id.' Such a religion, so far from 'binding together' and integrating, may all too easily become an instrument of repression, and so of individual and social disintegration.[26]

Conclusion

The repression of the feminine in religion and the return of the mother-goddess in disguised forms are phenomena that should be considered by theologians. Despite extensive discussion by psychotherapists during the past fifty years, theologians have avoided comment on either the absence of the feminine in the Judeo-Christian tradition or the distortions of the feminine which do appear. Protestants particularly have tended to avoid the problem. Only recently have feminist scholars begun to talk about the feminine and religion. However, even without their criticism, the phenomenon described by the psychotherapists is sufficiently important to require some response by the theological community.

Much feminist criticism of male theologians and churchmen has a polemical ring which stems from a sense of religious isolation. Many feminists feel their experiences of the divine are suppressed by the tradition and they resent being excluded from the church hierarchy. Frequently, however, they seek limited solutions to these problems, such as rediscovering the role of women in religion and pressing for ordination. No doubt these objections and suggestions are legitimate, but the presence of repression poses the problem at a much deeper level. Jung does not believe repression is bad for women; he believes it is bad for the human race. He appears to believe that if the feminine is not restored to its archetypal place in Western religion the results might be catastrophic. Although the repression of the feminine dimension of the divine creates especially poignant problems for women, its restoration may be necessary for the psychic health of all people.

By combining Jung's concept of archetypes with the more general psychoanalytic discovery of repression, it is possible to establish a broad base from which to begin a reinterpretation of the place of the feminine in the Christian tradition. I do not intend to introduce a makeshift feminine dimension into religion in order to silence feminist critics; rather, I propose to show: (1) actual historic representations of the archetypal feminine in religion; (2) how it was repressed in Judaism and early Christianity; and (3) how it returned in early church theology in disguised and distorted forms, which, heretofore, have eluded conscious recognition.

CHAPTER 4

The Hellenistic Goddesses: Demeter and Isis

Man is not organized like an archaeological mound, in layers; as he grows he makes the past part of all future.[1]

The Hellenistic Setting

The last time Western civilization recognized the feminine archetypes as goddesses was in the Hellenistic world.[2] This period was ushered in by the conquests of Alexander the Great, and its influences lasted at least until the establishment of Christianity as the religion of the Roman Empire. Suzerainty changed during this time from Greece to Rome and finally to Byzantium, but the religious, philosophical, and psychological ambiance remained quite constant. It was an era of change, characterized by anxiety;[3] it was also a high point of civilization, internationalism, and intellectualism which can be equaled only by our own times.

There are seven characteristics of this period which affected the attitudes of the Hellenistic world and, therefore, the religions of the goddesses. As Jung indicates, the archetype itself is essentially unconscious. When it does become conscious, it takes its "colour from the individual consciousness in which it happens to appear."[4] This phenomenon is also true historically of a culture. Therefore these seven characteristics constitute the "colour" of the Hellenistic consciousness in which the archetypal feminine was last seen as an explicit dimension of the divine.

First, Greek became the language of educated people throughout the ancient world. The language was carried originally by Alexander's army and administrators, and its use spread until it became the common tongue. With it came the Greek style of education and the wide assimilation of logic, science, and mathematics. Since a man became a Hellene not by birth but by education, an international community was forged out of disparate peoples. Political, philosophical, and cultural ideas flowed freely from one part of the empire to another. Language and education also transformed religious customs and beliefs which had previously been limited to small groups. Translation into Greek brought new insights and energy into old faiths and made them accessible to a wider audience.

Second, philosophy, which had already been firmly established in Greece under Plato and Aristotle, continued to expand. The Hellenistic period saw the creation of two new major schools—the Epicurean and the Stoic—and the further development of Platonism and Pythagoreanism. All of these contributed to the enthronement of reason which was a hallmark of this era. They also precipitated a shift in symbolic interpretation which can be seen in the writings of the Jewish philosopher Philo, as well as in Plutarch. This shift is particularly significant for an understanding of feminine symbolism, which became equated in this period with the body, the earth, the passive principle, passion, darkness, and irrationality.

Third, the conquests of Alexander and the subsequent organization of his empire helped bring an end to the provincial city-states. Although cities flourished throughout the era, they were no longer regarded as sovereign entities but as a part of a kingdom. Certain rivalries did develop between them, but the dominance of one city over another had ended. The breakdown of the city-states brought with it a reduction in the power of provincial religions and cults which had emphasized civic order and preservation. Although the traditional pantheons of Greece and Rome continued to survive, they were not as robust as they once had been.[5]

Fourth, there was a major increase in trade and travel. Alexander marched to the gates of India, but merchants went beyond to establish contact with China in the East and Britain in the West. Trade was facilitated by more common coinage, and an enormous market for commerce was rapidly developed. The caravans and ships opened up the world for the spread of ideas as well as goods, and international proselytizing was the norm among many religious groups long before the the ascendancy of Christianity.

Fifth, the rapid political and cultural changes that occurred in the early centuries of the Hellenistic age were accompanied by a growing sense of malaise and despondency.[6] One result was an upsurge of interest in religion, particularly religions that addressed individuals and what happened to them after death.

> We see for the first time in history bodies of men and women banded together, irrespective of nationality and social rank, for the purpose of religious observances, and religion becoming recognized as the affair of the individual rather than the state.[7]

With various alternatives available, it was not unusual for wealthy people to be initiated into several mystery religions. Only the Jews, and later the Christians, refused to dine from this religious smorgasbord.

Sixth, at the same time that religion turned toward the individual it was vitalized by the beginnings of theological abstraction.[8] Judaic, Babylonian, and Persian religions were greatly enhanced by such means. "The definite formulation of the systems of dualism, astrological fatalism, and transcendent monotheism came about with the help of Greek conceptualization"[9] because it facilitated the conveying of images and symbols in logical ways. One major factor abetting the development of theological abstraction was the use of allegory. This form of interpretation first arose with regard to the Homeric literature. The educated man of the Hellenistic world was offended by Homer's tales of the gods, yet he valued the ancient stories and wanted to retain them. The solution was the figurative interpretation of obscure or offensive passages. From these modest roots the use of allegory spread until it became a vital part of all major Hellenistic religions, including not only Judaism and Christianity but the religions of Egypt and Persia as well.[10]

Seventh, although the political and philosophical base of the Hellenistic world was located in Greece and Rome, the religions that ultimately dominated this period came from the Eastern half of the empire. Oriental cults from Egypt, Persia, Syria, Phrygia, and Israel captured the imagination of the people. Some of these cults were mystery religions, and temples to Isis and Mithra were erected throughout the Roman world. Other more philosophical religions based on the ideas of Zoroaster and of astrology were also widely accepted. Thus in the beginning Christianity itself probably seemed no more than one religion among many. The popularity of these new cults created a religious revival which emphasized personal salvation by means of mysterious and hidden knowledge communicated at the time of initiation. These new religions were often syncretistic; they absorbed a variety of features, but they were also unique in their own expressions of faith.[11]

Mystery Religions

The growth and popularity of the mystery religions was of singular importance for the worship of the feminine divine. As a genre these religions had much in common. They guaranteed individual salvation; they were international in appeal. Membership in the religions required initiation and since there were no class or sexual restrictions (except in Mithraism, which was limited to men), women and slaves were equal members with men. Individualism, democracy, and internationalism were the hallmarks of the mysteries. No doubt their wide acceptance helped prepare the way for the rapid expansion of Christianity on similar terms.

Unfortunately, much about the mystery religions is not known. They were secret, and there was substantial pressure to keep them that way. For instance, the details of the Eleusinian mysteries "can only be gathered from hints appearing in writers of a comparatively late date."[12] This shroud of secrecy makes it difficult to utter many unequivocal statements about what happened there. As Mylonas says, the secrets of Eleusis died with the last *hierophant.*[13]

It is necessary to reconstruct these religions from fragmentary and conflicting records. Much of the historical material was destroyed by enthusiastic and militant Christians after Christianity became the official religion of the Roman Empire. Unfortunately, few friendly sources survived.[14] On the other hand, Christian attacks on the mysteries have been preserved, as have the works of pagan satirists. Neither of these sources was without prejudice, and misunderstandings and misrepresentations have been discovered in both. Fragmentary sources make it difficult to trace the development of these religions and their form at crucial periods in history. For instance, historical dating is a particular problem for the mysteries of Isis. As a goddess, Isis appears in the funerary texts of the Old Kingdom, but it is difficult to discover when her mysteries began.

In spite of the secrecy and the fragmentary records, certain aspects of these religions are known. General statements can be made about the process of initiation and its results as well as the rituals of these popular cults.

Those who wished to be initiated into one of these religions underwent a period of preparation which included some, if not all, of the following features: confession, baptism, ascetic preparation, sacrifices, and a pilgrimage to the site of the cultic shrine.[15] While this part of the mysteries was often shrouded in secrecy, there is enough evidence to show that the advocates of these religions were serious-minded people who went to considerable expense and personal commitment to become initiated.

Initiation brought regeneration and salvation—a form of immortality.[16] It was symbolized as communion or union with the deity which could take the form of mystic identification with the divine, or a sense of divine indwelling, or of religious marriage with the deity. These experiences were accompanied by divine services, sacramental meals, and contemplative adoration.[17] In some of the mysteries there were probably orgiastic practices, such as those in connection with the earlier forms of the worship of Cybele during which male devotees castrated themselves. It would be erroneous, however, to suppose that such rituals were typical of all, or even most, of the mystery religions.

In summary, it can be said that mystery religions were a significant part of the spiritual life of the Hellenistic period. They expressed concern for the individual in the context of a cosmic or international perspective and thus differed from the established state religions with their elaborate pantheons. They promised redemption through a secret knowledge *(gnōsis)* of God, and they made wide use of liturgy, sacrament, symbolism, and allegory.[18] In general, the "mysteries seem to occur more usually in relation to the cult of women deities"[19] although there were examples of male mysteries such as the Orphic and Mithraic religions.

This overview of the religious currents of the Hellenistic world and the brief analysis of the role of the mystery religions may indicate the milieu in which the goddesses were last openly worshiped. Two of these, Isis and Demeter, were of particular renown. Enough evidence has been preserved to permit a general reconstruction of their myths, attributes, powers, and rituals. They have therefore been chosen as expressions of the feminine archetype in history prior to the period of repression which began almost two thousand years ago.

Demeter and the Eleusinian Mysteries

Demeter is one of the oldest representations of the feminine archetype in religion. Her origins are lost in time, but it is assumed that her prototype was worshiped in the Mycenaean-Minoan culture which preceded Greek society. Thus she was not originally part of the Olympian pantheon. Although she ultimately appears as Zeus's sister and one of his wives, her independence from the other Greek gods and goddesses is evident in both her myths and her rituals. She is generally regarded as an earth-mother figure. Her major festivals are connected with the changing of the seasons and with agriculture, particularly with grain and corn. The Eleusinian mysteries celebrated in her name add another dimension to her personality. It was believed that those who participated in them would have a better life after death than those who did not. This transformation of an agrarian festival into a mystery religion occurred quite early and was obviously well established in Greece by the seventh or sixth century B.C.E. The antiquity of these mysteries is indicated by the Homeric *Hymn to Demeter*, which is a poetic version of her myth and an expression of praise and thanksgiving for her mysteries.

This Homeric hymn is a major source of our knowledge. In one version or another it appears in almost every anthology of

Greek myths.[20] It is usually included to show how the Greeks explained the seasons. The myth, however, is far more important than that; it undergirds the Eleusinian mysteries. In essence it tells the story of two goddesses, a mother and a daughter. The daughter, Persephone, or the Kore, is abducted by Aidoneus while playing in the fields with other young goddesses. She is taken to Hades against her will and is told that Zeus, her father and king of the gods, had arranged this marriage. She wails and mourns and refuses to eat. Finally, Zeus relents and Persephone is returned to her mother, but since she ate a pomegranate seed at the last minute she is required to return to Hades for a third of every year.

While Persephone is away, Demeter searches everywhere for her daughter. Ultimately, Demeter arrives in Eleusis, where she goes to work as a nurse in the house of Celeus. While there, she sponsors the child Domophoon and would make him immortal except the goddess' power is doubted by his mother. Revealing her true identity, Demeter requires the people of Eleusis to build her a temple to which she then retires. Unable to persuade Zeus to allow Persephone to return to her, Demeter finally withdraws the fertility of the earth in order to prevent the people from sacrificing to the gods. This destructive act persuades Zeus to relent and restore Persephone to her mother, who remains unsatisfied and continues to avoid the company of the gods. Finally, Zeus sends Rhea to convince Demeter to return to Olympus, which she eventually does.

There are other myths connected with Demeter. One in particular seems to have been known to the author of the Homeric hymn although it is not related. Demeter apparently had sexual relations with other gods. Once she lay with Iasion in a thrice-plowed field and as a result bore Plutus, the god of wealth. He is mentioned at the conclusion of the hymn: "Greatly happy is the one of men on earth whom they [Demeter and Persephone] dearly love; straightway they send, as a guest to his great house, Plutus, who gives wealth to mortal man."[21]

In addition to relating the myth of the two goddesses, the Homeric hymn also explains the origins of the Eleusinian mysteries and certain features connected with them. It tells how Demeter broke her fast when she entered Celeus' house by drinking the *kykeon,* a combination of meal, water, and mint,[22] which "the great lady Demeter took . . . for the sake of the holy rite."[23] More important, the myth also tells how Demeter went to the "Kings who minister justice (Triptolemus, Diocles, the rider of horses, the mighty Eumolpus, and Celeus, the leader of the people) and showed them the performance of her holy rites and taught her mysteries to them all."[24] These kings of Eleusis passed on the teachings from generation to generation, and their families continued to preside over the mysteries until they ceased to be. Although there were other shrines to Demeter and Persephone, most notably in crevices in the earth and caves, there was only one place, Eleusis, to celebrate the mysteries.

Finally, the hymn extols the virtues which accrue to those who participate in the rites.

> Happy is the one of men on earth who has seen these things. But the one who is uninitiated into the holy rites and has no part never is destined to a similar joy when he is dead in the gloomy realm below.[25]

This hope of happiness impelled thousands of people to participate in the mysteries which "knew such a flowering that wherever Greeks lived its praises were sung; and a thousand years later, when Christianity put an end to the mysteries of Eleusis, Greek life itself seemed to have sunk into the grave with them."[26]

The images of Demeter and Persephone which emerge from the Homeric hymn are powerful. The attributes and powers associated with these goddesses are surprisingly diverse and strong. Demeter is not merely the weeping, grieving, searching mother; she appears as "awesome," "majestic," "venerable," practical, and highly principled. At times she is angry, wrathful, cruel, unyielding, and vindictive. Among her powers are the ability to bring the seasons and good harvests; she also protects, anoints, and immortalizes. She inaugurates the mysteries and brings the greatest blessing and joy to men and gods. She commands, she plans, and she schemes to achieve her purpose. And when she is thwarted or doubted, she destroys, curses, conceals, and deprives. She is an agent of fate.

A similar diversity can be found in the character of Persephone.[27] She is violated but she resists. She is also a gentle, loving virgin who is prudent, thoughtful, and venerable. In the end she is destined to "rule over all that lives and moves and . . . to hold the greatest honors among the immortals."[28] It is said that those who wrong her and do not propitiate her power by performing holy rites and sacrifices and offering appropriate gifts will find eternal retribution.

The mysteries at Eleusis may have grown out of another festival which honored Persephone and Demeter. Held in October, the Thesmophoria was only for women who were especially purified. They reenacted Persephone's descent into Hades by descending into crevices in the earth (or artificial crypts) and returning. Pigs were used in this ritual because they had been swallowed by the earth when Persephone was originally abducted. Apparently the festival was celebrated in honor of Demeter Thesmophoros, or Demeter the Law-Carrier or Law-Giver. The law brought by the goddess pertained to the transformation of Greece from a nomadic to a farming community. Nilsson points out how the peaceful nature of agriculture brought about new mores which replaced those of the warring knights of earlier times.[29] Thus, "with Demeter, it is said, came in agriculture, settled life, marriage and the beginnings of civilized law."[30] This connection between Demeter and the law is not a feature of the Homeric hymn but it was an attribute of her character which was widely known through other sources.

The Eleusinian mysteries have always fascinated scholars. Because of the careful archaeological work and research in recent times it is now finally possible to make some definitive statement regarding the actual ritual and cultic practices associated with them.[31] The Eleusinian mysteries were divided into two parts, the greater and the lesser mysteries. Initiation, a once and forever event, required participation in both ceremonies. The initiate, called a *mystes,* was under the direction of a sponsor, a *mystagogos,* who was present throughout the ritual. Thus initiation was always personal, despite the large numbers who went through the ceremony each year. A fee was charged to cover the cost of the initiation, and all the officials connected with the ceremony received a portion of it. The management of the mysteries was supervised by the chief magistrates of Athens. The priests of the mysteries, as was indicated in the Homeric hymn, were drawn from the hereditary families of Eleusis. For example, the *hierophant* was from the Eumolpid family. As the high priest he held office for life and proclaimed the holy truce. He was also the one who could refuse initiation to anyone considered unworthy, normally someone guilty of murder. In addition there was a priestess of Demeter and two *hierophantides* (women) who had important roles at the festival. Among the lesser officials (men and women) connected with the mysteries was a young child who had been initiated at the expense of the state in order to guarantee the favor of the goddesses to the city of Athens.

The lesser mysteries were held in the spring. Unfortunately, even our knowledge of these more public rituals is quite limited. It is only clear that they were necessary to prepare for the greater mysteries held in September. The greater mysteries were held once a year and every fourth year with particular pomp. Special messengers went throughout Greece to proclaim a holy truce, and to request a tithe of the firstfruits for the goddesses. The truce lasted fifty-five days and protected the participants who traveled to and from Eleusis from all over Greece, and later the world. The day before the greater mysteries a procession was led by the priests from Eleusis to Athens. The priestesses carried sacred objects called *hiera,* which were enclosed in baskets and unseen by the people. These objects were later carried back to Eleusis as part of the great procession of *mystai.*

The greater mysteries lasted nine days. The first day the people were invited to participate in the rites. They assembled at the Agora in Athens and were addressed to this effect: "Everyone who has clean hands and intelligible speech [i.e., Greek], . . . he who is pure from all pollution and whose soul is conscious of no evil and who has lived well and justly" is welcome to be initiated. Apparently this injunction was taken quite seriously and the warning may have been sufficient to keep the Emperor Nero from coming to Eleusis.[32]

The second day began with the words "To the sea, oh *mystai.*" It was a day of purification and the initiates cleansed themselves in the sea. Each of them carried a small pig which was also purified; later in the day it was sacrificed and eaten in a feast. This is reminiscent of the Thesmophoria, which had a different form of sacrifice with a pig.[33] The third day was given over to prayers for the city; the fourth day, to rites for latecomers. The fifth day saw the procession from Athens to Eleusis, with all the participants crowned in myrtle. It was led by Iacchos, a deity associated with the mysteries, who was the personification of the shouting and enthusiasm of the *mystai.*[34] In the evening there was probably singing and dancing in honor of the goddesses.

The sixth, and most significant day, was spent in resting,

fasting, purification, and sacrifice in preparation for the events of the evening. The fast, an imitation of Demeter's, was broken by drinking the *kykeon,* the drink of meal, water, and mint requested by the goddess. Then the major events began and the "initiates apparently went through certain experiences which left them . . . filled with awe and even confusion, but also overflowing with bliss and joy."[35] The evening was given over to the things that were enacted, *dromena;* to the things that were said, *legomena;* and to the things that were shown, *deiknymena.* The *dromena* included a sacred pageant dealing with the story of the abduction of Persephone, the wanderings of Demeter, and the reunion of the two goddesses. Mylonas does not believe there was a sacred marriage enacted at the mysteries; nor does he believe that the *mystai* wandered through a simulated Hell which he sees as part of the Orphic rather than the Eleusinian mysteries; and he is not convinced there was a sacramental meal eaten in conjunction with the holy rites. The *legomena* were probably short, significant liturgical statements, although what was actually said cannot be determined. Similarly, what was shown, the *deiknymena,* cannot be known, although this may have included the showing of the *hiera.* In sum, the *mystai* were witnesses to events which were not a play but a divine presence that realized the myth.[36]

The seventh day was spent in rest for the final night at the Telesterion which may have been reserved for the higher degree initiates known as *epopteia.* This second level of initiation was available for those who desired greater understanding, but it was not necessary for the blessings of Eleusis. The eighth day was probably given over to rites for the dead and general festivities prior to the ninth day which marked the return of the initiates to Athens or to their homes. After participating in the mysteries, the *mystai* had no special obligations to Demeter; they were not dedicated to her services, nor did they have to follow a special code of ethics.[37]

In general, there is a strong agrarian element in the mysteries and until recently "scholars felt tempted to explain the whole Eleusinian mystery on this basis."[38] Certainly Demeter's major festivals, Eleusis and the Thesmophoria, came in the fall and probably began as simple feasts of thanksgiving for the new grain and the renewal of life. However, it seems equally clear that even by the seventh or sixth century B.C.E. they involved more than that and despite apparent parallels, they are "ultimately unique, [and] require a very special explanation."[39] The complexity of these mysteries, coupled with their obvious popularity, has led many thinkers to speculate on their significance. Literary figures, psychoanalysts, and students of comparative religion have attempted to probe their meaning. But as Pater has recognized, all that we have are some fragments of poetry, some fragments of sculpture, and our great curiosity[40] which cannot be satisfied by "the mere application of philological method and a little modern psychology."[41] Nevertheless, it does seem possible to make some statements about the archetypal feminine contents of the myth and the mysteries.

It is easy to see Demeter as the classic *Mater Dolorosa,* the mother who mourns and grieves over the death of her child. Bereft of youth and beauty, she wanders over the earth hoping to find her child and to be reconciled with her. In the case of Demeter, however, another dimension is added to this picture: Demeter's rage. This rage stems from the forcible separation of mother and child and is directed primarily at the gods, particularly at Zeus, who is "wrapped in clouds." It is also apparent in her treatment of the child Domophoon and his mother. The barrenness of the earth is merely the last manifestation of her anger. Both Zeus and Aidoneus feel that Demeter is unreasonable because Aidoneus is so suitable as a son-in-law. Yet Demeter is not convinced by their argument. She rejects such illogic and responds to the fact that her daughter's virginity, her being one-in-herself, is violated by the abduction.

(Most versions of the myth indicate that Persephone was raped, although the Homeric hymn does not say that. But there is no question she loses her virginity in the wider sense.) Demeter then withdraws from the company of gods and lives among humans, seeking comfort by nursing another child whom she would make immortal. When that fails, she sits in her own temple and withdraws vegetation from the earth. It is this act of anger, not her grief, that moves Zeus to modify his agreement with Aidoneus and to allow Persephone to return to her mother. Demeter, in turn, must accept this partial reunion and return to the company of the gods and allow the earth to bloom again. This combination of grief *and* rage is usually missing in other prototypes of the *Mater Dolorosa* such as the Virgin Mary whose image is exclusively one of the grieving parent. In most cases the quality of rage is split off and projected onto witch-like figures. Clearly, Demeter retains both emotions. This great goddess embodies both the negative and the positive qualities of the maternal. The significance of this combination cannot be overestimated; it clearly precedes Neumann's understanding of the split between the good and the terrible mother.[42]

The figure of Persephone is equally complex. When the myth begins, she is a young child playing in the meadows with other young goddesses, dancing and collecting pretty flowers. After her abduction she mourns the separation from the earth and her mother. Nonetheless, she grows and matures and appears to become powerful during her sojourn in the lower world. Ultimately, it becomes difficult to reconcile the dimensions of her character. On the one hand she is the bright and lovely child mourning her mother; on the other she is the Queen of Hades, who appears in later Orphic mythology as "the dreaded Persephone."[43] She has been described as an *anima* figure. She is forever youthful, beautiful, playful, and alluring; but she also journeys to the depths and returns radically changed. Now equal to her mother in power she reigns over "everyone who lives."[44] Persephone is also identified with the human soul which survives death, and her myth symbolizes not only the changing of the seasons but the rescue of the human soul.[45] Certainly the mysteries seem to assure a happier time after death for those who had been initiated. The presence of Persephone seems pivotal for this blessing.

A third significant goddess connected with the Eleusinian mysteries is Hecate. Usually overlooked by analysts of the mysteries, she is nonetheless important. Once a moon goddess, she is now strongly connected with both Demeter and Persephone. First, she accompanies Demeter in the search for her daughter. Second, she reappears after Persephone returns from the underworld and accompanies her from that day forward. Hecate's attachment to the principal goddesses creates a trinity at Eleusis. Harrison indicates that three goddesses frequently develop from two, and in Greece the trinitarian form was exclusively "confined to the women goddesses."[46] In this particular case it is possible to see these three goddesses as aspects of the moon because both Hecate and Demeter wear the starry headband which symbolizes the night sky. Nilsson also believes there are connections between Hecate and Artemis, whom he calls the most popular goddess of Greece. He further perceives a relationship between Artemis and Diana of Ephesus, who was later replaced in the hearts of the Ephesians by the Virgin Mary.[47] This linking of Hecate-Artemis-Diana-Mary indicates the connections between some of the great goddesses of the Hellenistic world and Mary, who inherited certain attributes and powers traditionally belonging to these earlier feminine deities. Mary certainly inherits symbols from her sisters, most notably a bird, the epiphany of Artemis, and the dark (blue) cloak of Demeter.

This brief assessment of some of the archetypal feminine qualities inherent in Demeter, Persephone, and Hecate does not exhaust the potential for further study. Nor does it pretend to solve the enigma of the Eleusinian mysteries and their appeal to the Hellenistic world. It only indicates the extent of the power that goddesses were assumed to have had over this world, over the world of the dead, and ultimately over the gods themselves. This power appears to stem in part from the union of forces which later religious thinkers saw as mutually exclusive. Demeter's passive suffering and grief combine with active rage. Persephone's childish intoxication merges with queenship, judgment, and death. Hecate is a shadowy, chthonic person who yet carries the light. Connected with all of this is the ongoing cycle of death and rebirth which no doubt originated from the succession of the seasons, but which became a paradigm for the rebirth of the human soul—a paradigm initiated and presided over by the goddesses at Eleusis.

Isis

If Demeter is one of the best-known examples of the feminine archetype in religion, Isis is one of the most persistent. She appears in the oldest funerary texts from Egypt and she was the lead character in a modern television series for children. But in her five-thousand-year history, she was probably never more popular than during the Hellenistic period. After Alexander conquered Egypt, the Ptolemys adapted the religion of Isis to conform with Hellenistic views and eventually it spread throughout the Western world.[48] At this time Sarapis was created as a god and placed beside Isis as part of the Egyptian cult.[49] However, it was Isis who endured both in her native land and in the affection of the Hellenes.

The antiquity of Isis is without question. She apparently began as one of the gods of Heliopolis. Her mother is Nut, the great sky goddess, who is portrayed so often in Egyptian iconography as arching over her lover Geb, the earth. Among

Nut's children are Osiris, Nephthys, Set(h), and Isis. Their stories become the basis for much of the mythology of Egypt. Isis and Osiris apparently become lovers while still in their mother's womb and the child Horus is the result of that union. Set(h) is the enemy, first of Osiris and later of Horus. He is married to Nephthys, who is a generally neglected figure in the interpretations of Egyptian religion. Isis has a special relationship with each of these gods and goddesses, and is always portrayed as part of this family group.

The earliest representations show her with a special crown, a throne. In effect, she *is* the throne from which the pharaohs reign. They become Horus, the son of Isis, and their authority derives from this relationship. She is also closely associated with her sister and in this early period Isis and Nephthys appear together as the wailing women who sing songs of lamentation over the dead and carry out the process of embalming.

Other goddesses in pre-Hellenistic Egypt include Hathor, the great cow goddess of Abydos; Sakhmet, the lioness of Memphis; and Mut, the wife of Amun at Thebes. Also, there is Maat, the goddess of truth and right order whose crown is a simple feather. Because of the generally conservative nature of Egyptian religion, all of these goddesses could exist without conflict even though their areas of responsibility often overlapped.

Long before the Hellenistic period this theological conundrum was solved by coalescing the various goddesses. "The union is not a static or lasting one, but rather a dynamic inhabitation ('indwelling') by one of the other, which does not limit the independence or mobility of either partner."[50] Among the gods this appears in such constructions as Amon-Re where both names are retained. Among the goddesses it is often signified by borrowing regalia. Thus Isis takes over the crown of Hathor, although Hathor continues to exist as a separate deity. With this tradition, then, it is not surprising that the theologians of the Hellenistic Ptolemys endowed Isis with many of the attributes, powers, and symbols of her sisters. The Egyptians could continue to separate and identify the sources of this supra-goddess, but to the rest of the world she appeared as an individual deity who is honored by all "under various forms, with varied rites and by many names."[51] She is *Isis the Queen.*

There are many references to Isis in the Hellenistic period, and much of the information available about her myth and cult come from this time. However, there are numerous earlier sources, such as the mortuary literature (e.g., the Pyramid Texts and the Coffin Texts) and other documents, as well as artistic renderings from the tombs and temples. The best general account of her myth is found in Plutarch's *Moralia.* Written near the end of the first century C.E., it is dedicated to Clea, who was an initiate of the Isiac mysteries as well as a priestess of Delphi. The early part of the essay *Isis and Osiris* contains a brief recitation of the myth and a description of some of the cultic practices. The rest of this lengthy work is devoted to a philosophical and allegorical interpretation of the material. Here is a synopsis of her myth.[52]

After the children of Nut were born, Osiris became king of Egypt. He civilized the people and later the whole world, not by war but by persuasive speech. "When he was away Seth conspired in no way against him since Isis was on guard and kept careful watch. But on his [Osiris'] return he devised a plot against him." Seth built a chest to fit Osiris and tricked him into lying down in it.

> Then the conspirators ran and slammed the lid on, and after securing it with bolts from the outside and also with moulten lead poured on, they took it out to the river and let it go to the sea. . . . When Isis heard of it she cut off there and then one of her locks and put on mourning garments. . . . Isis, when she was

> wandering everywhere in a state of distress, passed by no one without accosting him, and even when she met children, she asked them about the chest.

While she was searching for Osiris she discovered that Nephthys had been intimate with Osiris, who had mistaken her for Isis. Nephthys had exposed the child of this union for fear of Seth, but when "Isis found it with the help of dogs which had led her on with difficulty and pain, it was reared and became her guard and attendant, being called Anubis."

Meanwhile, the chest containing Osiris washed ashore at Byblos and came to rest in a heath tree which grew around the coffin. The king admired the tree and had it cut down and used as a pillar to support the roof of his house.

> They say that Isis heard of this through the divine breath of rumor and came to Byblos, where she sat down near a fountain, dejected and tearful. She spoke to no one except the queen's maids, whom she greeted and welcomed, plaiting their hair and breathing upon their skin a wonderful fragrance which emanated from herself. When the queen saw her maids she was struck with longing for the stranger whose hair and skin breathed ambrosia; and so Isis was sent for and became friendly with the queen and was made nurse of her child. . . . They say that Isis nursed the child, putting her finger in its mouth instead of her breast, but that in the night she burned the mortal parts of its body, while she herself became a swallow flying around the pillar and making lament until the queen, who had been watching her (once), gave a shriek when she saw her child on fire, and so deprived it of immortality. The goddess then revealed herself and demanded the pillar under the roof. She took it from beneath with the utmost ease and proceeded to cut away the heath tree. . . . The goddess then fell upon the coffin and gave such a loud wail that the younger of the king's sons died. The elder son she took with her, and placing the coffin in a boat, she set sail. . . . As soon as she happened on a deserted spot, there in solitude she opened the chest and pressing her face to that

> of Osiris, she embraced him and began to cry. She then noticed that the boy had approached silently from behind and had observed her, whereupon she turned around and full of anger gave him a terrible look. The boy was unable to bear the fright, and dropped dead.

Isis then returned to Egypt and was reunited with her son Horus, who had been brought up in a hidden place. Some sources say he was nursed by Hathor. Isis set aside the chest containing the body of Osiris, but it was found by Seth, who chopped the body into fourteen pieces which he then scattered.

> When she heard this, Isis searched for them in a papyrus boat, sailing through the marshes. . . . From this circumstance arises the fact that many tombs of Osiris are said to exist in Egypt, for the goddess, as she came upon each part, held a burial ceremony. . . . The only part of Osiris which Isis did not find was his male member; for it had been instantly thrown into the river [and eaten by fish]. . . . In its place Isis fashioned a likeness of it and consecrated the phallus.

After that Osiris came to Horus from the underworld and trained him for battle against Seth. Many people came over to the side of Horus and, although the battle lasted for many days, Horus won.

> When Isis received Seth tied in bonds, she did not kill him, but freed him and let him go. Horus did not take this at all calmly, but laying hands on his mother he ripped the crown from her head. Thoth, however, put on her instead a cow-headed helmet. . . . [Later Isis] having sexual union with Osiris after his death, bore Harpocrates, prematurely delivered and weak in his lower limbs.

There are many similarities between Isis and Demeter. Both wander and grieve, hire out as nurses in a strange place, and would make a human child immortal except they are stopped by doubting mothers. Both have a great capacity for rage. However, there are also differences between the two goddesses. Isis is searching for her brother/husband, not her daughter. She buries her husband, but by making a phallus for him, bears a child after he is dead. Isis disputes with her own child and by releasing Seth brings upon herself the wrath of Horus. In the end, it is Thoth who helps her by restoring her crown.

One of the strongest features of the Isis myth is its portrayal of family relationships. First, there is Isis' husband/brother Osiris whom she protects and recovers. There is also her son Horus who ultimately becomes the king after Osiris is murdered. But Isis is also involved with her sister, whose illegitimate child she nurses, and with her brother, Seth, against whom she is on guard but whom she also frees. Her concern for people seems one of the most significant aspects of her personality. In *The Golden Ass,* by Apuleius, she takes pity on Lucius: "Behold, Lucius, I have come, moved by thy prayers. . . . I have come in pity for thy woes, I have come propitious and ready to aid. . . . For thee, by my providence, the day of salvation is dawning."[53] The kindness of Isis is also extolled in the prayer of thanksgiving which Lucius utters after being initiated into the Isiac mysteries.

> O holy and eternal guardian of the human race, who dost always cherish mortals and bless them, thou carest for the woes of miserable men with a sweet mother's love. Neither day nor night, nor any moment of time, ever passes by without thy blessings, but always on land and sea thou watchest over men; thou drivest away from the tempest of life and stretchest out over them thy saving right hand, wherewith thou dost unweave even the inextricable skein of the Fates; the tempest of Fortune thou dost assuage and restrainest the baleful motions of the stars.[54]

The prayer continues to name many of the powers of Isis, particularly her powers over the various elements.

> Thee the gods above adore, thee the gods below worship. It is thou that whirlest the sphere of heaven, that givest light to the sun, that governest the universe and tramplest down Tartarus. To thee the stars respond, for thee the seasons return, in thee the gods rejoice, and the elements serve thee. At thy nod the winds blow, the clouds nourish (the earth), the seeds sprout, the buds swell. Before thy majesty the birds tremble as they flit to and fro in the sky, and the beasts as they roam the mountains, the serpents hiding in the ground, and the monsters swimming in the deep.[55]

In addition to her powers over nature, Isis is a great queen of civilization. An aretalogy (or hymn of praise) found in Cyme dating from the second century C.E. attests to her activity in the world and her connection with law and justice. It also points up her complex nature: her capriciousness and her reasonableness.[56]

> I am Isis, the mistress of every land, and I was taught by Hermes, and with Hermes I devised letters, both the sacred (Hieroglyphs) and the demotic, that all things might not be written with the same (letters).
> I gave and ordained laws for men, which no one is able to change.
> I am eldest daughter of Kronos.
> I am wife and sister of King Osiris.
> I am she who findeth fruit for men.
> I am mother of King Horus.
> I am she that riseth in the Dog Star.
> I am she that is called goddess by women.
> For me was the city of Bubastis built.
> I divided the earth from the heaven.
> I showed the paths of the stars.
> I ordered the course of the sun and the moon.
> I devised business in the sea.
> I made strong the right.
> I brought together woman and man.

I appointed to women to bring their infants to birth in the tenth month.
I ordained that parents should be loved by children.
I laid punishment upon those disposed without natural affection toward their parents.
I made with my brother Osiris an end to the eating of men.
I revealed mysteries unto men.
I taught (men) to honor images of the gods.
I consecrated the precincts of the gods.
I broke down the governments of tyrants.
I made an end to murders.
I compelled women to be loved by men.
I made the right to be stronger than gold and silver.
I ordained that the true should be thought good.
I devised marriage contracts.
I assigned to Greeks and barbarians their languages.
I made the beautiful and the shameful to be distinguished by nature.
I ordained that nothing should be more feared than an oath.
I have delivered the plotter of evil against other men into the hands of the one he plotted against.
I established penalties for those who practice injustice.
I decreed mercy to suppliants.
I protect (or honor) righteous guards.
With me the right prevails.
I am the Queen of rivers and winds and sea.
No one is held in honor without my knowing it.
I am the Queen of war.
I am the Queen of the thunderbolt.
I stir up the sea and I calm it.
I am in the rays of the sun.
I inspect the courses of the sun.
Whatever I please, this too shall come to an end.
With me everything is reasonable.
I set free those in bonds.
I am the Queen of seamanship.

I make the navigable unnavigable when it pleases me.
I created walls of cities.
I am called the Lawgiver (Thesmophoros, a classical epithet
of Demeter).
I brought up islands out of the depths into the light.
I am Lord (note masculine form) of rainstorms.
I overcome Fate.
Fate harkens to me.
Hail, O Egypt, that nourished me!

It would be difficult to overemphasize the importance of this aretalogy which attributes to Isis those powers and interests usually associated with male gods: i.e., creation and the establishment of language, laws, justice, war, religion, and morality. Isis does all of this in addition to performing more traditional feminine functions. She originates and supervises family relationships; she is intimately connected with nature; and she is the merciful one who answers the supplicant. The wholeness of her personality is further reflected by the ambivalence of some of her attributes; her reasonableness apparently includes making the navigable *un*navigable when it pleases her, which would of course create chaos.

It is interesting to note that the Hellenes believed Isis was called by different names in different countries.[57] Thus she is Magna Mater (Cybele), Minerva, Diana, Proserpina (the Latin form of Persephone), Ceres (Demeter), Juno, Bellona, and Hecate. However, unlike these goddesses, Isis appears to have little or nothing to do with agriculture, grain, hunting, or the moon. The one goddess with whom she does seem to have much in common is Athena, although Isis does lack Athena's interest in crafts.

Initiation into the mysteries of Isis differed from initiation into the Eleusinian mysteries although both convey a sense of majesty. The primary account is from *The Golden Ass,* which describes many of the events in detail.[58] It should be noted that initiation was not a group experience at a fixed time but an individual one taking place on a day uniquely chosen by the goddess. Also, the world came to Eleusis to be initiated into the mysteries of Demeter, but the Isiac mysteries went into the world and apparently the rites could be held at any Isiac sanctuary, where they would be conducted by the local priests.[59] This is a brief synopsis of the initiation of Lucius:[60]

> I rendered attentive service at the daily observance of the sacred rites . . . but in the dark of night, by commands that were not in the least dark, she clearly signified to me that the day so long desired had come. . . . She also stated what amount I must provide for the supplications, and she appointed Mithras himself, her high priest, to administer the rites to me; for his destiny, she said, was closely bound up with mine by the divine conjunction of the stars. . . . [Lucius goes to Mithras, who says] "The day you have so long asked for by your unwearied prayers has come, when by the divine commands of the goddess of many names you are to be admitted by my hands into the most holy secrets of the mysteries." Then, taking my right hand in his, the gentle old man led me to the very doors of the huge temple; and after celebrating with solemn ritual the opening of the gates and completing the morning sacrifice, he brought out from a hidden place in the temple certain books whose titles were written in undecipherable letters. . . . At the same time he told me about the various preparations it was necessary to make in view of my initiation.
>
> I lost no time, but promptly and with a liberality even beyond what was required I either bought these things myself or had my friends buy them for me. . . . I entered the bath, where it is customary for the neophytes to bathe, he (Mithras) first prayed to the gods to be gracious to me and then sprinkled me with purest water and cleansed me. . . . Then, after confiding certain secret orders to me, those which were too holy to be spoken, he openly, before all who were present, bade me for ten successive days to abstain from all pleasures of the table, to eat no meat and drink no wine. . . . And at last came the day designated by divine

guarantee. . . . (In) the evening . . . came crowds of the initiates, flocking around me with various gifts. Finally . . . they put on me a new linen robe, and . . . led me to the very inmost recesses of the holy place.

Lucius says at this point that he knows the reader would like to know what was said and done there and "I would tell you if it were lawful for me to tell, and you would know all if it were lawful for you to hear." Since it is not, Lucius confines himself to the following statement:

I drew near to the confines of death, treading the very threshold of Proserpina. I was borne through all the elements and returned to earth again. At the dead of night, I saw the sun shining brightly. I approached the gods above and the gods below, and worshipped them face to face. . . .

As soon as it was morning . . . I came forth clothed in the twelve gowns that are worn by the initiate, apparel that is really most holy. . . . In the very midst of the holy shrine, before the image of the goddess, there was a wooden platform on which I was directed to stand, arrayed in a robe . . . so richly embroidered that I was a sight to behold. . . . It was adorned . . . with the figures of animals in various colors. . . . In my right hand I carried a flaming torch, and my head was decorated with a crown made of white palm leaves, spread out to stand up like rays. After I had been thus adorned like the sun and set up like an image of a god, the curtains were suddenly withdrawn, and the people crowded around to gaze at me.

Thereafter I celebrated this most joyful birthday of my initiation, and there were feasts and gay parties. The third day was likewise celebrated with formal ceremonies, with a solemn breaking of my fast, and the due consummation of my initiation. I remained a few days longer, enjoying the ineffable delight of being near the image of the goddess, to whom I was now pledged by blessings which I could never repay. But at length being admonished by the goddess, I offered up my humble thanks . . . and made a tardy preparation for my homeward journey.

After a final prayer of thanksgiving to Isis, uttered with tears in his eyes and in a voice broken by sobs, Lucius promises to treasure her image forever and to hide within his heart her divine face and her most holy deity.

> Having thus pleaded with the mighty deity, I embraced Mithras the priest, now my spiritual father, and hanging upon his neck with many a kiss I begged his forgiveness, since I could make no proper return for all the great benefits that he had conferred on me.

A year later Lucius is commanded by the goddess to undergo another consecration, which he does, as well as a third sometime later.

In addition to the mysteries themselves, there were other ways in which Isis was worshiped. There were daily services at her sanctuary; and her statue was carried through the streets at great festival occasions such as when she blessed the ships. She was served by tonsured priests who lived celibate and ascetic lives.

There are two major goddesses who coalesce with Isis during the Hellenistic period and who mingle their archetypal qualities with hers. The first is Hathor. The statues of Isis recovered from this time reveal the relationship between the two goddesses. Isis is now equipped with Hathor's regalia, including the sun disk crown, set between two horns;[61] the great knot, a symbol of "integral life and of wisdom";[62] and the sistrum, which has four rattles.[63]

Hathor is a major goddess of Egypt and her origins are lost in time. At a very early date she is portrayed as a great cow goddess and as the mother of Horus, a sky god identified with the king.[64] Throughout the years she is identified as a cow, or pictured as a woman with a cow's head. Her other appearances are as a woman with a crown consisting of the sun disk, which she carries between two cow's horns. In this guise she can be regarded as "the personification of the primeval, creative and divine power." However, Hathor is more than this, "she is truly an imposing figure" who functions as the guardian of the dead and "the manifestation of self-renewing life." Hathor's festivals were exuberant and joyful occasions as befits a goddess who loves music, dance, and beer. And "she could pride herself on her great popularity and her ability to win the love of her adherents, especially the women."[65]

These attributes of Hathor are affirmed in the "I am" statements of Isis. In the aretalogy she claims a role in creation when she says she "divided the earth from the heaven," "showed the paths of the stars," and "ordered the course of the sun and the moon." She also says, "I am she that is called goddess by women." This aspect of Isis is dramatized by her popularity among all women: wives and mothers as well as whores and women of easy virtue who could be found in or near her temples.[66] Finally, in *The Golden Ass* she claims to be "Queen of the dead" and ruler of the "mournful silences of the underworld." It does seem apparent that Hathor herself could not be a great goddess of the Hellenistic period because she is so strongly identified as a cow. The Greek repugnance for animal deities was widespread at that time,[67] so Isis, who is rarely portrayed as a sparrow hawk, would naturally be more popular. However, by means of coalescence, Hathor dwells within Isis and her attributes are preserved and acknowledged.

The second major feminine figure with whom Isis merges is Maat. However, Maat is more than a goddess; Maat is the principle of truth, justice, and right order in society.[68] The distinction between the two can be glimpsed in the paintings and hieroglyphics of Egypt. Maat, as a goddess, is shown as a woman who wears a feather in a band on her head. Frequently, however, the feather appears by itself, as on the scales where it is the counterweight against which the heart of the deceased is weighed. Or it can be combined with other signs to form symbols for morning and evening (which also stand for death and rebirth). Thus, Maat exists as a concept (the feather), although Maat can be embodied as a goddess (with a feather as her crown).

The concept of Maat is basic to any understanding of Egyptian religion. It is the principle which governs life both on this earth and after death. It is "brought into being by the primordial god and then constantly refreshed or restored by the king."[69] Maat is championed by the God Thoth, who as the administrator and chief scribe of Re "sees to it that Maat prevails in all fields of life and the world."[70]

> Maat is right order in nature and society, as established by the act of creation, and hence means according to the context, what is right, what is correct, law, order, justice and truth. This state of righteousness needs to be preserved or established, in great matters as in small. Maat is therefore not only right order but also the object of human activity. Maat is both the task which man sets himself and also, as righteousness, the promise and reward which awaits him on fulfilling it.[71]

Thus Maat is "not the modern scientific idea of a causality in nature, but the order of divine life creative in wisdom."[72] As a basic value rather than a series of explicit laws she has much in common with the Jewish concept of Hokhmah, or Wisdom, with whom she has often been compared.[73]

Although it may be more important to "keep Maat" than to worship her, she is personified in her own right and, in that guise, coalesces with Isis. One of the most striking aspects of the aretalogy is the frequent reference to law and justice. "I gave and ordained laws for men," "made strong the right," "ordained that the true should be thought good," "established penalties for those who practice injustice," "decreed mercy," "broke down the government of tyrants," "I am called the Lawgiver," "with me the right prevails." Even the establishment and the inspection of the courses of the sun, moon, and stars can be regarded as an aspect of Maat which governs nature as well as human activity. The power of judgment over the living and the dead, which is another characteristic of Maat, is now also an attribute of Isis.[74] Why Maat is not a universal goddess in her own right during the Hellenistic period is not known. It is interesting to note, however, that the coalescence of Maat, Hathor, and Isis is portrayed at the Ptolemaic temple of Dendera, where they accompany one another and are almost inseparable.

One unique aspect of Isis which is developed in this period is her ability to overcome fate. To this capacity some attribute her great popularity. Not only does Isis say in the aretalogy that she overcomes fate and that fate harkens to her, it is said of her by others. Thus the priests of Isis say that "Fortune has no power over those who have devoted themselves to serve the majesty of our goddess."[75] And Lucius thanks Isis for her "saving right hand, wherewith thou dost unweave even the inextricable skein of the Fates; the tempests of Fortune thou dost assuage and restrainest the baleful motions of the stars." In a period of upheaval and anxiety, this quality would have seemed almost more desirable than any other. This does not mean that Isis is not connected with the stars or with magic; rather, that she is their master. In fact, the presence of magical elements in her cult and the use of astrology are some of the most lasting elements of her worship and they reappear centuries later in alchemy and the rites of freemasonry which are presumably under her aegis.[76]

This overview of the archetypal features of the Hellenistic Isis shows certain parallels between her and the Eleusinian goddesses. They all combine opposites in their personalities. In the case of Isis, these include love and rage, reasonableness and capriciousness, as well as a strong relationship to both the sun and the chthonic powers. At Eleusis similar dualities are held separately by Demeter, Persephone, and Hecate. However, because of the Egyptian concepts of indwelling and coalescence Isis holds all these qualities within herself.

In addition to the dualities, Isis convincingly shows a deep connection between the feminine dimension of the divine and law, government, and justice. Although hinted at in Demeter Thesmophoros, this connection is a major aspect of the Egyptian goddess. This is particularly interesting because it reveals an attribute of the feminine which is usually denied and/or characterized as masculine.

By adding to herself the attributes of Hathor and Maat and by displaying both masculine and feminine qualities, she does seem entitled to say of herself:

> Behold . . . I have come . . . I, nature's mother, mistress of all the elements, earliest offspring of the ages, mightiest of the divine powers, Queen of the dead, chief of them that dwell in the heavens, in whose features are combined those of all the gods and goddesses.[77]

CHAPTER 5

The Expression and Repression of Sophia

Furthermore, being one, she can do all things,
And remaining in herself, she renews all things.
(Wisdom 7:27)

The concept of Wisdom[1] in ancient Judaism expresses the archetypal feminine in a different way from the goddesses of Greece and Egypt. Essentially, Sophia had no separate cult and apparently no independent status as a separate deity in the Jewish tradition. Rather, she emerged in the Hellenistic period as a hypostasis, that is, as a personification of an attribute of God.[2] Although hypostases in Judaism were common, the extent to which Sophia was personified and allowed to speak on her own behalf separated her from the others and made her unique. By the first century B.C.E. she had become such an influential figure in Hellenistic Judaism that she functioned virtually as a goddess in that culture, although her power was always somewhat restricted.

Most of the information available on Sophia in Judaism comes from the Wisdom literature, both the canonical material and that which has become part of the Apocrypha and the Pseudepigrapha of the Old Testament. Proverbs, chs. 1 to 9 (fourth and third centuries B.C.E.), Ben Sirach, or Ecclesiasticus (second century B.C.E.), and The Wisdom of Solomon (first century B.C.E.) are of greatest importance. Commentators on these books are aware that there are connections between Jewish and Egyptian concepts of Wisdom. There is disagreement, however, on whether or not Sophia was modeled on Isis/Maat or on any of the Semitic goddesses of neighboring countries. Some scholars minimize the direct links between those goddesses and Sophia, while others go out of their way to point to the similarities between them.[3] However, if Sophia is considered as an archetypal figure, then what characteristics were or were not borrowed from other cultures becomes less important. Since she emerged as a bearer of notions from the collective unconscious, she would quite naturally display many features in common with the other great goddesses.

In Judaism, however, at least two factors appear to have restricted her development and contributed to her remaining a hypostasis of God rather than emerging as a separated goddess with a cult to rival Yahweh. First, Judaism was strongly monotheistic and remained so. There are some scholars who believe Sophia was deliberately cultivated as a part of Judaism to provide a true Jewish alternative to Asherah, and other popular Canaanite goddesses, and Isis, who was attractive to the Hellenized Jews of the Diaspora, e.g., Alexandria. Regardless of origin and intent, the interest in and glorification of Sophia appeared to expand in the Hellenistic period. By the beginning of the Christian era there must have been a growing tension in Judaism between Yahweh and Sophia.[4] This tension appears to have been resolved by repression, as can be deduced from the writings of Philo. At least her power and prestige were radically curtailed at this time, and Sophia does not reappear as a major figure until the rise of Jewish mysticism in the Middle Ages.

Second, Jewish Wisdom literature separated the archetypal feminine into positive and negative images. This was accomplished by introducing the "strange woman," "foreign woman," or "Folly" as a destructive figure alongside the more affirmative Sophia. This is clearly the case in Proverbs, especially chs. 2, 4, and 9, where positive statements about Sophia are paralleled with negative statements about the strange or foreign woman who competes with Sophia for the hearts and minds of men. In Ben Sirach this splitting is intensified by flagrant mysogyny directed toward real women.[5] This separation of powers in the Jewish understanding of the feminine divine clearly distinguishes Sophia/Folly from either Isis or Demeter. Splitting her attributes between two competing female figures helped Israel limit the power of Sophia. That, in turn, helped assure the restriction of Sophia to a hypostasis. Yet in spite of the strict monotheism of the Jews, which was ultimately enforced by repression, and the creation of positive and negative female figures, the archetypal qualities of Sophia still emerged in highly articulate ways.

The power of Sophia can be clearly seen in the various aretalogies or "I am" statements she makes about herself and in those spoken by others on her behalf. The first of these critical passages is from Prov. 8:12–33.[6]

> I am Wisdom. My neighbor is intelligence.
> I am found in [company with] knowledge and thought.
> [To reverence the Lord is to hate evil.]
> Pride, arrogance, wicked behavior
> And perverse speech I hate.
> Mine are good counsel and power of achievement,
> I am discernment and the strength that goes with it.
> By me kings reign,
> And princes make just decrees;
> By me princes rule, and chieftains,
> And all who bear authority on earth.
> I love those who love me,
> And those who seek me earnestly find me.
> Riches and honor accompany me,
> Venerable dignity and approbation.
> My fruit is more precious than pure, fine gold,
> And my revenue than the choicest silver.

I walk firmly the way of right,
  Where the paths of justice meet,
Bestowing integrity on those who love me,
  And filling their treasuries.
The Lord possessed me, the first principle of his sovereignty
  Before any of his acts,
Ere then, from of old I was poured out,
  From the first, before the beginnings of the world;
I was brought forth when there were no watery deeps,
  No primeval sources or springs of the sea,
Before the mountains were settled on their bases,
  Before the hills, was I born,
When he had not yet made the wide world,
  Nor the first morsels of the earth's soil;
When he established the heavens, I was there,
  When he inscribed a circle on the face of the deep;
When he set the zenith firmly on high,
  And made the mighty fountains of the abyss;
When he made his statute for the sea—
  That the waters should not pass the bounds he
    commanded;
  When he laid the strong foundations of the earth—
Then I was beside him binding [all] together;
  I was his daily joy,
  Constantly making merry in his presence,
Rejoicing in the habitable world
  And delighting in the human race.
So now, O sons [of men], hear me!
  They will be fortunate who observe my ways.
Give heed to instruction and reject not wisdom!

The second citation is from Ben Sirach 24:1–31. Again, Wisdom is praising herself, describing her origin and how she came to settle in Israel.[7]

Wisdom praises herself,
  And is honoured among her people

She opens her mouth in the assembly of the Most High,
And is honoured in the presence of His hosts.
"I came forth from the mouth of the Most High,
And as a mist I covered the earth.
In the high places did I fix my abode,
And my throne was in the pillar of cloud.
Alone I compassed the circuit of heaven,
And in the depth of the abyss I walked.
Over the waves of the sea, and over all the earth,
And over every people and nation I held sway.
With all these I sought a resting-place,
And (said): In whose inheritance shall I lodge?
Then the Creator of all things gave me commandment,
And He that created me fixed my dwelling-place (for me);
And He said: Let thy dwelling-place be in Jacob,
And in Israel take up thine inheritance.
He created me from the beginning, before the world;
The memorial of me shall never cease.
In the holy tabernacle I ministered before Him,
Moreover in Zion was I established.
In the Holy City likewise He caused me to rest,
And in Jerusalem was my authority.
And I took root among an honoured people,
In the portion of the Lord (and) of His inheritance.
I was exalted like a cedar in Libanus,
And like an olive-tree on the mountains of Zion.
I was exalted like a palm-tree on the sea-shore,
And as rose-plants in Jericho;
And as a fair olive-tree in the plain;
Yea, I was exalted as a plane-tree by the waters.
As cinnamon and aspalathus have I given a scent of perfumes,
And as choice myrrh I spread abroad a pleasant odour;
As galbanum, and onyx, and stacte;
(I was) as the smoke of incense in the Tabernacle.

I as a terebinth stretched forth my branches,
  And my branches were branches of glory and grace.
I as a vine put forth grace,
  And my flowers are the fruit of glory and wealth.
Come unto me, ye that desire me,
  And be ye filled with my produce;
For my memorial is sweeter than honey,
  And the possession of me than the honey-comb.
They that eat shall still hunger for me,
  And they that drink me shall still thirst for me;
He that obeys me will not be ashamed,
  And they that serve me will not commit sin."
All these things are the book of the covenant of God Most High,
  The Law which Moses commanded (as) an heritage for the assemblies of Jacob,
Which fills (men) with wisdom, like Pison,
  And like Tigris in the days of new (fruits);
Which overflows like Euphrates, with understanding,
  And as Jordan in the days of harvest;
Which pours forth, as the Nile, instruction,
  And as Gihon in the days of vintage.
The first man knew her not perfectly,
  So also the last will not trace her out;
For her understanding is more full than the sea,
  And her counsel is greater than the deep.
And as for me, I (was) as a stream from the river,
  And I came forth as a conduit into a garden;
I said: "I will water my garden,
  I will abundantly water my garden beds";
And lo, my stream became a river,
  And my river became a sea.
Yet again will I bring instruction to light as the morning,
  And will make these things shine forth afar off.
Yet again will I pour forth doctrine as prophecy,

> And leave it for eternal generations.
> Look ye (and see), that I have not laboured for myself only,
> But for all those that diligently seek her.

The last citation is from The Wisdom of Solomon 7:22 to 8:1, in which Wisdom is praised by "Solomon."

> For there is in her a spirit quick of understanding, holy,
> Alone in kind, manifold,
> Subtil, freely moving,
> Clear in utterance, unpolluted,
> Distinct, that cannot be harmed,
> Loving what is good, keen, unhindered,
> Beneficent, loving toward man,
> Steadfast, sure, free from care,
> All-powerful, all-surveying,
> And penetrating through all spirits
> That are quick of understanding, pure, subtil:
> For wisdom is more mobile than any motion;
> Yea, she pervades and penetrates all things by reason of her pureness.
> For she is a breath of the power of God,
> And a clear effluence of the glory of the Almighty;
> Therefore can nothing defiled find entrance into her.
> For she is an effulgence from everlasting light
> And an unspotted mirror of the working of God,
> And an image of his goodness.
> And she, though but one, has power to do all things;
> And remaining in herself, renews all things:
> And from generation to generation passing into holy souls
> She makes them friends of God and prophets.
> For nothing does God love save him that dwells with wisdom.
> For she is fairer than the sun,
> And above all the constellations of the stars:
> Being compared with light, she is found to be before it;
> For to the light of day succeeds night,

But against wisdom evil does not prevail;
But she reaches from one end of the world to the other with
full strength,
And orders all things well.

The imagery of these magnificent hymns clearly identifies Sophia as an expression of the great feminine archetypes, and, as such, she has much in common with Isis and Demeter. There are strong similarities between what Wisdom claims for herself and what Isis claims for herself. Sophia, like Isis/Maat, is the source of royal authority and because she "orders all things well," is the source of right order and justice. She is the first of creation, and is poured out on the world from the time of its beginning. Furthermore, she is identified with the spirit of God and subsequently with the Torah. Sophia's throne is in the pillar of cloud which led the Israelites in the desert during the exodus; she is also in Jerusalem, where she ministered in the tabernacle.

It is also evident that Sophia possesses the duality of attributes shown to be typical of the goddesses. Like them, she wanders over the face of the earth as mist or water; she is also rooted like a tree or a vine. The wandering and searching of Sophia is dramatized by a brief summary statement in Enoch 42:1–2:

Wisdom found no place where she might dwell;
Then a dwelling-place was assigned her in the heavens.
Wisdom went forth to make her dwelling among the
children of men,
And found no dwelling-place:
Wisdom returned to her place,
And took her seat among the angels.

This could be as well a capsule commentary on the wanderings of Demeter. In addition, the duality of wandering and rootedness also appears in a less obvious way. The quotation that opens this chapter conveys Sophia's ability to remain within herself at the same time that she renews all things. And both Sirach and Proverbs refer to her being "poured out" continually generation after generation. Thus her wandering and rootedness is not merely physical—it is also spiritual. She is at home in herself at the same time that she is flowing and moving into holy souls.

Another duality begins to emerge in the foregoing selections. That is Sophia's definition as spirit on the one hand and her connection with the earth and sexuality on the other hand. She is clearly spirit emerging from the mouth of the Most High as a mist, breath, or effluence. She is also cloud; she is smoke; she is light. She is also concrete. Certainly the nature imagery in Ben Sirach is extensive—trees, spices, honey, fruit, wine, flowers, rivers, even the sea, are used to express her qualities. Mixing his metaphors, the author of Sirach draws out some of this imagery as he describes the man who meditates on Wisdom:

> Going forth after her like a spy
>   He looks stealthily upon her enterings-in.
> [Blessed is he] that peers into her window,
>   And harkens at her doors;
> Who encamps round about her house,
>   And fixes his pegs into her wall;
> Who pitches his tent close beside her,
>   And dwells in a goodly place;
> And builds his nest in her foliage,
>   And lodges among her branches;
> Seeking refuge from the heat in her shade,
>   He dwells within her habitations.
>
> (Sirach 14:22–27)

Here she is both house and tree. However, the most explicit connection between Sophia and a goddess of the harvest or the earth comes earlier in Sirach:

Draw nigh unto her as one that plows and sows,
  And wait for the abundance of her fruits.
For in cultivating her thou [needest to] toil but for a little,
  For to-morrow shalt thou eat her fruits.

(Sirach 6:19)

In addition to these references to the earth per se, there is as well a dimension of earthiness and sexuality connected with Sophia:

I purposed to do good (with her),
  And I was not put to shame, for I found her.
My soul was attached to her,
  And I turned not away my face from her;
I spread forth my hands to the heavens above,
  And for ever and ever I will not go astray from her.
My hand opened her gates,
  And I entered unto her, and looked upon her.
I set my soul aright after her,
  And I found her in her purity;
I got me understanding through her guidance.
  Therefore I shall not be forsaken.
My inward part was troubled like an oven to look upon her,
  Therefore have I gotten a good possession.
Jahweh gave me the reward of my lips,
  And with my tongue do I praise Him.

(Sirach 51:18–22)

It is true that such direct imagery is rare; usually it is merely implied in the descriptions of Sophia as a bride, such as those spoken by "Solomon":

Her I loved and sought out from my youth,
And I sought to take her for my bride.
And I became enamoured of her beauty.
She proclaims her noble birth in that it is given her to live
    with God,
And the Sovereign Lord of all loved her.

For she is initiated into the knowledge of God,
And she chooses out for him his works.
But if riches are a desired possession in life,
What is richer than wisdom, which works all things?
And if understanding works,
Who more than wisdom is an artificer of the things that are?
And if a man loves righteousness,
The fruits of wisdom's labour are virtues,
For she teaches self-control and understanding, righteousness, and courage;
And there is nothing in life for men more profitable than these.
And if a man longs even for much experience,
She knows the things of old, and divines the things to come:
She understands subtilties of speeches and interpretations of dark sayings:
She foresees signs and wonders, and the issue of seasons and times.
I determined therefore to take her unto me to live with me,
Knowing that she is one who would give me good thoughts for counsel,
And encourage me in cares and grief.
Because of her I shall have glory among multitudes,
And honour in the sight of elders, though I be young.

. . . .

Because of her I shall have immortality,
And leave behind an eternal memory to them that come after me.

. . . .

When I come into my house, I shall find rest with her;
For converse with her has no bitterness,
And to live with her has no pain, but gladness and joy.
When I considered these things in myself,
And took thought in my heart how that in kinship unto wisdom is immortality,

And in her friendship is good delight,
And in the labours of her hands is wealth that fails not,
And in assiduous communing with her is understanding,
And great renown in having fellowship with her words,
I went about seeking how to take her unto myself.
(Wisdom 8:2–18)

There are also places where Sophia is described as a mother as well as a bride; sometimes she is just portrayed as a woman of property:

For he that fears the Lord does this,
  And he that takes hold of the Law finds her.
And she will meet him as a mother,
  And as a youthful wife will she receive him;
And she will feed him with the bread of understanding,
  And will give him the waters of knowledge to drink.
(Sirach 15:1–3)

And:

Wisdom has built her house,
  She has erected her seven pillars;
She has slaughtered her sacrifice,
  She has poured out her wine,
  She has also prepared her table;
Having dismissed her maids, she proclaims
  From the summit of the upper town—
"Whoever is untutored, let him come hither!"
  To the ignorant she says,
"Come, feast on my food,
  And drink of the wine I have poured out;
Forsake your ignorance and find life,
  And set your feet on the road to understanding."
(Prov. 9:1–6)

The rival of Sophia, Folly, always appears in sexual garb. If it can be argued that the Jews separated the archetypal characteristics of the feminine divine into good and bad figures, it is then possible to refer to Folly or the Strange or Foreign Woman as a negative hypostasis of God. Ringgren supports this argument by pointing out the connections between Sophia and Spirit, and then by describing Spirit as both good and evil.[8] A parallel text about Folly follows immediately after the famous quotation about Wisdom just cited.

> Folly is [like] a woman,
>   Boisterous, ignorant, and shameless,
> Who sits in the doorway of her house,
>   [Or] on a seat in the upper town,
> Calling out to passers-by pursuing their own affairs,
> ["Whoever is untutored, let him come hither!"
>   To the ignorant she says,]
> "Stolen water tastes sweet,
>   Food eaten secretly is delightful";
> But he does not perceive that ghosts will be there,
>   That her guests are in the hollows of Sheol.
> (Prov. 9:13–18)

The seductive qualities of Folly are described even more explicitly in Prov. 7:10–27:

> See—a woman comes to meet him,
>   Dressed up as a prostitute and heavily veiled,
> Boisterous and bold, never at home,
> Now in the street, now in the square,
>   Lurking at every corner—
> She catches hold of him and kisses him,
>   And with brazen face says to him,
> "I have sacrificial meat on hand,
>   For today I discharge my religious vows;
> That is why I have come out to meet you,
>   I was looking for you and I have found you.
> I have spread coverlets on my couch,

Of gaily colored linen from Egypt;
I have sprinkled my bed with myrrh, aloes, and cinnamon.
Come, let us drink deep of love,
Till morning let us revel in love-making.
For my husband is not at home,
He has gone on a distant journey,
He has taken the moneybag with him,
He will not be home until the full moon."
She sways him with her many allurements,
And by her smooth words she persuades him.
All at once he is walking with her,
Like an ox being led to the slaughter,
Like a stag prancing into captivity,
Till an arrow pierces its heart;
Like a bird darting into a snare,
Not knowing its life is in danger.
So now, my son, listen to me,
And pay attention to what I say.
Do not toy with the thought of meeting her,
Do not stray into her paths;
For she has felled many victims,
And numberless are those she has slain;
Her house is the way to Sheol,
Descending to the chambers of Death.

It is certainly clear that by merging the two figures of Sophia and Folly, the archetypal feminine in Judaism can be shown to preside over both life and death. However, it is also possible to detect echoes of the same duality within the figure of Sophia herself. Sophia is not only positive, she can also be harsh, devious, angry, and condemning. One of the milder images is that of Sophia's yoke. Ben Sirach mentions it several times in ch. 51: "And her yoke was glorious to me" (v. 17), and "Bring your necks under her yoke, and her burden let your soul bear" (v. 26). However, he develops this imagery at some length in ch. 6:24–31:

Hearken, my son, and receive my judgement,
  And refuse not my counsel;
And bring thy feet into her fetters,
  And thy neck into her chain.
Bow down thy shoulder, and bear her,
  And chafe not under her bonds.
Draw nigh unto her with all thy heart,
  And keep her ways with thy whole power.
Inquire and search, seek and find,
  And take hold of her, and let her not go;
For at length thou wilt find her rest,
  And she shall be turned for thee into gladness.
And her fetters shall become a stay of strength for thee,
  And her bonds for robes of glory.
An ornament of gold is her yoke,
  And her fetters a cord of blue.
Thou shalt array thee with her (as with) robes of glory,
  And crown thee with her (as with) a crown of beauty.

It is evident from this extended treatment that the yoke of Sophia is originally unpleasant and that she herself will become a source of rest and gladness only after a long period of hardship and struggle. This harshness of Sophia is not minimized in the Wisdom literature; in fact, there are passages in which she can be described only as cruel and vindictive:

But I will walk with him in disguise,
  And at first I will try him with temptations.
Fear and dread will I bring upon him,
  And I will torment him with chastisements,
Until his heart is filled with me,
  And I try him with my ordinances.
(Then) will I lead him on again,
  And I will reveal to him my secrets.
If he turn away (from me), I will forsake him,
  And I will deliver him over to the spoilers.
(Sirach 4:17–19)

Faced with such a cat-and-mouse game, Sirach's later comment seems full of obvious irony:

How harsh is she to the fool,
  And he that is lacking in understanding cannot abide in her.
Upon him she is like a burdensome stone,
  And he is not slow to cast her off.
For Wisdom is according to her name,
  And to most men she is not manifest.
(Sirach 6:20–22, italics added)

The irony is even more pointed because this quotation immediately follows the statement "for in cultivating her thou [needest to] toil but for a little, for to-morrow shalt thou eat her fruits" (Sirach 6:19). However, the juxtaposition of these two descriptions of Sophia dramatizes the complexity of her nature.

There are also several statements in Proverbs that reflect this same duality:

For he who finds me finds life,
  And obtains the Lord's favor;
But the man who wrongs me hurts himself,
  And all who hate me love death.
(Prov. 8:35–36)

Again:

If you become wise your wisdom will be your own,
  If you scorn it, you alone will be responsible.
(Prov. 9:12)

However, none of these reveal Sophia's negative power with the grimness of Prov. 1:20–32 in which she judges and condemns, mocks and laughs, and is without mercy:[9]

Wisdom shouts aloud in the street,
  She makes her voice heard in the open squares,

From the top of the walls she cries out,
  Where the gates open into the city:
How long, you simpletons, will you prefer ignorance?
  The insolent ones delight in their insolence?
  The brazen hate knowledge?
If you would heed my warning I would pour out my thought
    to you,
  I would make you understand my words.
But, since I have called and you have refused [to listen],
  I have beckoned but no one has paid attention,
Since you spurn all my advice and will not accept my
    warning—
I in turn will laugh when sudden calamity strikes you,
  I will mock when terror overtakes you,
When panic strikes you like a squall wind,
  And disaster falls on you like a gale,
  When distress and anguish come on you.
Then men will cry out for me, but I will not answer.
  They will seek for me but will not find me.
Because they showed no love for knowledge
  Nor any wish to reverence the Lord,
Because they would have none of my counsel, derided my
    reproof—
Now they shall eat the fruit of their behavior
  And be gorged on their own devices.
Thus the waywardness of the witless will be the death of
    them,
  And the carelessness of fools will destroy them.

The destructive side of Sophia's character is balanced by descriptions of her benefits. Her love and protective nature are extolled, and life with her brings immortality and knowledge of all things:

Get wisdom! Get understanding!
  Neither forsake nor stray from what I tell you.
Forsake not Wisdom and she will protect you,

Love her, and she will preserve you.
[As the first of your wealth acquire wisdom,
And whatever you get, get understanding.]
Embrace her and she will exalt you,
She will bring you honor if you hold her fast.
She will provide for your head a graceful garland,
And will bestow on you a crown of beauty.
(Prov. 4:5–9)

And:

For in his hand are both we and our words;
All understanding, and all acquaintance with divers crafts.
For he hath given me an unerring knowledge of the things that are,
To know the constitution of the world, and the operation of the elements;
The beginning and end and middle of times,
The alternations of the solstices and the changes of seasons,
The circuits of years and the positions of stars;
The nature of living creatures and the ragings of wild beasts,
The powers of spirits and the thoughts of men,
The diversities of plants and the virtues of roots:
All things that are either secret or manifest I learned,
For she that is the artificer of all things taught me, even wisdom.
(Wisdom 7:16–22)

However, Sophia not only is able to explain nature, medicine, signs, wonders, and prophecies,[10] she also is directly linked to the laws of Israel and to the Torah:

And love of her is observance of her laws;
And to give heed to her laws is the assurance of incorruption;
And incorruption brings near unto God;
So then desire of wisdom promotes to a kingdom.
(Wisdom 6:18–20)

And:

> He that obeys me will not be ashamed,
> And they that serve me will not commit sin.
> All these things are the book of the covenant of God Most High,
> The Law which Moses commanded (as) an heritage for the assemblies of Jacob.
>
> (Sirach 24:22–23)

The final major duality evident in Sophia reveals both her hiddenness and her openness and availability. The aspect of hiddenness has already been described and it is seen to be part of her more negative features. On the other hand, Sophia is never more benign or loving than in those passages where she goes out, of her own will, to seek those who love her.

> Wisdom is radiant and fades not away;
> And easily is she beheld of them that love her,
> And found of them that seek her.
> She forestalls them that desire to know her, making herself first known.
> He that rises up early to seek her shall have no toil,
> For he shall find her sitting at his gates.
> For to think upon her is perfection of understanding,
> And he that keeps vigil for her sake shall quickly be free from care.
> For she goes about, seeking them that are worthy of her,
> And in their paths she appears unto them graciously,
> And in every purpose she meets them.
>
> (Wisdom 6:12–16)

This detailed analysis of Sophia taken from the Wisdom literature reveals many of the archetypal features already encountered in Isis and Demeter. Sophia is connected to the earth; she is seen as an intermediary between God and persons. Her character is distinguished by dualities which circumscribe life and death, rootedness and wandering, hiddenness and openness, love and rage, earthiness and spirituality. At the very least she is a hypostasis of God; psychologically, she is closer to being a pure goddess. Her power is certainly extensive.

In addition to the attributes already discussed, there are two interesting developments in the Sophiology of the first century B.C.E. First, the latter part of The Wisdom of Solomon describes Sophia as "the divine power, active in history."[11] Here, the history of the Jews is seen as guided by the movements of Wisdom in human life. In this book, Wisdom enters the broad stream of history itself; it is she who protects Adam, causes the death of Cain, and saves the world by assisting Noah. It is Wisdom who preserves Abraham, rescues Lot, and protects Jacob and Joseph. And it is Wisdom who "delivers a holy people and a blameless seed from a nation of oppressors . . . and guides them along a marvelous way, and becomes unto them a covering in the daytime and a light of stars through the night" (Wisdom 10:15–17). Thus it is Wisdom who saves the patriarchs and leads Israel out from bondage in Egypt.[12] However, at this point in the narrative "the grammatical subject changes imperceptibly and becomes God himself."[13]

Chapter 11 begins with Wisdom prospering the work of Israel and concludes with the Lord sparing all things because *he* loves the living. The remainder of The Wisdom of Solomon is a testimony to the works of God himself; however, even this shift in subject cannot detract from the earlier portrayal of Sophia as one equal with God in power who works in history to save her chosen people. Furthermore, at the same time as Wisdom is described as a savior, she is also described as judge. "At the resurrection Wisdom shall 'arise' from its place in Heaven and give itself unto the righteous. . . . Then she shall also be the judge of the whole earth" (Enoch 91:10 to 92:1).

These ascriptions mark the apex of Sophia's power and her development as a hypostasis of God. But, as Von Rad recognizes, she is no longer really a hypostasis but is "the primeval world order, . . . the mystery behind the creation of the world" who rules equally in "the non-human creation as well as in the sphere of human society." Furthermore, he observes that Wisdom speaks to men in a way that

> bears all the marks of divine address. It resounds everywhere; it is impossible to escape it; and the way in which it presents man with the decision between life and death is something like an outright ultimatum. Even the gifts which it promises can only be described as gifts of salvation, and here lies the problem: an "I," who is certainly not Yahweh, but who nevertheless summons men to itself.[14]

Von Rad concludes by pointing out that

> if one considers the ultimatum-like nature of this claim and the importance of the benefits promised, then it is difficult to imagine that this teaching about the self-revelation of creation could have accommodated itself, entirely free of tensions, to the old traditions about Yahweh.[15]

Undoubtedly Von Rad is correct. However, the tension created by the presence of an independent and powerful Wisdom figure was apparently broken, at least in part, by substituting a personified, masculine Logos for the feminine Sophia. The concept Logos was not new to Jewish theology; it appears in the first century B.C.E. where it is linked with Sophia as a secondary or complementary term. Commenting on The Wisdom of Solomon, for instance, Samuel Holmes notes that in the passage "O God, . . . who made all things by thy word; and by wisdom formed man" (9:1–2), one can see "the truth of the statement that the writer of Wisdom was a forerunner of Philo. Word and Wisdom are here synonymous. Our author chose Wisdom, Philo chose the Word as the intermediary between God and the world."[16]

Not only did Philo prefer Word over Wisdom, the authors of the New Testament did, too. Thus the transferral of attributes from Sophia to Logos was completed during the first few centuries of the Christian era in both Judaism and Christianity. This transformation was intensified in Christianity by the recognition that Jesus Christ was Logos incarnate. Although this phenomenon has been documented and discussed by numerous scholars, both from the Biblical point of view in the New Testament and from the philosophical works of Philo, one basic question has been overlooked. What happened to the feminine dimension of the divine, as represented by Wisdom, when Wisdom was subsumed under Word and Sophia became Logos? Obviously, the feminine was repressed and the divine female figure disappeared from the Judeo-Christian tradition. Furthermore, this repression was extremely successful. Although many of the attributes of Sophia were retained in Christology, direct access to the feminine dimension of the divine was effectively barred by the maleness of Jesus. The feminine figures which do appear in Christianity, i.e., *Mater Ecclesia* and the Virgin Mary, cannot qualify as replacements for Sophia as they do not have the scope of her attributes and powers, nor her divinity. Under the circumstances, the significance of the substitution of Logos for Sophia is far greater than had previously been thought, and, as such, deserves more complete documentation.

The Repression of Sophia in the Writings of Philo

Philo of Alexandria was a Jewish philosopher whose life spanned the changing of the millennium. In his works it is possible to see the elaboration and elevation of the concept of Logos as it was developed in tension with the older, established figure of Sophia. That is to say, both Logos and Sophia are present in his writings. Although their distinctions are not always clear, it is at least possible to sense a growing *preference* for Logos; and it is this preferred Logos which became so important in the Christological speculation of later theologians.

The relationship of Logos to Sophia in the work of Philo has elicited a variety of responses among modern scholars and their views often conflict. However, approaching the question from the viewpoint of the archetypal feminine, it appears that the basic conflict lies in Philo himself. It is the result of his desire to accomplish a number of different objectives at the same time. First, since Philo was a Jew and wanted to preserve Jewish tradition, he was obligated to retain Sophia in his interpretation of Jewish scripture.[17] At the same time, however, he wanted to enlarge the concept of Logos which was the more generally accepted term in the philosophical community of his day. He appears to have resolved his dilemma by assigning Logos to Sophia's most important roles in the cosmic scheme, and by reducing Sophia to a less significant position. This maneuver also permitted Philo to indulge his symbolic misogynism; this demotion of Sophia confined her to a station more befitting her sex.[18] In this manner he brought Jewish thought into greater conformity with the dominant philosophies of the Hellenistic world. Harry Wolfson, for instance, has shown how Philo used Platonism and Stoicism to support his cosmological views in favor of Logos. Burton Mack, on the other hand, has shown how Philo was also dependent on Egyptian myths, particularly those of Isis, Osiris, and Horus. There seems ample room in Philo's work to support both these theories.

Philo begins his transformation of Jewish thought by indicating the equivalence of Sophia and Logos. At times he uses parallel construction.[19]

> This issues forth out of Eden, the Wisdom [Sophia] of God, and this is the Reason [Logos] of God. (LA T,65)

> Nay, thou must change thine abode and betake thee to thy father's land, the land of the Word [Logos] that is holy and in some sense father of those who submit to training: and that land is Wisdom [Sophia], abode most choice of virtue-loving souls. (Migr, 28)

More frequently, however, Philo equates Logos and Sophia by comparing them to the same thing, although not necessarily in the same book.

> And who is to be considered the daughter of God but Wisdom, who is the first-born mother of all things and most of all of those who are greatly purified in soul? (QG IV, 97)

> For if we have not yet become fit to be thought sons of God yet we may be sons of His invisible image, the most Holy Word [Logos], for the Word is the eldest-born image of God. (Conf. 147)

In addition to calling both Sophia and Logos the firstborn of God, Philo compares each of them separately to Manna and to the number seven:

> We have proof of this in His feeding us with His own most "generic" word; for "manna" means "something," and this is the most generic of all terms. And the Word of God is above all the world, and is eldest and most all embracing of created things. (LA III, 175)

> Further, the heavenly food of the soul, Wisdom [Sophia], which Moses calls "manna," is distributed to all who will use it in equal portions by the Divine Word [Logos]. (Quis Rer, 191)

> By reason of this the Pythagoreans, indulging in myth, liken seven to the motherless and ever-virgin Maiden, because neither was she born of the womb nor shall she ever bear. (LA I, 14)

> This perfect Reason [Logos], moving in accord with the number seven, is the primal origin both of mind . . . and sense-perception. (LA I, 19)

On the basis of texts like these it is not surprising that Wolfson sees Logos and Sophia as synonymous words in Philo:

> This mind, created by God as the container of the intelligible world, is similarly called by him [Philo] Logos and sometimes also Wisdom. In the Logos or Wisdom, just as in the ideas which are contained in them, there are thus three stages of existence: first, a Logos or Wisdom which is eternal and is identical with God's essence; second, a Logos or Wisdom which is created as an incorporeal real being and is distinct from God's essence; third, an immanent Logos or Wisdom.[20]

Although he does indicate the synonymous use of the two terms, Wolfson also accurately reflects Philo's preference for Logos. Thus he says: "Wisdom is to him what he usually calls the Logos";[21] and "Wisdom, then, is only another word for Logos, and it is used in all the senses of the term Logos."[22]

Therefore, it is clear from Philo that Logos is in the process of usurping the role and function of the older and established Sophia, and that any synonymous usage of the two terms is meant to reinforce the right of Logos to replace Sophia. This is evident in other places where Philo describes Logos as the book of Moses of the Torah (LA I, 19), God's covenant (Somn II, 237), the glue and bond which "fastens and weaves together each separate thing" (Quis Rer, 188), leader of those who fall short of perfection, and as God's messenger who guards us, bringing us to the land God prepared, who should be heeded and not disobeyed, and who will not withdraw from us (Migr, 174). In sum, it is

> to His Word [Logos], His chief messenger, highest in age and honour, [that] the Father of all has given the special prerogative to stand on the border and separate the creature from the Creator.

> This same Word both pleads with the immortal as supplicant for afflicted mortality and acts as ambassador of the ruler to the subject. (Quis Rer, 205)

The detailed analysis of Sophia in the preceding section shows how Logos has here effectively taken over her function, although the negative qualities of Sophia or Sophia/Folly seem to be absent. Logos is now divine order, and law, the teacher of humans, firstborn of creation, the one who seeks out the virtuous and nurtures them and protects them from Folly.

It would seem that Sophia *qua* Sophia was no longer necessary since Philo was able to replace her with Logos. However, Sophia does not disappear from Philo's writings. Wolfson clearly indicates that Philo was influenced not only by the philosophical ideas of his day but also by his desire to preserve the Jewish scriptures. Because Sophia had already achieved a place for herself in that tradition, some place had to be found for her by Philo. In this regard, it is useful to examine the effect of Egyptian mythology on the work of Philo.[23] Philo was likely influenced by the Isis/Osiris/Horus stories and so was able to develop a comparison between Isis and Sophia and another one between Horus and Logos. The similarities between the goddess Isis and the figure of Sophia in The Wisdom of Solomon[24] helped prepare the ground for Philo's separation of Logos and Sophia and the establishment of Sophia as the mother of Logos. Thus in this aspect Logos and Sophia are *not* the same figure with interchangeable names. Because of the influence of Egyptian mythology, Logos can be provided with his own figure and mythological background.[25]

One of the clearest indications of the relationship between Isis and Sophia in Philo is his description of Sophia as "many-named": "By using many words for it Moses has already made it manifest that the sublime and heavenly wisdom [Sophia] is of many names" (LA I, 43). This was a major title for Isis as the selection from *The Golden Ass* makes clear. Furthermore, Sophia's role as goddess of light is reinforced by understandings of Isis, who, as the sun goddess, or goddess of the universe, penetrated everything by means of the sun's rays. Thus Philo can say: "But Wisdom [Sophia] is God's archetypal luminary and the sun is a copy and image of it" (Migr, 40). However, at the very time that Philo identified Sophia with Isis, he elevated Sophia into heaven, and separated her from the contamination of this world.

> The divine spirit is not a movement of air, but intelligence and wisdom. . . . Accordingly, this spirit comes into men but does not remain or long endure. But (Scripture) adds the reasons therefor, saying, "because they are flesh." For the nature of flesh is alien to Wisdom so long as it is familiar with desire.[26] (QGI, 90)

Sophia now becomes the goal of the way and is called land, or homeland; she represents salvation beyond this world, while Logos, her son, takes her place on earth.[27] Therefore, Philo can say:

> He gives the name Eden, which is by interpretation "delight" to the Wisdom [Sophia] of the Existent, because no doubt Wisdom is a source of delight to God and God to Wisdom. . . . The Divine Word [Logos] descends from the fountain of Wisdom like a river to lave and water the heaven-sent destined shoots and plants of virtue loving souls. (Somn II, 242–243)

Thus Sophia becomes the mother of Logos, who is identified as the high priest. Again evocative of Isis (and the incense which was offered at her temple three times a day) is the statement from Philo in which the whole world is seen as a "compound formed by the perfumer's art which is burnt as incense, in real fact it is the whole world, wrought by Divine Wisdom [Sophia] which is offered and consumed morning and evening in the sacrificial fire" (Quis Rer, 199). As Burton Mack indicates, this sacrifice is offered by the high priest. Thus Wisdom is elevated to heaven and Logos assumes her role on earth in the manner of Horus. Logos is also associated with King Solomon, Moses, Israel, or the Son of God. In these various capacities Logos assumes the role of Sophia in testing, disciplining, punishing, and judging human beings, as well as mediating the mysteries of the cosmos and of God. Because Logos now becomes law, one can also see mythological connections between Logos and Thoth, the companion of Maat. Thus it becomes the responsibility of Logos to lead human beings to the boundary of heaven and earth, where mystical union *(synusie)* with Wisdom takes place.[28]

For Philo, then, Sophia at least remains as a heavenly Wisdom. In this redefined role, she retains her feminine qualities. She is both the Mother of the world, its beginning, and the goal of human life in terms of union with her as bride in heaven. However, her role on earth is given over to Logos. Mack sees this transformation of the Isis/Horus myths into a Sophia/Logos concept of Wisdom as a further development of the Jewish Wisdom tradition:

> The attraction of the Egyptian concepts were obviously so great that new mythologems of the goddess Isis continually and increasingly penetrated into wisdom speculation to add features to the figure of Wisdom. In the end, motifs from Egyptian solar-theology, though in spiritualized form, were even accepted into the concept of God. Nevertheless, this Israelite-Judaic heritage was not abandoned by this act. For the use of concepts from Egyptian mythology in fact aimed at preserving the Jewish idea of God, at understanding the works of God and at heeding God's demand on Israel. That is precisely the concern (goal) of Jewish wisdom speculation.[29]

Nevertheless, comparisons between Isis and Philo's understanding of Sophia are far from exact. The most significant deviation is the picture of Philo's Sophia fleeing earth because she cannot bear to live with injustice and sinfulness:[30]

> And so though the divine spirit may stay a while in the soul it cannot abide there. . . . And why wonder at this? . . . Moses himself affirms this when he says that "because they are flesh" the divine spirit cannot abide. It is true that marriage, and the rearing of children, and provision of necessities, and disrepute following in the wake of poverty, and the business of private and public life, and a multitude of other things *wither the flower of wisdom before it blooms.* But nothing thwarts its growth so much as our fleshly nature. (Gig, 28–30; italics mine)

This Sophia is a pale and sickly copy of her sister Isis, who is a robust and powerful goddess, unlikely to be intimidated by the vicissitudes of earthly life. Philo's repression of the goddess led him to create a "dainty" Sophia who could only survive in the rarefied air of heaven and who needed to be protected from the contamination of the flesh. She is even a far cry from the Sophia of Proverbs who stands in the streets of Israel calling out to men to forsake the whore and to dine at her own table!

This reduction of Sophia's strength and fortitude reflects Philo's third objective. In general, he seems to have an unhappy view of the feminine. Not only does he create a delicate Sophia, he insists that the reason she must flee earth is because of the flesh, which is, interestingly, another feminine concept. This description of Sophia splits the feminine into two opposing images: the one to be sought and glorified, the other to be shunned and destroyed.

> Why is a sheep chosen? Symbolically, as I have said, it indicates perfect progress and at the same time the male. For progress is indeed nothing else than the giving up of the female gender by changing into the male, since the female gender is material, passive, corporeal and sense-perceptible, while the male is active, rational, incorporeal and more akin to mind and thought. (QE I, 8)

Philo's distaste for anything feminine is so strong that he even feels compelled to change the sex of Wisdom herself.

> For thou shalt find the house of wisdom a calm and fair haven, which will welcome thee kindly as thou comest to thy moorings in it; and it is wisdom's name that the holy oracles proclaim by "Bethuel," a name meaning in our speech "Daughter of God"; yea, a true-born and ever-virgin daughter, who, by reason alike of her own modesty and of the glory of Him that begot her, hath obtained a nature free from every defiling touch.
>
> He called Bethuel Rebecca's father. How, pray, can Wisdom, the daughter of God, be rightly spoken of as a father? Is it because, while Wisdom's name is feminine, her nature is manly? As indeed all the virtues have women's titles, but powers and activities of consummate men. For that which comes after God, even though it were chiefest of all other things, occupies a second place, and therefore was termed feminine to express its contrast with the Maker of the Universe who is masculine, and its affinity to everything else. *For pre-eminence always pertains to the masculine, and the feminine always comes short of and is lesser than it.*
>
> Let us, then, pay no heed to the discrepancy in the gender of the words, and say that the daughter of God, even Wisdom, is not only masculine but father, sowing and begetting in souls aptness to learn, discipline, knowledge, sound sense and laudable actions. (Fuga, 50–52)

Richard Baer comments on Philo's antipathy toward the feminine in a pointed fashion:

> In view of Philo's strong disparaging attitude toward woman and the female as well as his glorification of the male, but more particularly in the light of his identification of the female with sense-perception and the material world, and the male with the rational soul, it is not surprising to find that progress in the moral and religious life involve forsaking the realm of the female.[31]

Although the material world and the feminine may be passive, they nonetheless pose "a constant threat to man's existence."[32] One of the chief weapons of the female is pleasure, as Philo indicates when he says that the virtuous have not been reared in the woman's quarters and taught effeminate habits, but are "austere of life, reared by men, themselves too men in spirit, eager for what will do them good rather then for what is pleasant" (Somn II, 9). The threat constituted by the feminine to the masculine is real to Philo; thus it stands as an enemy to be defeated.

> For indeed our aims do not rest in peace like cities under a treaty, (but engage in war and deliver attacks) and counterattacks, in turn winning victory and suffering defeat. . . . Such is the cycle of *unceasing warfare* ever revolving round the many-sided soul.[33] (Somn II, 12–14)

It is clear from these statements that Philo must struggle with his distaste for the feminine whenever he deals with Sophia. It is not surprising, therefore, that he reduced her importance by elevating her to heaven and by reassigning her active role in creation and salvation to a male figure called Logos. It would be erroneous to assume, however, that Philo broke new ground in this regard, either philosophically or allegorically. His attitude toward the feminine was shared by other contemporaries and was formed by other philosophers, including Plato. The uniqueness of Philo, then, lies in his interpretation of Jewish scripture which later influenced early Christian theologians. His articulation of the problems influenced Christian attitudes toward the feminine dimensions of the divine in at least three ways.

First, Philo removed Sophia from the hurly-burly of this world and restricted her to heaven, where she is described as "ever-virgin," "Maiden," "daughter of God," "first-born Mother."

> We say, then, that the High Priest is not a man, but a Divine Word [Logos] and immune from all unrighteousness whether in-

> tentional or unintentional. For Moses says that he cannot defile himself either for the father, the mind, nor for the mother, sense-perception, because methinks, he is the child of parents *incorruptible and wholly free from stain,* his father being God, who is likewise Father of all, and his mother Wisdom, through whom the universe came into existence. (Fuga, 109)

The next time language such as this appears it is used to describe not Wisdom and God but the Virgin Mary. It is clear that Philo's elevation of Sophia helps prepare the way for the Mariology which is elaborated in the Christian tradition. But it also may suggest why Mary can never be a full-blown goddess figure in the style of Isis or Demeter, or even the Sophia of the Jewish Wisdom tradition. Philo's Sophia is already a truncated and weakened version of the goddess—remote and not immanent, heavenly and not earthly, unifaceted and not multidimensional.

Second, Philo's general attitude toward women and their equivalence to the material, corruptible world and sense perception results in open hostility toward the feminine. For Philo the feminine was something to be overcome. Therefore, he opened the way for the overt repression of all things regarded as feminine, either philosophically or physically. "It is precisely Philo's depreciation of woman that permits him to use her as a symbol of sense-perception, and, on the other hand, his castigation of female sense-perception and the material world that leads in turn to a further devaluation of woman."[34] Unfortunately, views similar to his come to predominate in Christian theology. The preeminence of the male was, and perhaps still is, regarded as normative in any area touching on the spiritual life.

Third, Philo follows his own advice and transforms significant feminine attributes into masculine ones, thereby changing the sex of the active, potent figure of Sophia which appears in Proverbs, Ben Sirach, and The Wisdom of Solomon. No longer female, it is the personified male Logos who now fills those roles and functions that were long associated with the goddess. This sleight of hand is reinforced in Christian theology by identifying the Logos with Jesus Christ; however, the underlying feminine nature of the Logos will strive for expression. Thus, the return of the repressed should be expected to emerge, disguised and hidden, in Christological and trinitarian speculation.

The Repression of Sophia in the New Testament

In the past ten to fifteen years the role of Wisdom in the Bible has received growing recognition. This includes interest in what has always been described as the Wisdom literature of the Old Testament, as well as a widening discussion of the affinities between Wisdom and Christ as they were developed in the New Testament.[35] Prior to this recent upsurge of attention, scholars had tended to treat Wisdom speculation as "tangential or eccentric traditions foreign to the purpose and theology" of the New Testament Evangelists and to relegate the Wisdom motif to "the footnotes of scholarly discussion, where it can be too quickly written off as an unexplained outburst of Johannine ideology."[36] New investigations, however, are once again opening up the Christian tradition to speculation about Wisdom which had been "one of the most exciting currents in early Christian history."[37]

The research of these Biblical scholars is pertinent to this study of the archetypal feminine in the Judeo-Christian tradition. Although their work does not comment on the repression of the feminine divine which was an important result of the transference of attributes from Sophia to Christ, their investigations do substantiate that theory by revealing how and when Christ replaced Sophia as personified Wisdom.

In essence, the New Testament writers accomplished this transformation in one of two ways. The first, typical of Paul and Matthew, involved the direct identification and then substitution of Christ for Sophia.[38] On the other hand, John favored a more indirect approach in which Sophia was superseded by Logos, and then Logos was identified as Christ. However, both methods indicate that speculation about Wisdom was moving in a new direction at the beginning of the Christian era. It was moving toward its transformation from a feminine hypostasis of God into a masculine one.

Paul

Paul does not dwell on the identification of Christ and Wisdom in his letters, but his few remarks on this subject are among the most significant in the New Testament. Most of them emerge from the early chapters of First Corinthians, in which Paul discusses worldly wisdom and the Wisdom of God. In this context he asserts that Christ is "the power of God and the wisdom of God" (I Cor. 1:24). This is amplified almost immediately by the statement that God made Christ Jesus "our wisdom, our righteousness and sanctification and redemption" (v. 30). In these passages, not only is Paul identifying Christ with Sophia by name, he is also by implication identifying Christ with her various roles in creation. In other words, Christ is now the same as that Sophia who "meets us continually in the Jewish Wisdom tradition from the third century B.C. onwards."[39] If they are the same, Paul can imply that Christ is with God at the beginning (cf. Prov. 8:22–31); he is sent to Israel (cf. Sirach 24:11–34); he is the savior (cf. Wisdom, ch. 10), the protector and preserver of the Godly (cf. Prov. 4:6), the law (cf. Sirach 24:23), and life itself (cf. Prov. 8:35). These are certainly among the attributes that stand behind Paul's affirmation about Christ which would have been easily recognized by Hellenistic Jews. Furthermore, it would have been an appropriate identification for them, just as it was for many of the early church fathers, such as Justin Martyr, Clement, and Origen.

Several other passages in this section of Corinthians also press the point. One identifies Christ as "a secret and hidden wisdom of God, which God decreed before the ages for our glorification" (I Cor. 2:7). This passage repeats the theme of the preexistence of Wisdom who was with God, who was poured out on his creation and sent to live in Israel. The somewhat parallel statement from Colossians (Col. 2:2–3) illustrates an additional theme. That author, who may have been Paul, hopes his readers "have all the riches of assured understanding and the knowledge of God's mystery, of Christ, in whom are hid all the treasures of wisdom and knowledge." The passage recalls the power of Wisdom to teach all things "either secret or manifest" and to give "an unerring knowledge of the things that are" (Wisdom 7:16–22).[40] In both these cases Christ can be identified as Wisdom and as the one who reveals the Wisdom and knowledge of God, i.e., himself. In other words, we are dealing with the self-revelation of Wisdom/Christ.

Another interesting feature of this section of Corinthians is the "paradoxical contrast between 'wisdom' and 'folly' . . . that pervades the entire passage." Pearson attributes this to an "apocalyptic reversal of values."[41] It is also extremely reminiscent of the first nine chapters of Proverbs in which Wisdom and Folly contend for the hearts of men. Paul's entire discussion emphasizes the identification of Christ with Wisdom. At the same time he counsels his readers against being deceived by Folly, which he equates with the wisdom of the world. Certainly Paul knew that Folly persuades the innocent one "with much seductive speech" and compels him "with her smooth talk. All at once he follows her . . . ; he does not know that it will cost him his life" (Prov. 7:21–23). Thus, in many ways, the first three chapters of Corinthians could be described as an explication of Proverbs, chs. 1 to 9, and it is unlikely that the parallel was lost on his readers.

In addition to his straightforward identification of Christ with Sophia, Paul also equates the two by allusion. In I Cor. 10:1–4 he says:

> Our fathers . . . were baptized into Moses in the cloud and in the sea, and all ate the same supernatural food and all drank the same supernatural drink. For they drank from the supernatural Rock which followed them, and the Rock was Christ.

Thus Paul, perhaps drawing on an earlier tradition, identifies Christ as the one "who must accompany Israel on its journey through the wilderness as the 'spiritual rock.' . . . [However,] according to Wisdom 10:17, it was the divine Wisdom which guided Israel on its miraculous journey."[42] The description of Christ as the Rock is intended to call to mind the figure of Wisdom and to indicate that now Christ has assumed her functions.

A similar parallelism can be found in Col. 1:15–16. (Although Colossians is now commonly regarded as Deutero-Pauline rather than Pauline, it is appropriate to discuss it here.) Christ "is the image of the invisible God, the first-born of all creation; for in him all things were created." The reference is to both Prov. 8:22–31 and Wisdom 7:26 which describe Sophia as the firstborn of creation and "an unspotted mirror of the working of God and an image of his goodness." As Hengel says: "In Paul Christ is also the *eikon,* the 'image of God,' " and in this concept the ideas of "the mediator of revelation and . . . the mediator at creation are combined."[43] Thus Paul again borrows language from Sophiology and applies it to Christ. In fact, it can be said that Paul "appropriates concepts and literary forms developed in the Wisdom schools of Hellenistic Judaism" and uses them to provide a "conceptual framework for the Christian faith."[44]

To summarize the position of Paul, it is clear that he identifies Christ with (and substitutes him for) Sophia in terms of agency and efficacy. Hengel believes that Paul is not expressing a new idea, but repeating one that had become established in the early church within a few years after Christ's death.[45] This development had an inner consistency about it, as well as an "inner necessity." "The connection between Jesus and Wisdom had been prepared for by Jesus' own preaching during his ministry, the form of which was very much in the wisdom tradition."[46] After his death, he was recognized as the preexistent one because of his claims to make all things new. "The beginning . . . *had to* be illuminated by the end."[47] Thus Christ became the confidant of God, the firstborn who was with God at creation.

> Once the idea of pre-existence had been introduced, it was obvious that the exalted Son of God would also attract to himself the functions of Jewish Wisdom as a mediator of creation and salvation. Even Wisdom, which was associated with God in a unique way from before time, could no longer be regarded as an independent entity over against the risen and exalted Jesus and superior to him. Rather, all the functions of Wisdom were transferred to Jesus.[48]

Paul reflects this transference clearly and accurately, not only in Corinthians but whenever he discusses the law. Prior to Paul, pious Jews had ascribed the functions of salvation to Wisdom/Torah. But when Christ appropriates the role of Wisdom, he shatters "to pieces the function of the law in the ordering of the world and the salvation of men."[49] This was undoubtedly a "fatal scandal" to many of his contemporaries, but it is a consistent part of Paul's Christology. Hengel's insights on this point are interesting. Perhaps as other Biblical scholars begin to explore the role of Wisdom in Paul's Christology, they will shed more light on the significance of Law and Gospel for his theology.

Matthew

Even a cursory reading of Matthew reveals many parallels between Christ and Sophia. The origin of these references to Wisdom appears to come from the source known as Q, which, as reconstructed, is a precursor to the first Gospel and to Luke. Although the Q tradition, which is developed in Matthew, ultimately ends up with a type of Sophia Christology, it did not begin that way.[50] Apparently, Q originally identified both Jesus and John the Baptist "as the last of Wisdom's messengers,"[51] who were sent to Israel by Sophia in the manner of Adam, Abraham, Jacob, Joseph, and Moses. A remnant of this earlier tradition is still evident in Matt. 11:18–19:

> For John came neither eating nor drinking, and they say "He has a demon"; the Son of man came eating and drinking, and they say "Behold a glutton and a drunkard, a friend of tax collectors and sinners!" Yet wisdom is justified by her deeds.

In keeping with this understanding of Jesus as the latest of the prophets sent by Wisdom, the parables of Christ originally form part of the general Wisdom-saying tradition.[52] "The primitive Palestine community collected the unique wisdom teachings of the Messiah in the nucleus of the Logia source, just as earlier the wise sayings of King Solomon, David's son, had also been collected together."[53] The *logoi,* or sayings of Christ, play an important role in Matthew's Gospel, and actually continue to be developed by both orthodox and gnostic Christians until the time of Polycarp when the expansion of the sayings collections was restricted, probably because of their misuse "by gnosticizing heretics."[54]

There are two additional legacies from Q which carry through into Matthew. First, the Son of Man motif is seen as belonging to Wisdom.[55] This Gospel identifies the Son of Man with Wisdom rather than seeing the Son as the mediator of revelation or as the idealized *Sophos.*[56] Second, Matthew still reflects traces that suggest that Q apparently regarded Sophia/Spirit more highly than Christ Jesus. Hence the enigmatic statement (Matt. 12:32): "And whoever says a word against the Son of man will be forgiven; but whoever speaks against the Holy Spirit will not be forgiven." There is no question that this tradition regarding Sophia/Spirit ultimately gives way to an identification of Jesus with Sophia, in the sense that Jesus becomes Sophia incarnate.[57]

The Sophia Christology of Matthew is evident in a number of other passages. The most obvious one is Matt. 11:28–30:

> Come to me, all who labor and are heavy laden, and I will give you rest. Take my yoke upon you, and learn from me; for I am gentle and lowly in heart, and you will find rest for your souls. For my yoke is easy, and my burden is light.

The yoke of Sophia has been discussed in the preceding section. It is worth noting, however, that Christ's yoke appears to be less burdensome than Sophia's, and that Christ does not try the believer with temptations, or "torment him with chastisements" (Sirach 4:17–18). Nevertheless, the demands that Christ makes on his followers are set in strong, if not harsh, language in this Gospel (Matt. 10:34: "I have not come to bring peace, but a sword"); and Matthew is the only Gospel, except Mark, to record Christ's fit of rage against the barren fig tree (Matt. 21:19).

Another example of the Evangelist's dependency on Wisdom speculation appears in the following passage:

> O Jerusalem, Jerusalem, killing the prophets and stoning those who are sent to you! How often would I have gathered your children together as a hen gathers her brood under her wings, and you would not! Behold, your house is forsaken and desolate. For I tell you, you will not see me again, until you say "Blessed is he who comes in the name of the Lord." (Matt. 23:37–39)

This lament, analogous to the laments of Wisdom, can be broken into three parts. First is the oracle of doom which precedes this passage: "Woe to you, scribes and Pharisees, hypocrites!" (Matt. 23:29); then is the lament itself; finally there is the invitation to come to Wisdom for salvation.[58]

Biblical scholars also point out that "speculation about the pre-existent Sophia constituted an important element in Matthew's understanding of Christ" in the same way it did for Paul and later for John.[59] Furthermore, they note that Matthew identified Christ with the law (Matt. 5:17ff.) which, of course, is regarded in traditional Wisdom literature as Sophia. Christ is seen as both fulfilling the law and assuring that the law will be in effect until the Last Day.[60] Finally, Christ is substituted for Sophia because he now takes over her activity of sending prophets. The prophets of Christ are the disciples whom he chooses and sends out as "sheep in the midst of wolves." They, like the messengers of Sophia, will be persecuted, but those who lose their life for Christ's sake will find it. Note the similarity between this passage and Prov. 8:35: "For he who finds me [Sophia] finds life, and obtains the Lord's favor."

In summary, the Gospel of Matthew not only reflects the earlier Q tradition but extends it by creating a Christology that depends in large measure on the Hellenistic understanding of Sophia, whose powers and attributes are now seen as incarnate in the man Jesus.

John

The Gospel of John accomplishes the transformation from Sophiology to Christology in a different way from Paul or Matthew. John transfers the powers and attributes of Sophia to the Logos and then identifies Christ as incarnate Logos—the Word made flesh. This analysis of John hinges primarily on the treatment and origin of the Logos motif in the Prologue which I see emerging from Judaism as a disguise for the older Sophia tradition. This position, derived from the study of the archetypal feminine and its expression in divine form as goddesses, differs from that of Rudolf Bultmann and, to a lesser extent, of C. H. Dodd. On the other hand, my views are almost identical to those of Raymond Brown.

In analyzing the Gospel of John, Bultmann states that "the mythological figure of the Logos has its home in a particular understanding of the world, namely, the Gnostic," particularly a "relatively early oriental Gnosticism" which stresses soteriology rather than cosmology.[61] In addition to positing the root of Johannine Christology in a pre-Christian gnosticism, he explicitly denies that a potent Wisdom myth existed in earlier Judaism. "The Wisdom myth was not as such a living force in Judaism." What mythology did exist was "only a variant on the *Revealer-myth,* which is developed in Hellenistic and Gnostic literature; and the kinship of the Johannine Prologue to the Judaic Wisdom speculation is due to the fact that both go back to the same tradition for their source."[62] Bultmann believes it is this Revealer-myth which is presupposed by both Philo and the Pauline and Deutero-Pauline writers. He does not see how Logos can be understood on the basis of Old Testament Sophiology: "If the absolute use of the concept *ho logos* shows how far the Prologue is from the Old Testament, the same holds good of its relation to *Judaism.*"[63] Nor does Bultmann believe John was influenced by Stoic or Greek philosophy, because the

Logos never appeared as a mythological figure in those traditions. Crucial to understanding the Gospel of John is the decisive idea of the Gnostic myth "and in particular the idea of the intermediary, that mediates divine powers to the world" which is of *pre-Gnostic origin.*[64] If this view of Bultmann is correct, there need be no direct connection between Sophia and Logos, and, therefore, Logos can hardly be described as a masculine substitute for Sophia.[65]

In *The Interpretation of the Fourth Gospel,* C. H. Dodd gives a different explanation for the origin of the Logos motif. "Rabbinic Judaism, Philo and the Hermetica remain our most direct sources for the background of thought" in John, although Johannine Christians transformed those very ideas they held in common with other traditions.[66] Obviously, Dodd holds much the same view of John as Suggs does of Matthew: he recognizes the Wisdom background in John, but stresses the uniqueness of John's incarnational development. Dodd believes that John borrows the pre-incarnate and immanent nature of the Jewish Sophia and combines it with the cosmological understanding of Logos in Philo, which can be described as "the rational principle in the universe, its meaning, plan or purpose, conceived as a divine hypostasis in which the eternal God is revealed and active."[67] Both Philo and John understand the Logos to be the Way to God, and they identify the Logos with the heavenly man, or Son of God, or Son of Man. However, the difference between them is that John believes in Logos incarnate.

Dodd never tires of stressing the unique contribution of John—the incarnation.

> Although it would be idle to look for any real anticipation of the Johannine doctrine of incarnation, the idea of the immanence of Wisdom in men, making them friends of God, provides a kind of matrix in which the idea of incarnation might be shaped.

Nevertheless, despite the contributions from Sophiology and the additional understanding that the "functions assigned to Wisdom are often clearly those which are elsewhere assigned to God Himself," Dodd believes "we are still far from anything which could justify the statement *theos en ho logos.*"[68] According to Dodd, this is John's gift to Christology and it has no precedent.

The analysis of the Gospel of John by Raymond Brown comes closest to reflecting the view held by this writer. Brown believes that "the Wisdom literature offers better parallels for the Johannine picture of Jesus than do the later Gnostic, Mandean or Hermetic passages sometimes suggested."[69] Furthermore, he argues "that the most decisive influence in the form and style of the discourses of Jesus in the Fourth Gospel comes from the speeches of divine Wisdom in books like Proverbs, Sirach, and Wisdom of Solomon."[70] Brown notes that John has sharply modifed the presentation of Wisdom by introducing a clearer historical perspective, which culminates in seeing Jesus as "the supreme example of divine Wisdom active in history, and indeed divine Wisdom itself."[71] But even Brown recognizes that "this demythologizing of the Wisdom concept by incorporating it into salvation history is not totally new, for one encounters the same tendency in the very late Wisdom literature."[72] Finally, Brown perceives certain similar tendencies in the Synoptic Gospels such as those already discussed in the section on Matthew.

> The Synoptic evidence is not overwhelming, but there is enough of it to make one suspect that the identification of Jesus with personified Wisdom was *not* the original creation of the Fourth Gospel. Probably here, as with other Johannine themes like "the hour," and the "I am" sayings, John has capitalized on and developed a theme that was already in the primitive tradition.[73]

These views of Brown completely coincide with my own analysis of the Prologue, but there are additional factors in John which contribute to my belief that behind the portrait of Jesus as incarnate Logos is the identification of Jesus with Sophia.

Of primary importance are the "I am" statements which run throughout the Gospel. The knowledgeable Hellene would immediately recognize the similarities between those statements and those of Isis in the aretalogy previously cited. In addition, Hellenistic Jews could identify them with the first person discourses of Wisdom in Proverbs and Ben Sirach.[74] In this case, not only is the style alike, so also is the symbolism. "The explicit use of symbolism is an obvious characteristic of this gospel—living water, bread of life, the true vine, the good shepherd, etc."[75] Clearly these images were used in pre-Christian times to describe Sophia. Even Dodd notes that "the water which comes down from above" and the bread are symbols for Torah or Wisdom or the Holy Spirit.[76] Also Jesus' statement "I am the light of the world" (John 8:12) resonates strongly with those remarks made about Sophia in The Wisdom of Solomon 7:26,29:

> For she is an effulgence from everlasting light
> And an unspotted mirror of the working of God,
> And an image of his goodness.
>
> . . . .
>
> For she is fairer than the sun,
> And above all the constellations of the stars:
> Being compared with light, she is found to be before it.[77]

In addition to the "I am" statements which draw attention to the relationship between Jesus and Sophia, John continually portrays Jesus as a caring, nurturing person in a way that is evocative of the great virgin goddesses Demeter and Isis. This feminine dimension is expressed by the many stories about

Jesus that appear only in this Gospel. It is immediately evident in his relationship to women: his mother (at Cana and the crucifixion); Mary (at the tomb); the Samaritan woman at the well; the woman taken in adultery; and to Mary and Martha, the sisters of Lazarus. His care for them is characterized by respect, awareness, sensitivity, compassion, and love. More than once his attitude is a cause for surprise and hostility from others. This attitude is hardly restricted to women; it is equally present in his dealings with men, for example, the disciples John and Thomas, and Lazarus at whose death Jesus wept. Nowhere is the nurturing Christ described more vividly than in the Johannine account of the Last Supper, which begins with the physical act of caring—washing the disciples' feet—and ends with a spiritual act—Jesus' prayer to God the Father:

> I am praying for them. . . . I have guarded them, and none of them is lost but the son of perdition. . . . I do not pray that thou shouldst take them out of the world, but that thou shouldst keep them from the evil one. . . . And for their sake I consecrate myself, that they also may be consecrated in truth. I do not pray for these only, but also for those who believe in me through their word. (John 17: 9–20)

This presentation of Jesus culminates in the last chapter when Jesus passes on this nurturing role to Peter. Three times he enjoins Peter: "Feed my sheep . . . feed my lambs . . . feed my sheep."

It can be seen by this analysis that the Gospel of John identifies Christ with the archetypal feminine in three ways. First, by means of the Prologue, Jesus is defined as the incarnate Logos, which is a masculine substitute for Sophia. Second, the "I am" statements and their symbols—e.g., light, water, vine—evoke the "I am" statements of Wisdom and, therefore, support the Evangelist's understanding of Jesus as incarnate Wisdom. Third, the picture of Jesus as a divine figure who is particularly nurturing and caring endows him with at least some of the attributes of the great virgin goddesses of that day. It is because of these three techniques that John can ultimately be characterized as the most feminine of the Gospels.

Conclusion

The purpose of this chapter has been to demonstrate the expression and repression of Sophia in the Judeo-Christian tradition. Beginning as a personified hypostasis of God, Wisdom grew in stature and importance for the Jews from the fourth to the first century B.C.E., until her power was virtually equivalent to that of any Hellenistic goddess. She combined in herself positive and some negative qualities, although she was often paired with another feminine figure called Folly, or the strange or foreign woman, who was entirely negative in character. By the beginning of the Christian era Sophia was portrayed as acting in history and assuming the roles of judge and savior of the Jewish people. At this point there can be no question that she rivaled the power of Yahweh himself and spoke to men in such a way that her words bear "all the marks of divine address." She commanded men to choose between life and death, and the gifts she promised "can only be described as gifts of salvation."[78]

Within a hundred years Sophia's power was broken and she was superseded by a masculine figure who took over her roles. In Hellenistic Judaism the personified Logos of Philo's philosophy became the firstborn image of God who was with God at creation, the principle of mind and rational order, and the intermediary between God and men. However, in deference to Jewish scripture, Sophia was not totally discarded, but was elevated to heaven, where she was relegated to a minor part in the divine/human drama. At the same time, the early Christians replaced her with Jesus and within a few decades of his crucifixion, all her powers and attributes had been ascribed to Christ. This was either done directly, as in Paul's letters and Matthew's Gospel, or indirectly, as in John which identified Christ with the Logos, a masculine figure similar to the one developed by Philo. Ultimately, Sophia's powers were so totally preempted by Christ that she herself completely disappeared from the Christian religion of that time.

It is difficult to say why Sophia was replaced by Logos/ Christ. Philo's work indicated the presence of a symbolic misogynism which might have come from a psychocultural need to replace Mother with Father. However, Hengel also makes a provocative statement in his book *The Son of God:*

> The Logos Christology of the Johannine prologue about fifty years after Paul is therefore only the logical conclusion of the fusion of the pre-existent Son of God with traditional Wisdom, though of course the concept of "*sophia*" which was always threatened by mythological speculation, had to give way to the clear "Logos," the Word of God.[79]

Unfortunately, he does not elaborate on why Sophia was "always threatened by mythological speculation," or why she had to be replaced by the "clear" Logos. One wonders if it is because Sophia is feminine. Whatever the reason, it is nevertheless apparent that Sophia reached her pinnacle and was then abruptly replaced by a masculine figure. As a result of this transference of attributes, overt access to the feminine dimension of the divine in the Judeo-Christian tradition was cut off or repressed. This laid the groundwork for the return of the great feminine archetypes in disguised and hidden forms in the theology of the early church.

CHAPTER 6

The Return of the Repressed

> The instinct has either retained its forces, or collects them again, or it is reawakened by some new precipitating cause. Thereupon it renews its demands.[1]

With the repression of the feminine dimension of the divine in the first centuries of the Christian era, the stage was set for the ultimate return of the repressed. Using Freud's general analysis of this phenomenon, it is possible to predict that the repressed feminine will return in one of two ways. First, certain elements of the feminine might evade the initial repression and "remain accessible to memory and occasionally emerge into consciousness." These fragments, however, would still be "isolated, like foreign bodies out of connection with the rest." Or, second, since the material that is repressed retains its "upward urge," it will eventually enter consciousness in disguised form. The fact that it cannot return "smoothly and unaltered" testifies to the resistance of the ego which cannot be entirely overcome.[2]

An analysis of the theology of the early church enables us to see that the feminine dimension of the divine does return to consciousness in both these ways. Although it may eventually be important to document all the appearances of the repressed feminine in Christianity, I confined my own search to the three major areas of Christian doctrine that seem most promising: Mariology, Ecclesiology, and Christology. Mariology and Ecclesiology are the two overt feminine motifs in Christian theology. The preceding analysis of New Testament Christology has already shown that Christology contains an initial dependency on, and a transformation of, the Sophiology of Hellenistic Judaism.

Mariology

The Mariology of the first centuries of the Christian era focused on five major themes. All of these originally grew out of Mary's position as the mother of Jesus. Whatever powers and attributes were ascribed to her were given to her because she played such a preeminent role in her son's life. In other words, it would be fallacious to assume that Mary was introduced into Christianity extraneously and at a late date. On the contrary, she appears from the time of the Gospels as an integral part of the Christian mystery and as part of God's plan for the salvation of the human race.[3] But within a few hundred years, her role in the divine mystery was substantially embellished. Three of the themes that came out of the patristic period pertained to Mary's own personal life. First was the story of Mary's own miraculous conception. Second was the belief in her perpetual virginity. Third was the description of her bodily assumption into heaven after her death. The other two Mariological motifs dramatize the importance of her relationship to her son. The first was expressed in the title *Theotokos,* or Mother of God, conferred on Mary at the Council of Ephesus in 431 C.E. The second emerged from the portrait of Mary as co-redemptrix in the theology of some of the patristic fathers.

Each of these five themes attributes to Mary certain suprahuman qualities and indicates the presence of archetypal features heretofore found only in the goddesses of the Hellenistic world. The evidence for this Mariology comes from three sources: the Apocrypha, early iconography and hymnology, and the theology of the early church.

The Apocrypha

The major apocryphal works written about Mary during this early period are The Protoevangelium of James, The Gospel of Pseudo-Matthew, The Gospel of the Nativity of Mary, The Passing of Mary (or The Assumption of Mary), and The Falling Asleep of Mary.[4] Collectively they attest to the miraculous birth of Mary, her perpetual virginity, and her bodily assumption into heaven. While describing her holiness, her miraculous powers of healing, and her power as an intercessor with Christ, they also draw out parallels between her death and that of Christ in a pointed, if not startling, fashion. It is evident, therefore, that "devotion to Mary had made considerable advances" even by the second century and that "attributes reserved in the primitive tradition for Jesus were ascribed also to Mary."[5]

The Protoevangelium of James and Pseudo-Matthew set forth the story of Mary's birth and early life. Mary was the daughter of Anna and Joachim, two pious Jews who were childless until their old age. Her miraculous birth, similar to Isaac's, resulted from an angelic visitation. At the age of three Mary went to live with the virgins at the Temple. Her parents "set [her] down upon the third step of the altar, and the Lord God sent grace upon her; and she danced with her feet, and all the house of Israel loved her."[6] While there she lived as a dove, fed "from the hand of an angel." From her earliest childhood she walked and spoke with maturity and spent her time praising God and weaving. There was

> no one more learned in the wisdom of the law of God, more lowly in humility, more elegant in singing, more perfect in virtue. She

> was indeed stedfast *(sic),* immovable, unchangeable, and daily advancing in perfection. . . . The angels of God were often seen speaking with her, and they most diligently obeyed her. If anyone who was unwell touched her, the same hour he went home cured.[7]

When she reached the age of twelve, the priests decided it was time for her to leave the Temple. Mary had vowed to remain a virgin, so at God's command she was betrothed to Joseph, an elderly widower with children of his own. While she lived in Joseph's house she took on the task of weaving the purple thread for the Temple veil. This was also the time of the Annunciation and the beginning of Mary's pregnancy. During this period Joseph lived apart from her and so was distraught when he discovered her condition. However, after an angel assured him Mary's child was from God, not man, he remained with her and together they faced the trial in the Temple which further attested to the miraculous nature of her pregnancy. On the way to Bethlehem, Mary gave birth in a cave, without pain or bloodshed, and although Joseph brought midwives to assist her, Jesus was born before they arrived. Nevertheless, these two women verified her perpetual virginity: "a virgin has conceived, a virgin has brought forth, and a virgin she remains."[8] After the visit of the Magi, the family fled to Egypt to avoid the wrath of Herod. On the way there, lions and panthers accompanied them and Mary was afraid, until Jesus said, "Be not afraid, mother; for they come not to do thee harm, but they make haste to serve both thee and me."[9] Pseudo-Matthew concludes with stories from the early childhood of Jesus. Among other events, it relates how Mary persuaded her son to restore to life an evil boy Jesus himself had killed.

The death of Mary and her bodily assumption into heaven are described in The Passing of Mary and The Falling Asleep of Mary. Before Christ died, Mary asked her son to receive her soul and to notify her three days before she was to die. Christ honored her request, calling her "O palace and temple of the living God, O blessed mother, O queen of all saints, and blessed above all women."[10] Two years after Christ's ascension, an angel appeared to Mary to announce her impending death. Shortly thereafter John and the other disciples were transported by a cloud to Mary's side. She blessed them and called upon them to watch and pray with her through the night. On the third day, at the third hour, Christ descended and took away Mary's soul, "and as the clouds went up the whole earth shook, and in one moment all the inhabitants of Jerusalem openly saw the departure of St. Mary."[11] Mary's shining body was washed by three virgins and prepared for the tomb. During the procession to the grave "there appeared above the bier a cloud exceeding great, like the great circle which is wont to appear beside the splendour of the moon."[12] Then her "spotless" body was transferred to paradise, where all the saints (Elizabeth, Anna, Abraham, Isaac, Jacob, and David) adored her holy relics. The disciple Thomas was not present at her ascension, but when he saw her rising through the heavens, he asked her for a blessing and she threw him her girdle. Finally Thomas joined the other disciples and revealed to them her empty tomb and her girdle. Both books contain a prayer that the faithful would be worthy to receive her prayers and good offices and to be "under her shelter, and support, and protection" both in this world and the next.[13]

This brief summary of the apocryphal material can hardly do justice to the wealth of imagery and information contained in these books. Among the titles, powers, and attributes ascribed to Mary are the following: Ever-virgin; Queen; Mother of God; Merciful; Holy; Wonder-working; Giver of comfort, support, confidence, shelter, protection, and mercy; Blessed; Steadfast; Immovable; Unchangeable; Glorious; Sweet-smelling; Palace and Temple of the living God; Most Precious Pearl. She is surrounded by light; she is learned in wisdom. She commands the angels and is served by animals and birds. She influences her son and acts as an intermediary between Christ and sinners. Her assumption is "venerated and worshipped,"[14] and her relics are adored by the saints. These are qualities previously associated with goddesses, not mortal women. Some of them echo feminine attributes found in the myths of Demeter and Persephone, or in the aretalogy of Isis, or in the hymns to Sophia. In addition, Mary's virginity, her superb ability as a weaver, and her epiphany the dove, would have reminded the Hellenes of Athena. In the same way the appearance of the moon cloud over her bier would have suggested a kinship between Mary and the great moon goddesses of that day.[15]

Iconography and Hymnology

The artistic and poetic renderings of Mary from this period are somewhat scant. The earliest paintings from the catacombs depict her by herself in the posture of an *orante,* that is, with her arms upraised and the palms of her hands facing outward. The other most common pose is the Virgin seated with the infant Jesus on her lap. Sometimes the picture is informal, showing Jesus nursing at her breast; in others, Christ sits on her lap as though it were a throne. These latter paintings evoke comparisons with the iconography of Isis/Horus, and because of the popularity of Isis during these early centuries it can be assumed that the similarities were intentional. After the declaration of Mary as *Theotokos,* this pose dominated all others in Marian art.[16]

Another popular theme in this period depicted the adoration of the Magi. Usually Mary holds the infant on her lap allowing confusion to arise whether or not Christ alone is adored. Achilles Stubbe believes it is possible to distinguish between the art which venerates Mary as the mother of Jesus and that which was a product of her independent cult. Mary is venerated when she is pictured with her son, but the iconography which illustrates Mary's own life apart from Jesus is the product of her cult.[17] Nevertheless, there is a hidden motif even in the Mary/Jesus pictures which, by association, indicate that Mary is a goddess similar to Isis.

Latin hymnology of this period tells "only the simple narrative of the life of Jesus and contains merely the reflection of the Virgin's praise in its earliest forms."[18] These early hymns emphasize the nativity, crucifixion, and resurrection of Christ in which Mary is almost exclusively portrayed as the Virgin mother. Messenger believes that when asceticism was recognized as the basis of the consecrated life, "the Virgin came into her inheritance of devotion."[19] Saint Ambrose particularly emphasizes her virginal qualities and uses her as a model for all Christians.[20]

In the second century, however, the Virgin Mary is portrayed at least once with more archetypal qualities. The Odes of Solomon, particularly the nineteenth, present her as more independently powerful. This Jewish-Christian hymn tells how the Holy Spirit (described as feminine) took the milk of the Father and gave it to Mary.

> The womb of the Virgin took (it)
> And she received conception and gave birth.
>
> So the Virgin became a mother with great mercies.
>
> And she laboured and bore the Son but without pain,
> Because it did not occur without purpose.
>
> And she did not require a midwife,
> Because He caused her to give life.
>
> She brought forth like a strong man with desire,
> And she bore according to the manifestation,
> And acquired with great power.

And she loved with redemption,
And guarded with kindness,
And declared with grandeur.

Hallelujah![21]

It is apparent that the author is familiar with the apocryphal material because he cites information lacking in the Gospels, for example, that Mary gave birth without pain or midwife. Furthermore, the Ode praises Mary as merciful, protective, and loving not only toward her son but toward all humanity. These are abilities which give Mary redeeming power. This Mary shares certain qualities with Sophia, who was so familiar to Hellenistic Jews.

Theology

There are three Mariological themes that emerge from the theology of the early church fathers: Mary as Virgin; Mary as mother and *Theotokos;* and Mary as co-redemptrix. The term "Virgin" was an honored title applied to Mary from the beginning of Christianity. By the second century this word appeared prominently not only in the Apocryphal tradition but also in the writings of such theologians as Irenaeus, Origen, Athanasius, Ambrose, Cyril of Alexandria, Gregory of Nyssa, and John Chrysostom. In the opinion of most of these authors, Mary was not only a virgin when she conceived, she was a virgin even after she gave birth. "The womb of the Holy Virgin which ministered to an Immaculate Birth, is pronounced blessed in the Gospel, for that birth did not annul the Virginity, nor did the Virginity impede so great a birth."[22] This concept of Mary's perpetual virginity was made dogma at a Lateran Council in 649 C.E., but it had been generally accepted long before that time.[23]

No doubt this emphasis on Mary's perpetual virginity results from a desire to testify to the miraculous nature of Christ's birth. Nevertheless, the picture of Mary that thus evolves is quite similar to that of the great goddesses of the Hellenistic world, who were called Virgin because they were one-in-themselves. It is interesting to observe that in order to preserve her virginity Mary never becomes subject to Joseph in any way, either before or after Christ's birth. Neither is she under the control of her father or any other man.[24] She appears in the Gospels to come and go as she pleases. Even in her relationship with her son, she is remarkably independent. This unusual picture of a young virgin free of parental or connubial control makes Mary quite unique; it conveys the image of a woman of power which could only intensify her veneration. Thus her description as Perpetual Virgin allows archetypal feminine qualities of the goddesses to appear in a humble girl from Jerusalem.

Mary's role as mother is also important to the early church fathers. First, she is regarded as the mother of all Christians. "No one can apprehend the meaning of it except he have lain on Jesus' breast and received from Jesus Mary to be his mother also."[25] This statement refers to Jesus' words from the cross when he says to Mary, "Woman, behold, your son!" and to John, "Behold, your mother!" (John 19:26–27). Origen clearly understands this passage as a testament to the universal motherhood of Mary; however, this aspect of her motherhood is eclipsed when she is designated Mother of God during the Nestorian controversy. As with the title "Virgin," the primary reason for naming Mary *Theotokos* was to glorify Christ. The theological issue concerns the dual nature of Jesus: the fact that he was both God and man from the moment of his incarnation until his death. By the fifth century there were a variety of heresies that denied this article of Christian faith and Mary was called Mother of God to reinforce the orthodox position. Nestorius appealed to the church to find another title for her because he was afraid it would make the Virgin a goddess. Nevertheless, the fathers of the church rejected the alternative *Christotokos,* as well as the title *Anthrotokos,* and declared Mary Mother of God at Ephesus in 431.[26]

Cyril of Alexandria cannot imagine this title will pose any problem for the church:

> We . . . who call her Mother of God, have never at all deified any one of those that are numbered among creatures, . . . and we know that the Blessed Virgin was woman as we.[27]

Although Cyril attests that Mary is Mother of God because she gave birth to God and was the source of Christ's flesh, he does not shy away from calling her "Holy," "all pure Virgin," "augustly crowned." These titles, certainly when taken together, describe a woman who is not "as we." Even Cyril's careful theology cannot restrain the wellspring of Mary's powerful attraction which was so evident to the jubilant crowds at Ephesus.

The third, and most revealing, example of the return of the repressed feminine divine occurs in the designation of Mary as the "new Eve" and the resulting double typology of salvation which emerges in the theology of Justin Martyr and Irenaeus. "Typology . . . is the essential and permanent ingredient in patristic exegesis."[28] Because it has as its basis the relationship of the Old and New Testaments, typology also lies at the heart of the idea of recapitulation which was first expressed by Paul in Rom. 5:12–21:

> Then as one man's trespass led to condemnation for all men, so one man's act of righteousness leads to acquittal and life for all men. For as by one man's disobedience many were made sinners, so by one man's obedience many will be made righteous. (Rom. 5:18–19)

This original theme subsequently expanded in patristic theology to include Adam and Eve and Christ and Mary, or the church.[29]

Justin Martyr makes the analogy clear:

> [Christ] is born of the Virgin, in order that the disobedience caused by the serpent might be destroyed in the same manner in which it had originated. For Eve, an undefiled virgin, conceived the word of the serpent, and brought forth disobedience and death. But the Virgin Mary . . . gave birth to Him . . . by whom God destroys both the serpent and those angels and men who have become like the serpent.[30]

The height of the recapitulation theory of Christ, however, occurs in Irenaeus and it is accompanied by a fully articulated double typology of salvation.

> For as by one man's disobedience sin entered, and death obtained (a place) through sin; so also by the obedience of one man's righteousness having been introduced, shall cause life to fructify in those persons who in times past were dead . . . so did He who is the Word, recapitulating Adam in Himself, rightly receive a birth enabling Him to gather up Adam (into Himself) from Mary who was yet a virgin.[31]

> And thus also it was that the knot of Eve's disobedience was loosed by the obedience of Mary. For what the Virgin Eve had bound fast through unbelief, this did the Virgin Mary set free through faith.[32]

If there is any doubt about Irenaeus' intention, he restates his argument in even stronger terms by placing Mary's contribution first:

> And thus, as the *human race* fell into bondage to death by means of a virgin, so *is* it *rescued by a virgin*, virginal disobedience having been balanced in the opposite scale by virginal obedience. For in the same way the sin of the first created man receives amendment by the correction of the First-begotten.[33]

In these texts, Irenaeus is clearly stating that the human race is saved by *both* Mary and Christ. As humanity fell by the disobedience of Adam and Eve, it is raised through the obedience of Christ and Mary. Obviously this is a striking development in the theory of recapitulation as it proposes Mary as a co-redemptrix with Christ. This role, which is suggested in the Nineteenth Ode, places Mary in the company of goddesses who, wandering the earth, reveal the mysteries of the divine, and bring salvation and immortality to humankind. Nowhere does the repressed feminine break through more clearly than in this double typology of salvation.

Conclusion

The preceding analysis has shown that the basic themes of Mariology were established during the first few centuries of the Christian era. They appeared in both popular piety—the Apocrypha, iconography, and hymnology—and in theological speculation. In the main, the purpose of glorifying Mary was to increase the glorification of her son, Jesus Christ. However, despite this lofty motivation, the process yielded an unexpected result: Mary emerged as a powerful figure in her own right with many attributes formerly associated with the Hellenistic goddesses. Clearly this is an example of the return of the repressed feminine which found a weak spot and, by opening another path for itself, came to light without the acquiescence of the ego and without its understanding.[34] Thus when Cyril said Mary was a woman "as we" at the same time that he conferred upon her several titles, he undercut his conscious intention.

Mariology is also an example of the return of the repressed because the archetypal qualities are distorted. Mary is always referred to as a creature, and the attributes assigned to her are one-dimensional. Thus Mary is always good, merciful, and supportive. She has no dark side and is never angry, demanding, or cruel. For these reasons her theology is fraught with conflicting messages and the image that results is confused. She is and is not a goddess or a representative of the feminine dimension of the divine.

Ecclesiology

The Ecclesiology of the early church is similar in many ways to the Mariology which was developed in the same period. In fact, they share so many feminine motifs that it is easy to slip imperceptibly from talking of one to talking of the other. Roman Catholic theologians articulate this phenomenon as follows: "that which is said 'universally' of the Church . . . is said of Mary 'specially' and of the faithful soul 'singularly'—that is to say 'individually.' "[35] Thus, much that will be described in this section has already been discussed previously in the context of Mariology. Nevertheless, Ecclesiology is such an important part of theology that it warrants its own treatment.

There are three important feminine motifs in Ecclesiology: the church as Wisdom, the church as Mother, and the church as the Bride of Christ. The latter two themes are widely acknowledged, but the understanding of the church as Wisdom, particularly as preexistent Wisdom, has not yet received enough recognition.[36]

The figure of the church in The Shepherd of Hermas is one of the first reflections of the church as Wisdom. In this treatise the church is described as established in God's wisdom and providence: it is said that her home is in the east; that she sits on a throne; and that she holds the book of heaven and is its revealer. The church is deeply concerned with Hermas and his entire family, and the whole book revolves around what Hermas must do to live the good life. The Shepherd contains many elaborate parables which must be explained; and the Mandates, which begin with the phrase "he said to me," could just as easily start with "my son." These various motifs and literary devices are similar to those in the Wisdom literature of the Jews and evoke the image of Sophia contained therein. If there is any doubt as to the purpose of the allusions in The Shepherd, it is dispelled by the explanation that the church is elderly "because she was created before all things . . . and for Her sake the world was erected."[37] Not only does this statement clearly identify the church with Sophia, it dramatizes the entire thrust of this second-century manuscript which indicates that the church has taken over the teaching function of Sophia.

Clement of Alexandria affirms the same connection but in an oddly negative way. In discussing the commandment to honor father and mother, he says:

> The Creator of the universe is their Lord and Father; and the mother is not, as some say, the essence from which we sprang, nor, as others teach, the church, but the divine knowledge and wisdom, as Solomon says, when he terms wisdom "the mother of the just," and says that it is desirable for its own sake.[38]

Here Clement affirms the basic paradigm Mother = Wisdom, although he recognizes that it has already begun to shift to Mother = Wisdom = Church.

The concept of the preexistence of the church also appears in the homily ascribed to Clement.

> If we do the will of God our Father, we shall be of the first Church, that is spiritual, that hath been created before the sun and the moon. . . . The male is Christ, the female is the Church. And the Books and the Apostles *plainly declare* that the Church is not of the present, but from the beginning. For she was spiritual, as our Jesus also was.[39]

However, it is Methodius who draws the most telling analogy between Sophia and *Mater Ecclesia.* He describes the church as a mother but also as *"a power by herself, distinct from her children;* whom the prophets . . . have called sometimes Jerusalem, sometimes a bride, sometimes Mount Zion, and sometimes the Temple and Tabernacle of God."[40] This could be an elegant description of Sophia, who, although she enters holy souls to make them friends of God and prophets, remains One in herself (cf. Wisdom 7:27). By calling the church "a power by herself" and describing her as the "Temple and Tabernacle of God," Methodius clearly infers that the church has taken over the role of Sophia, complete with its archetypal qualities.

The second major feminine motif in Ecclesiology is that of Mother. It was first articulated by Paul in Gal. 4:26: "But the Jerusalem above [the church] is free, and she is our mother." But even "independent of Scripture citation . . . the full popular personification was 'in the air' well before the middle of the second century."[41] Furthermore, it is a "commonplace with patristic writers everywhere."[42] There are three characteristics of the church as mother: she is virgin, she is fruitful, and she is sorrowing.[43] One of the first images of the church as virgin occurs in the Odes of Solomon. The Thirty-third Ode portrays her as vying with the Devil for the souls of men in much the same way as Sophia competed with Folly.

> However, the perfect Virgin stood,
> Who was preaching and summoning and saying:
>
> O you sons of men, return,
> And you their daughters, come.
>
> And leave the ways of that Corruptor,
> And approach me.
>
> And I will enter into you,
> And bring you forth from destruction,
> And make you wise in the ways of truth.

Be not corrupted
Nor perish.

Obey me and be saved,
For I am proclaiming unto you the grace of God.

And through me you will be saved and become blessed.
I am your judge;

And they who have put me on shall not be falsely accused,
But they shall possess incorruption in the new world.

My elect ones have walked with me,
And my ways I will make known to them who seek me;
And I will promise them my name.[44]

Although the full imagery of the Virgin Mother is usually associated with Mariology, it also appears in Ecclesiology. At least Clement of Alexandria can declare: "And one alone, too, is the virgin Mother. I like to call her the Church."[45] However, generally, it is the simple term "Mother" that appears as a synonym for the church. For instance, in Tertullian's analysis of the Lord's Prayer, he insists that the word *pater* implies the presence of *mater.* "Nor is even our Mother, the Church, passed by, if, that is, in the Father and the Son is recognized the mother, from whom arises the name both of Father and Son."[46] Methodius is also fond of the concept of the church as Mother. He says that Christ is born in men who have seen the "manifold Wisdom of God." Those who receive the mystery of grace "will be born in knowledge and understanding. Therefore from hence the Church is fitly said to form and beget the male Word in those who are cleansed (in the baptismal font)."[47]

The Shepherd of Hermas uses the image of a Mother Church who is supported by seven additional feminine figures, daughters, who stand for the seven virtues of the Christian life: faith, continence, simplicity, innocence, reverence, knowledge, and love. These are called the powers of the Son of God. However, there are also seven negative feminine figures who stand for the vices. These beautiful women in black seduce some of the Christians who "clothed themselves with their power, and shed the power of the virgins. Therefore they were ejected from the house of God and handed over to the women."[48] Surprisingly, God uses these same women to punish the sinners, either by killing them or by devising evil against them. These women in black seem to have an affinity with the figure of Folly encountered in Proverbs and, thus, may be remnants of the negative hypostasis of the feminine divine which is part of the Jewish tradition.

The Motherhood of the Church implies fruitfulness, i.e., she gives birth to Christians. However, she also mourns over her children who are killed in the persecutions, as well as over those lost to schism, heresy, and apostasy.[49] Both these themes are used by Cyprian in his essay "On the Dress of Virgins." In discussing virgins, he says:

> The glorious fruitfulness of Mother Church rejoices by their means, and in them abundantly flourishes; and in proportion as a copious virginity is added to her number, so much the more it increases the joy of the Mother.[50]

On the other hand, when virgins go astray the church "groans" and "mourns."[51]

The final image, the church as Bride, likewise appears first in Paul. In II Cor. 11:2: "For I betrothed you [the church of Corinth] . . . as a pure bride to her one husband [Christ]." And in Eph. 5:31–32: " 'For this reason a man shall leave his father and mother and be joined to his wife, and the two shall become one.' This is a great mystery, and I take it to mean Christ and the church." These statements establish the protocol of calling the church Bride. This image becomes increasingly popular as the result of its further elaboration in allegorical interpretations of the Song of Songs, such as the one by Origen.[52] These same passages also form the basis for a typology that calls the church the New Eve. This aspect of Ecclesiology is identical to the Marian typology which has already been discussed.

These three major feminine themes in Ecclesiology are supported by secondary images previously encountered in the analysis of the goddesses and Sophia. Thus the church is frequently compared to objects in nature such as a garden, earth, vine, fountain, tree of paradise, or dove. At other times the symbolism evokes architectural figures such as a tower, house, sanctuary, gate, fortress, tabernacle, or ark. Furthermore, she can be described as light, or in terms of royal authority complete with throne, crown, and scepter.

The three images of the church as Wisdom, Mother, and Bride, in addition to the lesser archetypal symbols, indicate that the repressed feminine divine has returned in the figure of the church in early Christian theology. For instance, her role as Wisdom clearly shows that the church has taken over many of the functions as well as the attributes ascribed to Sophia at the height of her power. Perhaps the most significant function is that of the teacher who trains, punishes, and chastises those who would reap her rewards. Because this divine prerogative now belongs to the church, enormous power is now conveyed to its magisterium. Even the church as Mother evokes the image of goddesses, such as Demeter and Isis, who were also virginal, fruitful, and sorrowing.

Nevertheless, at the same time as these divine images were applied to *Mater Ecclesia,* the fathers also described the church as earthly, as a creature. Origen reminds his readers of this even in the midst of his commentary on the Song of Songs when he says the "Church is we ourselves."[53] This understanding leads to a split image of the church which Origen calls Mother/daughter. The preexistent and heavenly church is Mother; the earthly church, which has no archetypal power, is the daughter.[54] This double image is, at best, confusing. It is somewhat similar to Philo's treatment of Sophia which has already been discussed as an example of repression. In Ecclesiology, however, the distortions of the feminine are more likely to be examples of the return of the repressed. Not only is this evident in the creatureliness of the church, but also in her totally benign and one-dimensional character.

Thus Ecclesiology and Mariology are both examples of the return of the repressed. While both theological motifs are preeminently feminine and contain imagery, attributes, and powers normally associated with the goddesses of that day, these characteristics are isolated and disconnected from the full spectrum of qualities previously associated with the feminine dimension of the divine. Furthermore, the doctrines in which they appear are separated from the mainstream of theological speculation, particularly in the Protestant tradition. Although some aspects of the feminine divine eluded the initial repression of the first century C.E., these qualities have been distorted and remain conscious only in a disguised or spurious way.

Christology

Repression of the feminine dimension of the divine in the early church seems to be based on what I have come to call Philo's law of preeminence: "Pre-eminence always pertains to the masculine, and the feminine always comes short of and is lesser than it."[55] In other words, anything feminine cannot be divine and anything divine must be masculine. This symbolic misogynism creates difficulties for those who are forced to discuss motifs that had been or could have been traditionally thought of as both feminine *and* divine. Early Christians, however, seem to have solved this problem either by relegating that feminine figure to the status of a creature, e.g., Mary and the church; or by changing its sex, e.g., turning Sophia into

Christ/Logos. Regardless of method, the return of the repressed material can be expected in disguised and troublesome forms. This appears to be one of the roots of the Christological disputes of the third and fourth centuries.

In the main, the Christology of the early church continued to develop along lines previously established by the New Testament authors. Sophiology was an important component of Biblical Christology in that qualities of Sophia were ascribed to Jesus. Matthew and Paul did this directly. In John the attributes of Sophia were assigned to the Logos, who was then identified as Jesus. In either case, the end result was the same: the male figure Jesus assumed the power of Sophia, while Sophia, a female God-figure, disappeared.

This process is sustained and reinforced by the church fathers and, as a result, the place of Wisdom in early Christianity is of more consequence than has "hitherto been recognized" and its "significance goes far beyond the first few centuries."[56] In Christological speculation the significance of Wisdom is both positive and negative. In their eagerness to describe Jesus as the incarnation of Sophia,[57] the early Christians overlooked the fact that in Jewish scripture Sophia had been officially subordinated to Yahweh. The development of a transcendent and preexistent Sophia created problems in Judaism which were solved in such a way as to preserve strict monotheism. The Jews restricted Sophia by describing her as the firstborn of creation. She was not regarded as co-equal with Yahweh, nor was she truly co-creator with him. Therefore, when the early Christians began to call Jesus the Wisdom of God, they inadvertently placed the Son in the same position vis-à-vis the Father that Sophia had occupied with Yahweh. In other words, since Jesus and Sophia were equivalent and since Sophia was less than God, therefore Jesus was less than God. The ramifications of this equivalence eventually acted as a brake against the development of a complete trinitarianism.

Grillmeier pinpoints the problem quite accurately:

> It becomes clear in [The Shepherd of Hermas] that an absolutely closed Judaistic monotheism *necessarily* brings adoptionism in its train. We have reached the point where church teaching had to develop trinitarian and Christological dogma side by side if it was to maintain the divine Sonship of Christ *in the true sense.* This connection first became clear in the third century, and at the same time the difficulties which accompany it are revealed.[58]

The major difficulty was subordinationism, which included adoptionism among its various manifestations, and it appears that a major source of these ultimately heretical views can be traced to the very equation of Jesus and Sophia.[59] Certainly Sophiology became an undertow, dragging Christ away from any true equivalence with God Father. Thus, what promised to be such a fruitful addition to Christological thinking proved to be disastrous. In fact, the danger of misunderstanding the relationship between Father and Son seemed to increase the more Sophiology was used as a basis for Christology. Had Sophia been recognized in Jewish writings as co-equal with Yahweh, the opposite would have been true: then the identification of Christ with Sophia would have reduced the tendencies toward subordinationism. Since this was not the case, the early church fathers eventually had to redefine their Christology by abandoning all reference to Jesus as the incarnate Wisdom of God. This redefinition amounts to a second repression of Sophia. The feminine dimension of the divine was initially repressed by ascribing her attributes to Jesus. During the second and third centuries, Wisdom returned as a more overt component of Christology until it became apparent that her status was a severe handicap to the development of a trinitarian Christianity. At this point Sophia was re-repressed in orthodox circles and disappeared from the Western theological tradition.

The custom of identifying Christ and Wisdom, which began with the New Testament authors, was intensified during the early patristic period. It appears first among Jewish Christians, or Christians trying to convert Jews, who believed their task was to awaken faith in Jesus as the Christ. Both The Shepherd of Hermas and Justin Martyr's *Dialogue with Trypho* identify Jesus with Sophia. The Shepherd does this indirectly through the use of analogy. In the Eighth Parable, Christ is identified with the law.

> This tree that covers plain and mountain and the whole earth is the law of God, given to the whole world. This law is the Son of God proclaimed to the ends of the earth. The persons under its shelter are the persons who have heard the proclamation and believed in Him.[60]

To Jews the law is identified with Sophia, but here the law is Christ, the Son of God. In the Fifth Parable, The Shepherd identifies Christ with "the holy, pre-existent Spirit, that created every creature" which God made to dwell in the flesh.[61] This spirit

> is regarded not as a divine person, but as a divine power, in some way analogous to the Biblical *Sophia.* . . . The "Son of God" in Sim, V, 5 emerges as the servant chosen by God, in whom the spirit of God has dwelt and who because of his faithfulness is permitted to share in the privileges of the divine spirit.[62]

But, as Grillmeier recognizes, there is a danger in this analogy because it leads to Christologies of "indwelling" and "merit" which are later "used as labels to denote heresy."[63] This is the first glimmer of the problems that will arise from the identification of Christ and Wisdom.

Justin Martyr is more specific in his comparisons than the author of The Shepherd of Hermas and clearly identifies Jesus with Sophia. "But this Offspring, who was truly begotten of the Father, . . . this Son, who is called Wisdom by Solomon, was begotten as a beginning before all His works, and as His Offspring."[64] In another place, as well, Justin declares that in the words of the prophets Jesus "is called Wisdom."[65] Both these statements indicate that "the incarnation is merely the conclusion in an immense series of manifestations of the Logos which had their beginning in the creation of the world."[66] Of course, this ultimately subverts the understanding of Christ as unique and different from the prophets and holy souls into which Sophia entered in every generation (cf. Wisdom of Solomon 7:27).

The similarities between Christ and Wisdom are continued most emphatically by the great Alexandrians, Clement and Origen.[67] For Clement, Christ appears in the role of teacher, a role commonly ascribed to Wisdom in the Jewish writings. For example, in *The Stromata,* Christ, the first-begotten, "is called Wisdom by all the prophets. This is He who is the Teacher of all created beings, the Fellow-counselor of God who foreknows all things; and He . . . trains and perfects."[68] At the same time, Clement also specifically refers to the power of Christ to reveal the mysteries, the "things of old . . . the things to come . . . signs and wonders . . . the issues of seasons and times" (Wisdom of Solomon 8:8). This power had formerly belonged to Wisdom, but Clement confers it on Christ because Christ is Wisdom.

> If, then, we assert that Christ Himself is Wisdom, and that it was His working which showed itself in the prophets by which the gnostic tradition may be learned, as He Himself taught the apostles during His presence; then it follows that the *gnosis,* which is the knowledge and apprehension of things present, future and past, and which is sure and reliable, as being imparted and revealed by the Son of God, is Wisdom.[69]

Here Christ is identified as the bringer and revealer of a Christian *gnōsis* which draws on the role and power of Sophia for its authenticity.

Although the feminine nature of Sophia is generally ignored by the early church fathers, Clement does recognize it, at least tangentially, by acknowledging that if Christ is Wisdom he is androgynous. This is dramatized in a charming manner in the Hymn to the Instructor which comes at the end of *The Paedagogue.* Here, Christ is endowed with breasts from which flow milk, the gift of Wisdom.

> Milk of the bride,
> Given of heaven,
> Pressed from sweet breasts—
> Gifts of Thy Wisdom—
> These Thy little ones
> Draw for their nourishment;
> With infancy lips
> Filling their soul
> With spiritual savor
> From breasts of the Word.[70]

Thus it can be seen that both Justin and Clement drew from the personification of Wisdom in Judaism certain qualities which enhanced the position of Jesus. Justin did this in the *Dialogue with Trypho,* the Jew, in order to show that Jesus Christ was the incarnation of the Wisdom of God, who was with God before creation. On the other hand, Clement borrowed from Sophia in order to set forth a superior Christian *gnōsis* as compared with the teachings of the heretical Gnostics. Thus, for Clement, Christ is divine reason and "essentially the teacher of the world and lawgiver of mankind."[71] The motives of both men were undoubtedly laudatory. But in identifying Jesus and Sophia they were probably unaware of the full consequences of their analogy.

The most complete identification of these two figures occurs in the writings of Origen. In his systematic treatment of theology, *First Principles,* he devotes the second chapter to Christology. Throughout this analysis Christ is repeatedly referred to as Wisdom; this is carried to the extent that that word appears to be a surrogate for the word Christ. Origen begins by ascertaining that the only-begotten Son of God is (1) "Wisdom, according to the expression of Solomon"; (2) "First-born . . . not by nature a different person from the Wisdom, but one and the same"; and (3) "The power of God and the wisdom of God," according to Saint Paul. Origen takes the position that Christ, the "Son of God is His wisdom hypostatically existing." In summary, Origen says the following:

> Whatever, therefore, we have predicated of the wisdom of God, will be appropriately applied and understood of the Son of God, in virtue of His being the Life, and the Word, and the Truth, and the Resurrection: for all these titles are derived from His power and operations.[72]

Origen bases his theology on the authority of Holy Scripture and he places both Saint Paul and The Wisdom of Solomon in that category. Therefore, he can describe Christ as the image of the invisible God and the true light. Quoting The Wisdom of Solomon he calls Wisdom/Christ the breath of the power of God, the purest efflux of the glory of God, the spotless mirror of the working of God, and the image of God's goodness. In every case Wisdom is a synonym for Christ.

Origen's heavy reliance on Sophiology, directly and indirectly, produces a Christology which clearly contains subordinate tendencies. Thus, it is finally possible to detect both the positive and negative ramifications of the Christ/Wisdom equivalence. Origen is accused of being a subordinationist because he openly used the attribute "the first born of creation" to describe Christ. He also makes statements that apparently understand Christ as an intermediary between God and humans. "We worship . . . the one God and His only Son, . . . and we offer our petition to the God of the universe *through* His only-begotten Son. . . . Our faith is directed to God *through* His Son, who strengthens it in us."[73] Indirectly and perhaps unconsciously, Origen has the Son appear subordinate to the Father. Hellenistic Christians and Jews familiar with the full text of The Wisdom of Solomon would know that Wisdom was subordinate to Yahweh. Thus, Origen's dependency on Sophiology confuses his Christology enough at least to give support to the subordinationists and later to the Arians.[74]

The Arian heresy, which was the apotheosis of all the subordinationist heresies, divided the church for over sixty years.[75] It stubbornly survived the Council of Nicea in 325 C.E. which had been called to settle the issue of the relationship of Christ to God Father. It was not put to rest until Constantinople in 381.[76] Basil, the great Cappadocian, describes the bitterness of the struggle by portraying it as a fratricidal battle which was destroying the church.[77] Certainly, the polemic in the *Four Discourses Against the Arians* by Athanasius underscores Basil's comments.

The fundamental basis of all Arianism is the belief that Christ is a creature and as such had a beginning. In other words, there was a time when the Son was not. As J. N. D. Kelly indicates, the issue was not the unity of the Godhead but "the Son's co-eternity with the Father, which the Arians denied, His full divinity in contrast to the creaturely status they ascribed to Him."[78] The Arians took support from Scripture, specifically from passages such as Rom. 8:29, where Christ is referred to as the firstborn among many; and from Col. 1:15, in which Christ is said to be "the image of the invisible God, the first-born of all creation." However, perhaps the most pivotal text came from Prov. 8:22: "The Lord created me at the beginning of his work, the first of his acts of old." Athanasius devotes almost all of his second discourse to a discussion of this text and a refutation of the Arian interpretation of it. With the exception of the last passage, these citations are descriptions of Jesus taken from the New Testament; however, it should be noted that *all* of them were originally descriptions of Sophia uttered by herself which were then later applied to Christ. Thus, in many ways, it is possible to characterize the Arian controversies as Sophia's revenge. The theft of her attributes, powers, and functions now contaminated Christology by casting Jesus in the same relationship with God the Father that she had been confined to by the scrupulous monotheism of the Jews.

There is no question that the Arians made a significant contribution to the development of the Christological and trinitarian dogmas of the orthodox church by bringing to consciousness this hidden, negative dimension of the Christ/Wisdom analogy. The confrontation forced the fathers to clarify their understanding of the relationship between Christ and God Father, and to define in new language what Paul meant by his statement in First Corinthians that Christ is "the wisdom of God." Thus, for instance, although Athanasius continues to call Christ Wisdom in his second discourse against the Arians, he never mentions The Wisdom of Solomon or any other text related to Sophia. The implication is that Christ is called Wisdom because he is God. What is rejected is that Christ is (or is not) God because he is Sophia.

This second repression of Sophia brings to an end the effort to see Wisdom as God beside God. In the early stages of Christianity Jesus gained stature by being identified with Sophia and by taking over her attributes and powers. But because she had never really achieved the official status of a goddess in Judaism, this identification finally became a deterrent to the full development of *homoousios.* The Arian controversy brought the problem into the open and it was apparently solved by (1) rejecting the earlier identification of Sophia and Christ; (2) rejecting the hypostatic status of Sophia and relocating her powers and attributes in God Father; and (3) then identifying Christ with God Father. Because Christ is God and God is Wisdom, Christ can once again be called Wisdom without fearing any contamination from Sophiology. What was lost in this process was direct access to the feminine dimension of God which had struggled so long for recognition in the guise of Sophia. Naturally, there will always be a trace of Sophiology in Christology; the New Testament and the writings of the Ante-Nicene fathers would assure it. However, after this early period it remains as nothing more than an elusive and haunting factor in the subsequent development of Christian doctrine.

CHAPTER 7

Conclusion

> Today, the goddess is no longer worshipped. Her shrines are lost in the dust of ages while her statues line the walls of museums. But the law or power of which she was but the personification is unabated in its strength and life-giving potency.[1]

The patterns for the repression of the feminine dimension of the divine in the Christian tradition were set in the first five centuries of the Christian era. So also were the patterns for the return of the repressed. Since that time there have been few changes or variations on these original themes. Philo's assertion of masculine preeminence has been accepted by most philosophers and theologians in the Western tradition. To be sure, the doctrines concerning Mary, the Church, and Christ were elaborated and refined, but their basic elements remained intact; the fragments and distortions of the feminine divine continued to be unrecognized. However, something has happened in the last ten or twenty years to alter human consciousness. It is now possible to detect the patriarchal nature of the Christian tradition in a way that would have been literally unthinkable before.

This new awareness probably has its own roots in the eighteenth or nineteenth century in such disparate philosophers as Nietzsche and Feuerbach.[2] However, the full impact of the absence of the feminine in Western religion did not emerge until after the promulgation of the Dogma of the Assumption of the Virgin Mary in 1950 and the beginnings of the feminist movement in the 1960s. The result is not so much a raising *of* consciousness as a raising *into* consciousness of material that previously had been repressed. Why this has happened now is probably as unanswerable a question as why the feminine was repressed in the first place. It may very well be, as psychotherapists suggest, that both are the result of psychic necessity. If that is true, there is little point in either congratulating ourselves for our current insight or in blaming those in the past for their repressive attitudes. What does seem necessary is to explore and evaluate the new gestalt which now seems to be emerging.

This new consciousness is not yet completely clear. It already enables us, however, to recognize that certain presumed philosophical truths or givens concerning the nature of woman and/or the feminine are neither true nor given. Thus, the symbolic misogynism which has dominated Western religion and philosophy for two thousand years is recognizable as a product of patriarchal bias and not as a scientific "fact." For similar reasons, the virtues of man *qua* man are no longer regarded as the quintessence of human development from which the female is basically excluded. Most important, the feminine ground which the masculine overshadowed is now becoming evident. For many centuries the male aspect was dominant in Western thinking to the point that the female was virtually unnoticed. Literally and figuratively she was background; she was the darkness. Now, however, the focus has shifted so that attention has begun to fall on the shadow and the boundary between what was thought to be light, clear, positive, and masculine and what was thought to be dark, mysterious, negative, and feminine. To date, this new noticeability of the feminine is the most significant result of the emerging gestalt. This awareness has made it possible to observe that the feminine dimension of the divine was repressed and accordingly had to return in distorted ways. Until now such an analysis would have been unimaginable, even though the data has been present for more than fifteen hundred years.

Despite these new insights regarding the feminine, I believe even greater changes lie before us. Our present awareness is focused more on observing an old pattern and watching it dissolve than on recognizing or forming a new pattern. As a result, it is extremely difficult to predict with any degree of accuracy what theology will be in the future. When the new picture does emerge, it will probably incorporate the various elements in a totally different way: what was at the boundary will become an integral part of the new configuration. Yet until that happens, I believe that everyone is limited by the interregnum which comes between the breakup of one pattern and the emergence of another. Women are no more exempt from the tensions and anxieties created by this situation than men, although they are probably more highly motivated to anticipate the beneficial aspects of a change in the relationship between what has always been regarded as masculine and feminine.

Bearing in mind these limitations, I would still anticipate that there are at least five areas in systematic and practical theology which will be affected by any future shift in theological symbolism. These are the areas which either presently contain elements of the repressed feminine or those which prior to the dominance of Christianity were overtly feminine.

Two aspects of systematic theology which I imagine will be most affected by the emerging consciousness are trinitarian speculation, and the question of the origin and nature of evil. Theologians generally confine their study of the essential development of the doctrine of the trinity to the early centuries of the Christian era. As argued above, however, it is apparent that there is an important relationship between Sophia in Judaism and Jesus in Christianity. Therefore, it might be more proper to begin any analysis of the trinity with a discussion of the appearance of the tensions that beset Jewish monotheism in the fourth to the first centuries B.C.E. The most important question may be, How is monotheism to be given image? In other words, does belief in One God require belief in only one image of God? In Judaism, traditionally that answer has virtually always been yes, and that one image has virtually always been male. The first threat to that understanding came from within Judaism itself in the form of Sophia, a female God-figure, who was described as teacher, savior, and judge. At the turn of the age, she was subsumed in both Judaism and Christianity by a male figure, the Logos or Jesus Christ. However, this transformation did not settle the question of the monotheistic image. On the contrary, it split the protagonists into two camps. For the most part, those who yearned for multiple images of One God, or what I would call *inclusive* monotheism, became Christians. Those who preferred one image of the One God, or *exclusive* monotheism, remained Jews or later turned to Islam. Thus, the doctrine of the trinity ultimately owes a great deal to the original desire of human beings to image God as both male and female. Unfortunately, this desire could not be fulfilled in an overt way at that time, although it did survive in distorted forms in the image of Christ/Sophia. Now, however, it may be possible to rectify that omission and allow the feminine dimension of God to come to expression.

The role of Sophia in the development of the Christian trinity is important for a retrospective understanding of the origins and final expression of that important doctrine. It cannot in itself, however, supply an answer for any future theology which may want to allow for clear and ready access to the feminine divine. As that situation develops, the feminine image of God might be expressed in one of three different ways. First, it might be possible to describe one member of the trinity as feminine. Because the Holy Spirit is the least sexually defined member of the trinity, and because it is often symbolized by feminine images—by fire and the dove—I imagine that the Spirit would be chosen.

A second solution might be possible: the feminine aspect of all three members of the trinity could be developed. For instance, since Sophiology plays a large part in Christology, that element could be made explicit. In an age that has begun to recognize the androgynous nature of all human beings, this alternative way of disclosing the feminine nature of the divine is less bizarre than it sounds. Furthermore, there are some early precedents for it in the theology of Clement of Alexandria and in the Odes of Solomon.

A final choice, and the most radical, would be the addition of a feminine image of God and the creation of a quaternity. Jung raises this possibility in his analysis of the promulgation of the Dogma of the Assumption of Mary.[3] Since this would entail recognizing the Virgin Mary as a divine figure, I imagine it would be strenuously opposed by most Protestants who have clearly excised her from their own tradition.

Of course, it is possible that none of these choices will be found viable. I do foresee, nevertheless, that some approach will be found which will assist us in lifting the repression of the feminine, and permit the development of a feminine image of God. The center of that storm will probably be the doctrine of the trinity and the definition of monotheism just as it was in the early centuries of the Christian era.

The second area of systematic theology which will probably be affected by any recognition of the feminine dimension of the divine is the question of evil. It has been shown that prior to the Christian era, the character of the great goddesses of the Hellenistic age was distinctly inclusive. Among the dualities they combined were love and rage, law and chaos, light and dark, youth and age, openness and hiddenness, rootedness and wandering, earth(iness) and spirit(uality). Thus, while they were described as awesome, majestic, and caring, they were also characterized as wrathful, unyielding, and vindictive. They were, in fact, a combination of Sophia and Folly. Because these dualities are a hallmark of the goddess, similar dualities are likely to emerge in any new representation of the feminine in the Christian trinity. Unfortunately, half of the dualities that are indicative of the feminine divine are not presently regarded as qualities of God. On the contrary, rage, chaos, darkness, and earthiness are usually identified as properties of Satan. Thus it can be anticipated that the appearance of a feminine aspect of God will necessitate a new analysis of the problem of evil—what it is and who is responsible. Clearly, this would be a move away from the form of theological dualism in which God and the devil vie for the human soul. Moreover, this more inclusive awareness of the divine character is likely to lead Christians to experience God as more mysterious and enigmatic than had previously been thought.

The deep symbolic connection between the feminine and evil cannot be avoided; although they are not identical, they do seem inseparable. This is even suggested by Jung himself in his analysis of the quaternity. He begins his discussion by referring to the Assumption, but in the next sentence he moves to his main point, the problem of evil:

> The *Assumptio Mariae* paves the way not only for the divinity of the Theotokos (i.e., her ultimate recognition as a goddess), but also the quaternity. At the same time, matter is included in the metaphysical realm, together with the corrupting principle of the cosmos, evil.[4]

This second sentence sets the tone for the rest of his essay which concerns the need to recognize the fourth member of the quaternity, the devil, as part of the divine image. As far as I know, Jung never indicates that Mary and the devil are synonymous; nevertheless, in his thinking they have something in common. This same connection will probably arise for theologians who are willing to discuss the feminine dimension of the divine. Those courageous enough to struggle with this problem can find comfort from Biblical precedents which imply that the One God is the source of both good *and* evil. These can be discovered in the descriptions of God's Spirit in the Old Testament. "If the Old Testament has taken the power out of all cosmic and earthly dominions and powers, it has anchored the demonic firmly in the Almighty power, that is to say in the Spirit of God . . . [which] can become active as an evil spirit."[5] This ancient insight can encourage those who hesitate to open what appears to be another Pandora's box. Whatever the final theological resolution, access to the feminine dimension of the divine and the accompanying negative aspects of God's power should stimulate a new sense of awe for the Holy One who cannot be predicted or confined by human standards of morality.

There are several additional theological themes that could be affected by a recognition of the feminine dimension of the divine. Most of them fall in less formal areas of theology. Some have already been suggested by other scholars; many have already become emotionally charged; and all of them need further study before they can be resolved.

First, Catholic attitudes concerning Mary and the church can be expected to change once they no longer have to carry the burden of the repressed feminine. Doctrinally, these theological motifs may still retain certain archetypal elements; however, when a feminine image of God is openly acknowledged, these same motifs may not attract the fervor of devotion which Protestants have always found so distasteful. At the same time, open access to a female God-figure should help Protestants overcome their outspoken antipathy to *any* expression of the feminine aspects of the divine, which is an attitude Catholics find so puzzling. A moderation of both the Catholic and the Protestant positions regarding Mariology and Ecclesiology could only facilitate the movement toward church unity which presently seems snagged on the interpretation of these two theological issues.

Second, the recognition and elaboration of a feminine image of God should affect the image of real women reflected in Christian anthropology. Such an explication would act as an antidote to the notions of masculine preeminence. Furthermore it could give women a sense of dignity previously unknown and provide support for their requests for ordination and full participation in the priesthood. In addition, an image of God with both masculine and feminine dimensions would dramatize the *intra*sexual harmony of the divine which human beings could emulate in their own *inter*personal relationships.

Third, recognition of a female God-image should expand our awareness of the majesty and mystery of God. Our prior dependency on a relatively narrow image of the divine as male, particularly as male parent, may have stifled our faith and limited our experience of God. At worst it may have become a form of idolatry created by mature men who have made God in their image. When the *ikon* of God as father is replaced by a multiplicity of images, including the feminine, Christianity may undergo a rebirth which might expand, rather than diminish, its appeal.

Taken together, these conclusions point out our prior dependence on a masculine understanding of God and indicate the growing recognition of the feminine background which is only now emerging from the obscurity into which it was placed by our preoccupation with the masculine. Finally, they demonstrate that recognition of the feminine dimension of the divine will have wide significance for our faith. It will affect our understanding of the trinity and the doctrine of evil as well as certain practical and pragmatic expressions of the Christian religion in ways we cannot yet fully anticipate.

Notes

Chapter 1. THE ARCHETYPE

1. Erich Neumann, *The Great Mother: An Analysis of the Archetype*, trans. Ralph Manheim (Pantheon Books, 1955), p. 93.

2. Carl Gustav Jung, *Collected Works*, ed. Herbert Read and others, trans. R. F. C. Hull (Pantheon Books; Princeton University Press, 1966–), 7:65. All further references to Jung's *Collected Works* consist of volume number, part number where applicable, and page number.

3. Jung, 11:15.

4. Jung, 9, 1:43.

5. Jung, 7:64–65.

6. Freud also recognized these same motifs. Cf. Sigmund Freud, "The Interpretation of Dreams," in *The Standard Edition of the Complete Psychological Works of Sigmund Freud*, translated under the editorship of James Strachey in collaboration with Anna Freud, assisted by Alix Strachey and Alan Tyson, Vols. 4 and 5; hereafter cited as *Psychological Works* with volume and page.

7. Jung, 11:50.

8. Neumann, *The Great Mother*, p. 13.

9. Jung, 11:103–104.

10. Jung, 9, 1:183.

11. Jung, 9, 1:38.

12. Jung, 9, 1:48. For this reason Jung says, "It is no use at all to learn a list of archetypes by heart" (Jung, 9, 1:30).

13. Jung, 9, 1:38.

14. Antonio Moreno, *Jung, Gods, and Modern Man* (University of Notre Dame Press, 1970), p. 8.

15. Jung, 9, 1:93.

16. Jung, 9, 1:23.

17. Jung, 9, 1:8.

18. Neumann, *The Great Mother,* p. 10. Erich Neumann puts the case strongly when he stresses the fact that archetypes determine human behavior "unconscious" (*ibid.,* p. 4).

19. Jung, 9, 1:93.

20. Neumann, *The Great Mother,* p. 8. See full discussion in Chapter 2.

21. Jung, 9, 1:38.

22. Jung, 9, 1:12–13.

23. Neumann, *The Great Mother,* p. 3.

Chapter 2. The Feminine Archetypes

1. Mary Esther Harding, *Woman's Mysteries, Ancient and Modern: A Psychological Interpretation of the Feminine Principle as Portrayed in Myth, Story and Dreams* (G. P. Putnam's Sons, 1972), p. 96.

2. See Jung's comments in his essays "Psychological Aspects of the Mother Archetype" (9, 1:75–110), "The Psychological Aspects of the Kore" (9, 1:185–203), and "Women in Europe" (10:113–133).

3. Jung, 9, 1:203.

4. Of course, Esther Harding is a woman and there are some differences between her work and that of Jung and Neumann, but basically she does not challenge their insights. The first post-feminist critiques have been made by Ann Belford Ulanov and Naomi Ruth Goldenberg, but the great popularity of Adrienne Rich's *Of Woman Born* (1976) and Nancy Friday's *My Mother/My Self* (1977) indicate that the time may be ripe for even more detailed analysis of the feminine archetypes. Such a study will probably require a more careful differentiation of these archetypes than men have thought necessary or possible. For example, is there a female hero, or hera, archetype which can be distinguished from either mother or maid? Furthermore, since the *anima* is part of the male psyche, women may wish to forgo analyzing this archetype in favor of exploring the *animus,* which is the male counterpart in the female psyche. Certainly there is a need to go beyond what has already been done and to expand our understanding of these archetypes. My own insights in this area have emerged somewhat along the lines Jung anticipated and are reflected in my analysis. However, it should be noted that I am approaching the archetypes as a theologian, not as a psychotherapist.

5. Esther Harding, on the other hand, gives more attention to the *mater,* or elemental mother.

6. Jung, 9, 1:83.

7. Jung, 9, 1:81–82.

8. Jung, 9, 1:82.

9. Neumann, *The Great Mother,* p. 25. It is easy to see why he prefers the mode of the *anima;* he appears hostile to and afraid of the great mother as *mater.*

10. *Ibid.*, p. 33.
11. Erich Neumann, *Amor and Psyche: The Psychic Development of the Feminine: A Commentary on the Tale by Apuleius,* trans. Ralph Manheim (Pantheon Books, 1956), p. 116.
12. Neumann, *The Great Mother,* p. 79.
13. See chart, Neumann, *The Great Mother,* p. 82.
14. *Ibid.*, pp. 39, 42.
15. *Ibid.*, p. 31.
16. *Ibid.*, p. 59; italics added.
17. *Ibid.*, pp. 291–292.
18. *Ibid.*, p. 55.
19. *Ibid.*, p. 47.
20. *Ibid.*, p. 285.
21. *Ibid.*, p. 59.
22. Harding, *Woman's Mysteries,* p. 46. See also Sir James George Frazer, *The Golden Bough: A Study in Magic and Religion,* 3d ed. (Macmillan Co., 1935), Vols. 5 and 6, for discussion of Osiris and Attis and the significance of trees in rituals connected with the goddesses.
23. Harding, *Woman's Mysteries,* p. 49.
24. The complex nature of these animal figures is seen in an interpretation of the serpent image. There is a close association between serpents and the moon. Both have the power of self-renewal: the snake through its ability to shed its skin, and the moon through its ability to disappear and reappear each month. Furthermore, both are associated with the underworld. As Mary Esther Harding says in *Woman's Mysteries:* "Snakes live in dark holes and go down through cracks in the earth. . . . For these reasons they have always been considered to be related to the underworld and to the shades of the dead. In its dark phase the moon, also, has to do with the underworld and with chthonic powers, and in this aspect the divinities of the moon can appear . . . in the form of snakes" (p. 53).
25. *Ibid.*, p. 189.
26. Exceptions are found in Japan and Egypt, where the goddess is connected with the sun, e.g., Isis.
27. Harding, *Woman's Mysteries,* p. 106.
28. The term "hera" is used to designate the female hero and should not be confused with the Greek goddess Hera.
29. Neumann, *The Great Mother,* p. 50.

Chapter 3. The Repression of the Feminine

1. Erich Neumann, "Narcissism, Normal Self-Formation and the Primary Relation to the Mother," *Spring* (1966): 100–101.
2. Freud, "Moses and Monotheism," in *Psychological Works,* 23:127.
3. *Ibid.*, pp. 94–95.

4. Jung, 11:75.

5. Freud, "Moses and Monotheism," in *Psychological Works,* 23:185.

6. *Ibid.,* pp. 129–130. This identification of the development of civilization with the development of the male child betrays a deep patriarchal bias that runs through the work of psychotherapists. Once one moves from analyzing male neurosis to analyzing culture as a whole, their comments must be scrutinized with great care. At the very least they pose enormous problems for women regarding their self-understanding and their role in society. Nevertheless, the parallels discovered by these psychotherapists seem most apt. This reflects and dramatizes the observation that culture has been developed by men to suit their own needs and fantasies rather than the needs and fantasies of women. There can be no question that men have controlled society and thus have had the necessary political, economic, and religious power to shape it along their own lines. Of course there have been exceptional women in all these areas, but their power has been transitory when compared to the consistency of the male establishment. See comments by Neumann, *Amor and Psyche,* pp. 130–132.

7. Arthur B. Brenner, "The Great Mother Goddess; Puberty Initiation Rites and the Covenant of Abraham," *Psychoanalytic Review* 37 (October 1950): 325.

8. Neumann, "Narcissism," pp. 100–101. All quotations up to the next citation are from this same source.

9. Freud, "Moses and Monotheism," in *Psychological Works,* 23:133.

10. *Ibid.,* pp. 134–135.

11. Richard L. Rubenstein, *The Religious Imagination: A Study in Psychoanalysis and Jewish Theology* (Bobbs-Merrill Co., 1968), p. 97.

12. Ernest Jones, *Essays in Applied Psycho-Analysis* (London: Hogarth Press, 1951), 2:209.

13. *Ibid.*

14. *Ibid.,* 2:371.

15. *Ibid.,* 2:367.

16. *Ibid.,* 2:366.

17. Erich Fromm, *The Dogma of Christ and Other Essays on Religion, Psychology and Culture* (Holt, Rinehart & Winston, 1963), pp. 90–91.

18. Freud, "Moses and Monotheism," in *Psychological Works,* 23:88.

19. Erik H. Erikson, *Young Man Luther: A Study in Psychoanalysis and History* (W. W. Norton & Co., 1958), p. 263.

20. Rubenstein, *The Religious Imagination,* pp. 97–98.

21. *Ibid.,* p. 93.

22. The treatment of living women in this tradition, and their lack of position in the religious hierarchy, is certainly one aspect of this situation; however, because I am focusing on the symbolic and theological expressions of the feminine, it is not possible for me to discuss it here. Fortunately, there are a number of books that do. *Religion and Sexism,* edited by Rosemary

Ruether, provides an admirable historical introduction to the general problem. See also *Women in Church and Society,* by Georgia Harkness; *Beyond God the Father,* by Mary Daly; and *The Bible and the Role of Women,* by Krister Stendahl.

23. Victor White, *Soul and Psyche: An Enquiry Into the Relationship of Psychotherapy and Religion* (London: Harvill Press, 1960), p. 141.

24. David Bakan, *The Duality of Human Existence: Isolation and Communion in Western Man* (Beacon Press, 1966), p. 90.

25. Jung, 11:465.

26. White, *Soul and Psyche,* pp. 122–123.

Chapter 4. The Hellenistic Goddesses: Demeter and Isis

1. Erikson, *Young Man Luther,* pp. 117–118.

2. Among the numerous sources for this period I have relied most heavily on Eva Matthews Sanford, *The Mediterranean World in Ancient Times* (Ronald Press Co., 1938); Hans Jonas, *The Gnostic Religion: The Message of the Alien God and the Beginnings of Christianity,* 2d ed., rev. (Beacon Press, 1963); Samuel Angus, *The Mystery-Religions and Christianity: A Study in the Religious Background of Early Christianity* (Charles Scribner's Sons, 1925); Francis Legge, *Forerunners and Rivals of Christianity: Being Studies in Religious History from 330* B.C. *to 330* A.D. (Cambridge: University Press, 1915); Frederick C. Grant, *Hellenistic Religions: The Age of Syncretism* (Liberal Arts Press, 1953); M. P. O. Morford and Robert J. Lenardon, *Classical Mythology* (David McKay Co., 1971); Harold Rideout Willoughby, *Pagan Regeneration: A Study of Mystery Initiations in the Graeco-Roman World* (University of Chicago Press, 1929); and two books by Martin Persson Nilsson, *Greek Popular Religion* (Columbia University Press, 1940), and *A History of Greek Religion,* trans. F. J. Fielden, 2d ed. (Oxford: Clarendon Press, 1949). In addition I have consulted Frazer, *The Golden Bough,* and Robert Briffault, *The Mothers: A Study of the Origins of Sentiments and Institutions* (Macmillan Co., 1927). The most helpful introductions to the religions of Demeter and Isis are by George Mylonas, *Eleusis and the Eleusinian Mysteries* (Princeton University Press, 1961), and by Reginald Witt, *Isis in the Graeco-Roman World* (Cornell University Press, 1971). I would like to call attention to several art books that have also been very helpful: Jean Charbonneaux, Roland Martin, and François Villard, *Hellenistic Art (330–50* B.C.),trans. Peter Green (George Braziller, 1973); Kurt Lange and Max Hirmer, *Egypt: Architecture, Sculpture, Painting in Three Thousand Years,* trans. R. H. Boothroyd, 4th ed., rev. and enl. (London: Phaidon Press, 1968); Eberhard Otto, *Egyptian Art and the Cults of Osiris and Amon,* trans. Kate Bosse Griffiths (London: Thames and Hudson, 1968). I would also like to indicate the general usefulness of the series published by Brill in Leiden, *Études préliminaires aux*

religions orientales dans L'Empire Romain.

3. "In calling it 'an Age of Anxiety' I have in mind both its material and its moral insecurity" (E. R. Dodds, *Pagan and Christian in an Age of Anxiety* [W. W. Norton & Co., 1970], p. 3).

4. Jung, 9, 1:5.

5. Willoughby, *Pagan Regeneration,* p. 9. Cf. Legge, *Forerunners and Rivals of Christianity,* p. xxiv.

6. Dodds, *Pagan and Christian in an Age of Anxiety, passim.*

7. Legge, *Forerunners and Rivals of Christianity,* p. 21.

8. Grant, *Hellenistic Religions,* p. xxx.

9. Jonas, *The Gnostic Religion,* p. 21.

10. See John Gwyn Griffiths, "Allegory in Greece and Egypt," *The Journal of Egyptian Archeology* 53 (1967): 79–102. Plutarch used allegory extensively in his commentaries on pagan religious symbolism. Philo did the same in his analysis of Judaism and Jewish scripture. It was also a mainstay of the patristic fathers. This form of allegory was used to facilitate the understanding of more ancient and established texts and should not be confused with more modern allegory—such as that of Jonathan Swift—which was originally written to be understood figuratively. In other words, the Hellenistic theologians did not write allegory; they allegorized the work of earlier authors.

11. Most scholars regard syncretism to be a major feature of the Hellenistic world. Certainly it was actively practiced by Plutarch and others. However, pointing out the "syncretistic" aspects of non-Christian religions seems to have been one of the most favored techniques of Christians who wished to cast aspersions on "pagan" religions while claiming a uniqueness for their own. Because this latter practice seems unnecessarily defensive and since there are ample distinctions between each of the major Hellenistic religions, I would prefer to give this term a rest. Angus has a long discussion of the differences between the various mystery religions (*The Mystery-Religions and Christianity,* pp. 236–247) and says: "We should remember too—what the church fathers sometimes forgot—that the many ancient mysteries cannot be reduced to one common denominator" (p. 236).

12. Legge, *Forerunners and Rivals of Christianity,* pp. 39–40.

13. Mylonas, *Eleusis and the Eleusinian Mysteries,* p. 285.

14. Frederick Grant has collected a number of these friendly sources, particularly those from the Orphic, Isiac, and Mithraic mysteries. Some were written by authors such as Plutarch and Apuleius, others appear as inscriptions on stone. See Grant, *Hellenistic Religions,* pp. 103–149.

15. Angus, *The Mystery-Religions and Christianity,* pp. 80–91.

16. *Ibid.*, pp. 137–143.

17. *Ibid.*, pp. 111–135.

18. *Ibid.*, pp. 121–132.

19. Jane Harrison, *Prolegomena to the Study of Greek Religion,* 3d ed. (Meridian Books, 1960), pp. 150–151.

20. Literal translations of the Homeric hymn are the most accurate. They can be found in Morford and Lenardon, *Classical Mythology*, pp. 199–209; and in Charles Boer's poetic rendering in his book *The Homeric Hymns* (Swallow Press, 1970), pp. 91–135. The version in Edith Hamilton's *Mythology* (Little, Brown & Co., 1942) is also quite good. Robert Graves, however, takes great liberties with this myth. Since variations in the basic story occur in other collections as well, it is preferable to rely on the actual Homeric hymns whenever possible.

21. Morford and Lenardon, *Classical Mythology*, p. 209.

22. A student of mine experimented with barley, water, and mint. The mixture fermented, and within a few days turned into a mild beer. Whether the *kykeon* drunk by the participants in the mysteries was also a beer cannot be known.

23. Morford and Lenardon, *Classical Mythology*, p. 203.

24. *Ibid.*, p. 209.

25. *Ibid.*

26. Eranos-Jahrbuch, *Papers from the Eranos Yearbooks* (Pantheon Books, 1954–), Vol. 2: *The Mysteries*, p. 14. This article is by Walter Friedrich Otto.

27. Persephone also plays a part in the Orphic mysteries. In that tradition she is described as a great queen who brings forth all things and slays all things. Cf. Grant, *Hellenistic Religions*, p. 110.

28. Morford and Lenardon, *Classical Mythology*, p. 207.

29. Nilsson, *Greek Popular Religion*, pp. 57–58.

30. Harrison, *Prolegomena*, p. 136.

31. The most detailed account is contained in Mylonas, *Eleusis and the Eleusinian Mysteries*. Another description can be found in the chapter on Demeter in Morford and Lenardon, *Classical Mythology*, but it is quite dependent on Mylonas.

32. Mylonas, *Eleusis and the Eleusinian Mysteries*, pp. 247–248.

33. Nilsson believes the pig was sacred to Demeter. This animal is often associated with earth-mother goddesses as a symbol of fertility. See Nilsson, *Greek Popular Religion*, p. 49.

34. Mylonas points out that this god is often assumed to be Dionysus, but he can find no evidence to support that assumption. He believes Dionysus was never one of the gods worshiped at Eleusis (p. 238). Mylonas is almost alone in this opinion, as most other commentators believe Dionysus did have a place at the mysteries. Certainly there are similarities between Demeter and Dionysus. They are both pre-Greek in origin, less remote and more closely related to the people than the Olympian gods. Also both are related to fertility and agriculture. However, Dionysus was so important to the Greeks that it does seem likely his connections with the Eleusinian mysteries would have been specifically stated. Since he is not mentioned in the Homeric hymn nor portrayed in the temple art at Eleu-

sis, I am inclined to agree with Mylonas on this point.

35. Mylonas, *Eleusis and the Eleusinian Mysteries,* p. 261.

36. Eranos-Jahrbuch, *Papers,* Vol. 2, p. 29.

37. Mylonas, *Eleusis and the Eleusinian Mysteries,* p. 280. Cf. Erwin Rohde, *Psyche: The Cult of Souls and Belief in Immortality Among the Greeks,* trans. from 8th ed. by W. B. Hillis (Harper & Row, 1966), Vol. 1, p. 228. The mysteries were without moral influence, dogma, or ethics.

38. Eranos-Jahrbuch, *Papers,* Vol. 2, p. 15.

39. *Ibid.*, p. 16. One of the unique aspects of the mysteries is the relationship between mother and daughter. As far as I know, it is the *only* example of this type in religion. Usually, mothers have sons. Jung is very aware of this. He says "the Demeter-Kore myth is far too feminine to have been the result of an anima-projection. . . . In fact, the psychology of the Demeter cult bears all the features of a matriarchal order of society, where the man is an indispensable but on the whole disturbing factor" (Jung, 9, 1:203). Certainly the myth is saturated with women: Demeter, Persephone, Hecate, Rhea, Iambe, the daughters and wife of Celeus, the playmates of Persephone; yet I am unaware of any attempt to interpret it from the feminine perspective.

40. Walter Horatio Pater, *Greek Studies: A Series of Essays,* prepared for the press by Charles L. Shadwell (Macmillan Co., 1899), p. 112.

41. Eranos-Jahrbuch, *Papers,* Vol. 2, p. 30.

42. Neumann in *The Great Mother* only sees their combination in the primordial goddess and clearly Demeter is far too sophisticated to be that. It is interesting to note that not until Elisabeth Kübler-Ross (*On Death and Dying* [Macmillan Co., 1969]) have human beings again generally accepted the great connection between grief and rage which appears at the time of death or any enforced separation.

43. Nilsson, *A History of Greek Religion,* p. 138.

44. See "The Psychological Aspects of the Kore," Jung, 9, 1:182–203.

45. Rohde, *Psyche,* 1:224–225.

46. Harrison, *Prolegomena,* p. 286.

47. Nilsson, *A History of Greek Religion,* pp. 28–29, 204–205.

48. See Witt, *Isis,* for a detailed discussion; especially pp. 21–22.

49. *Ibid.*, pp. 52–53. Cf. Siegfried Morenz, *Egyptian Religion,* trans. Ann E. Keep (Cornell University Press, 1973), p. 246.

50. Morenz, *Egyptian Religion,* p. 140. Morenz is speaking here of male gods, particularly of relationships such as those involving Amon-Re. However, since he believes these liaisons were created between deities of the same sex, his argument would apply equally to goddesses. Claas Jouco Bleeker makes much the same observation in his book *Hathor and Thoth: Two Key Figures of the Ancient Egyptian Religion* (Leiden: Brill, 1973), pp. 24–27.

51. Apuleius, *The Golden Ass,* in Grant, *Hellenistic Religions,* p. 138. This is a collection of ancient sources and hereafter will be cited as Grant.

52. This is my own condensation of Plutarch's rendition of the myth. It

is thought that Plutarch assembled the myth from a variety of sources and, in fact, there is no Egyptian version. The direct quotations are taken from Eberhard Otto's synopsis which appears in his book *Egyptian Art and the Cults of Osiris and Amon,* pp. 61–63. He has substituted Egyptian names for the Greek ones used by Plutarch. The full myth can be found in Plutarchus, *Plutarch's Moralia,* Vol. 5: *Isis and Osiris,* trans. Frank Cole Babbitt (London: William Heinemann; Cambridge, Mass.: Harvard University Press, 1928–).

53. Apuleius, *The Golden Ass,* in Grant, p. 138.

54. *Ibid.,* p. 143.

55. *Ibid.*

56. *The Aretalogy from Cyme,* in Grant, pp. 131–133. I have quoted the aretalogy in its entirety because it is difficult to locate and because all of it is so relevant to this study of the archetypal feminine. Note the use of Greek names throughout the aretalogy. See the lengthy analysis in Jan Bergman, *Ich bin Isis. Studien zum memphitischen Hintergrund der griechischen Isisaretalogien* (Uppsala: Universitet; Stockholm: Almqvist & Wiksell, 1968).

57. Apuleius, *The Golden Ass,* in Grant, p. 138.

58. This section of *The Golden Ass* is regarded as autobiographical and differs substantially from the rest of the "novel." See the introductory remarks by Harry Schnur in *The Golden Ass,* trans. William Adlington (Collier Books, 1962), p. 10.

59. Lucius' initiation apparently took place in Cenchreae, "the most famous town of all the Corinthians" (Book X, ch. 46).

60. This synopsis is culled from the "The Initiation of Lucius," in Grant, pp. 140–144.

61. In *The Golden Ass* this is described as "a round disc like a mirror, or rather like the moon." Because of the connections between goddesses and the moon I never questioned this understanding until I read the analysis of the symbolism by N. Rambova which shows that the disc in Hathor's crown is the sun. See *Mythological Papyri,* trans. with an introduction by Alexandre Piankoff, ed., with a chapter on the symbolism of the papyri, by N. Rambova (Pantheon Books, 1957). It is also clear from the aretalogy that Isis has stronger ties to the sun than to the moon. Originally, then, she was associated with the sun, but it would appear that in the Hellenistic period she may have been occasionally identified with the moon.

62. Bleeker, *Hathor and Thoth,* p. 59.

63. Plutarchus, *Moralia,* No. 376. Plutarch gave the sistrum a special interpretation: The four rattles represent earth, air, fire, and water and the sistrum itself shows that "all things in existence need to be shaken." Perhaps it is by means of the sistrum that she "whirls the sphere of heaven" and tramples down evil. It is said that a rattle is given to children so they may ward off evil.

64. This Horus should not be confused with Horus the son of Isis.
65. Bleeker, *Hathor and Thoth,* pp. 102–103.
66. Witt, *Isis,* pp. 85–86.
67. Plutarchus, *Moralia,* No. 379. "The great majority of the Egyptians in doing service to the animals themselves and in treating them as gods have not only filled their sacred offices with ridicule and derision, but this is the least of the evils connected with their silly practices. There is engendered a dangerous belief which plunges the weak and innocent into sheer superstition, and in the case of the more cynical and bold, goes off into atheistic and brutish reasoning." Let Plutarch speak for the Hellenes; it is doubtful he spoke for the Egyptians or understood the powerful symbolism of the animalistic and zoomorphic deities.
68. Bleeker, *Hathor and Thoth,* p. 12.
69. Morenz, *Egyptian Religion,* p. 114.
70. Bleeker, *Hathor and Thoth,* p. 156. For instance, Thoth as a baboon can be found sitting above the scales of justice which are used to weigh the hearts of the dead. He is usually holding a book or scroll and records the verdict.
71. Morenz, *Egyptian Religion,* p. 113.
72. Bleeker, *Hathor and Thoth,* p. 69.
73. See Witt, *Isis,* pp. 194–195; Morenz, *Egyptian Religion,* pp. 119–125. Typically, "It has been pointed out that personified Maat was also familiar to the Jews who lived in the Upper Egyptian town of Elephantine and that this led, by way of the Aramaic Words of Ahiqar . . . to the hypostatization of 'wisdom' in the book of Proverbs" (Morenz, *Egyptian Religion,* p. 125).
74. The vignette in Plutarch's myth which describes Isis releasing Seth, losing her crown because of Horus' rage, and receiving from Thoth the crown of Hathor may be a glimmer of the relationship of Isis and Maat. Freeing Seth is actually an act of divine order and it is Thoth, Maat's agent, who restores the dignity of Isis.
75. Apuleius, *The Golden Ass,* in Grant, p. 139.
76. See the fascinating discussion in Jacques Chailley, *The Magic Flute, Masonic Opera: An Interpretation of the Libretto and the Music,* trans. Herbert Weinstock (London: Victor Gollancz, 1972).
77. Apuleius, *The Golden Ass,* in Grant, p. 138.

Chapter 5. The Expression and Repression of Sophia

1. Wisdom is called *hokhmah* in Hebrew and *sophia* in Greek. Here it will be called Sophia because that was the more widely used term in the Hellenistic world, among both Jews and Christians.
2. Helmer Ringgren, *Word and Wisdom: Studies in the Hypostatization of Divine Qualities and Functions in the Ancient Near East* (Lund: H. Ohlssons boktr., 1947).

3. Von Rad is typical of the former and Ringgren of the latter.

4. Gerhard von Rad, *Wisdom in Israel* (Abingdon Press, 1972), pp. 161–164. Unfortunately, Von Rad discusses this problem in terms of Logos and Yahweh, which is an anachronism, because the substitution of Logos for Sophia occurred only after the Wisdom literature to which he refers had already been written.

5. "Better is the wickedness of a man than the goodness of a woman" (Sirach 42:14). In their notes Box and Oesterley quote Edersheim: " 'The misogyny of the author here reaches its climax' " (R. H. Charles, ed., *The Apocrypha and Pseudepigrapha of the Old Testament in English* [Oxford: Clarendon Press, 1913], 1:471). Sirach also blames women for the fall. "From a woman did sin originate, and because of her we all must die" (Sirach 25:24).

6. R. B. Y. Scott, tr., *Proverbs. Ecclesiastes,* The Anchor Bible, Vol. 18 (Doubleday & Co., 1965), pp. 67–68. All quotations from Proverbs are from this translation.

7. All the citations from Ben Sirach and The Wisdom of Solomon are taken from Charles, *The Apocrypha and Pseudepigrapha of the Old Testament,* 1:268–568. In most instances the verb forms have been modernized to facilitate reading. The more widely available Revised Standard Version of the Old Testament Apocrypha was not selected because of the euphemistic (rather than explicit) language used in several of the critical texts.

8. Ringgren, *Word and Wisdom,* pp. 165–171. Specifically, "Another interesting detail should be observed here. Yahweh's *ruah* is not always good or benevolent" (p. 168).

9. This passage is reminiscent of the fury of a woman scorned; however, it is interesting that none of the analysts of Wisdom whom I read cared to comment on or discuss this negative aspect of Sophia's character although it is obviously a significant facet of her personality. They apparently prefer to regard her as entirely benign.

10. Cf. Wisdom 8:8.

11. Ringgren, *Word and Wisdom,* p. 115.

12. Cf. Wisdom 9:18: "And men were taught the things that are pleasing unto thee; and through wisdom were they saved."

13. Ringgren, *Word and Wisdom,* p. 115.

14. Von Rad, *Wisdom in Israel,* pp. 161–163. As I have indicated before, Von Rad does not use the word "Sophia" in these passages although he should because he is referring to her deeds and powers as they are described in the Wisdom literature. He has substituted the word "Logos" and refers to it as "it."

15. *Ibid.,* p. 164.

16. Charles, *The Apocrypha and Pseudepigrapha of the Old Testament,* 1:549.

17. Harry Austryn Wolfson, *Philo: Foundations of Religious Philosophy in Judaism, Christianity, and Islam,* 4th printing, rev. Structure and Growth

of Philosophic Systems from Plato to Spinoza, No. 2 (Harvard University Press, 1962), 1:188.

18. Philo, *Fuga* 50–52. This symbolic misogynism is also evident in Plutarch's *Isis and Osiris,* No. 374, in which the father is described as good, wise, and self-sufficient in all things. The mother is described as helpless, without means, utterly lacking of herself in the good, but being filled by the male. Plutarch also states that the seed of woman does not supply power or the origin of the child but only the material and nurturing part of the process of generation. Thus Isis becomes the passive receptive partner and Osiris the active creative one. Obviously, this interpretation flies in the face of the myth.

19. All the following quotations from Philo are taken from the Loeb Classical Library edition in twelve volumes published by the Harvard University Press from 1929 to 1962.

20. Wolfson, *Philo,* 1:291; see also 1:258–282.

21. *Ibid.*, 1:184.

22. *Ibid.*, 1:258.

23. Wolfson totally disregards Egyptian religion as an influence on Philo; in fact, he debunks it. He maintains that the religious philosophy of the Egyptians shows no "essential difference from the religious philosophy of the Stoics of that time." Wolfson claims that the Egyptians themselves syncretized their religion with that of the Greeks and believes that Plutarch's account of the Isis/Osiris legend reflects how the Egyptians saw their own religion; for instance, "the Egyptian goddess Isis is nothing but the Greek word for 'knowledge' " (1:7). Wolfson never mentions the role of Maat.

24. Burton Lee Mack, *Logos und Sophia: Untersuchungen zur Weisheitstheologie im hellenistischen Judentum* (Göttingen: Vandenhoeck & Ruprecht, 1973), pp. 64–65.

25. *Ibid.*, pp. 153–154.

26. See also Gig, 28–30.

27. Mack, *Logos und Sophia,* pp. 119–121, 141.

28. *Ibid.*, pp. 141–157.

29. *Ibid.*, p. 185; trans. M. Torza.

30. See Mack's discussion of this point on p. 177, although in a different context.

31. Richard Arthur Baer, *Philo's Use of the Categories Male and Female* (Leiden: Brill, 1970), p. 45.

32. *Ibid.*, p. 44.

33. Bultmann maintains that Philo's interest in the dualities of male/female, soul/body is due to his Neo-Platonic leanings (Rudolf Bultmann, *Primitive Christianity in Its Contemporary Setting,* trans. R. H. Fuller [London: Thames and Hudson, 1956], pp. 98–99). This leaves untouched, however, the origin of warfare between the dualities. Certainly this is one of the most depressing developments in theology and philosophy as it sets forth the

"battle of the sexes" as a normative condition of human existence.

34. R. A. Baer, *Philo's Use of Categories Male and Female,* p. 40.

35. This would include the work by James Robinson and Helmut Koester, *Trajectories Through Early Christianity* (Fortress Press, 1971), as well as those by Gerhard von Rad, Helmer Ringgren, and Burton Mack already cited. Other scholars also enter this discussion through their analysis of the Prologue to the Gospel of John. See Rudolf Bultmann, *The Gospel of John: A Commentary,* trans. G. R. Beasley-Murray (Oxford: Basil Blackwell; Philadelphia: Westminster Press, 1971); C. H. Dodd, *The Interpretation of the Fourth Gospel* (Cambridge: University Press, 1953); Raymond Brown, *The Gospel According to John,* The Anchor Bible, Vol. 29 (Doubleday & Co., 1966). See also Wilfred Knox, *St. Paul and the Church of the Gentiles* (Cambridge: University Press, 1939). As one of the principal advocates of the exploration of Wisdom in the New Testament, James Robinson has developed the idea of "trajectories" to explain the evolution of trains of thought in Biblical and post-Biblical theology. He conceives this word to reflect a "dynamic, historic, existence/process-oriented new metaphysics" and believes it should replace words such as " 'background' or 'environment' or 'context' " (Robinson and Koester, *Trajectories,* pp. 9, 13). The latest work on Wisdom as a trajectory is edited by Robert Wilken, *Aspects of Wisdom in Judaism and Early Christianity* (University of Notre Dame Press, 1975).

36. M. Jack Suggs, *Wisdom, Christology, and Law in Matthew's Gospel* (Harvard University Press, 1970), p. 2. A typical example of the discussion of Wisdom prior to this new interest can be found in *The Interpreter's Bible,* Vol. 10 (1953), in the exposition of I Cor. 1:24 by John Short in which the Wisdom theme is dismissed as unimportant.

37. Suggs, *Wisdom,* p. 1.

38. This is also found in Luke's Gospel inasmuch as he is dependent on Q. Q, as reconstructed, is a source used by both Matthew and Luke which was put together after Christ's death and contained many sayings of Jesus. For a detailed discussion, see Suggs, *Wisdom,* pp. 5–29; and Robinson and Koester, *Trajectories,* pp. 71–113.

39. Martin Hengel, *The Son of God: The Origin of Christology and the History of Jewish-Hellenistic Religion* (Fortress Press, 1976), p. 48.

40. Cf. the article by Birger Pearson, "Hellenistic-Jewish Speculation and Paul," in Wilken, *Aspects of Wisdom in Judaism and Early Christianity.*

41. *Ibid.,* p. 49.

42. Hengel, *The Son of God,* p. 72. Cf. Harry Austryn Wolfson, *The Philosophy of the Church Fathers,* Structure and Growth of Philosophic Systems from Plato to Spinoza, No. 3 (Harvard University Press, 1956–), p. 164; here he points out that Philo also equated both the rock and manna with Sophia and Logos.

43. Hengel, *The Son of God,* p. 14.

44. Pearson, "Hellenistic-Jewish Speculation and Paul," p. 43.

45. Hengel, *The Son of God,* p. 77. Cf. p. 2: "More happened in this period of less than two decades than in the whole of the next seven centuries."

46. *Ibid.,* p. 71.

47. *Ibid.,* p. 74.

48. *Ibid.,* p. 72.

49. *Ibid.,* p. 73.

50. James Robinson, "Jesus as Sophos and Sophia," in Wilken, *Aspects of Wisdom in Judaism and Early Christianity,* p. 10. Robinson adds that Matthew "seems to carry forward the Q trajectory more than does Luke."

51. Suggs, *Wisdom,* p. 19; also pp. 40–41.

52. These sayings can be identified by their need for further explanation in order to be fully understood. See Robinson and Koester, *Trajectories,* p. 89.

53. Hengel, *The Son of God,* p. 74.

54. Robinson and Koester, *Trajectories,* p. 98. This statement of Robinson does lead one to wonder whether one reason for the general repression of the Wisdom/Christ tradition was the abuse of that association in gnosticism. It does appear that overt Sophia Christology drops away at about the time the Gnostic heresies come into full flower.

55. Suggs, *Wisdom,* p. 50.

56. *Ibid.,* p. 96.

57. *Ibid.,* p. 58. Cf. Robinson, "Jesus as Sophos and Sophia," in Wilken, *Aspects of Wisdom in Judaism and Early Christianity,* pp. 11, 15.

58. Suggs, *Wisdom,* p. 100. The sorrowing mother motif is now ascribed to Christ.

59. *Ibid.,* p. 97; see Matt. 11:17.

60. Suggs, *Wisdom,* pp. 115–116.

61. Bultmann, *The Gospel of John,* pp. 24, 30.

62. *Ibid.,* p. 23.

63. *Ibid.,* p. 21. In discussing Logos and Sophia in Philo, Bultmann indicates that the Sophia figure in Philo is an "oriental figure" transformed through Isis theology (p. 23, n. 4).

64. *Ibid.,* p. 27.

65. It is interesting to note, however, the following comment: "It is *remarkable* [italics mine] that in the Odes of Solomon where normally the 'Word' embodies the Revelation, in Ode 33 the 'pure virgin,' which is identical with the Sophia, stands alongside the Word" (Bultmann, *The Gospel of John,* pp. 23–24, n. 4).

66. Dodd, *The Interpretation of the Fourth Gospel,* p. 133.

67. *Ibid.,* p. 280.

68. *Ibid.,* p. 275.

69. Brown, *The Gospel According to John,* p. cxxiv.

70. *Ibid.,* p. lxi.

71. *Ibid.*, p. cxxiv.
72. *Ibid.* Cf. Wisdom, ch. 10; Sirach 24:23.
73. *Ibid.*, p. cxxv. See earlier discussion on the Pauline letters.
74. *Ibid.*, pp. 537–538. For a lengthy analysis of the "I am" statements, see Appendix IV, pp. 531, 538.
75. Dodd, *The Interpretation of the Fourth Gospel,* p. 134.
76. *Ibid.*, pp. 137–138. Bultmann categorically denies this connection and quotes with approval E. Schweizer, who "has shown that the vine in John 15 does not have its origin in the OT-Jewish tradition, but in the myth of the tree of life" (Bultmann, *The Gospel of John,* p. 530, n. 5).
77. Again, Bultmann insists that the "Rabbinic statements which call God, the law, Israel, or individual teachers a 'light' or 'lamp' . . . are in no way parallel. Rather the use here is based on Gnostic usage" (Bultmann, *The Gospel of John,* p. 342, n. 5).
78. Von Rad, *Wisdom in Israel,* p. 163.
79. Hengel, *The Son of God,* p. 73.

Chapter 6. The Return of the Repressed

1. Freud, "Moses and Monotheism," in *Psychological Works,* 23:127.
2. *Ibid.*, 23:94–95.
3. According to Hengel, the Christological themes of preexistence, mediation at creation, and the sending of "the son into the world were all developed chronologically *before the legends of the miraculous birth of Jesus.* The tradition behind the prologue to the Fourth Gospel is 'earlier' than the infancy narratives of Matthew and Luke in the present form" (Hengel, *The Son of God,* p. 72). Nevertheless, this still marks the appearance of Mary at a very early date in the Christian tradition.
4. Although the apocryphal material about Mary is somewhat difficult to date, scholars generally agree that the Protoevangelium comes from the second century and the content of The Passing of Mary emerged by the fifth. Rather than discuss each work separately, I have conflated the stories for the sake of brevity. All the quotations are taken from *Apocryphal Gospels, Acts, and Revelations,* trans. Alexander Walker, Ante-Nicene Christian Library, Vol. 16 (Edinburgh: T. & T. Clark, 1873). For a detailed discussion of the various traditions, histories, and dates of each of these works, the reader is advised to consult the critical comments in *New Testament Apocrypha,* ed. Wilhelm Schneemelcher, trans. A. J. B. Higgins *et al.*, 2 vols. (Westminster Press, 1963, 1966); and *The Apocryphal New Testament,* trans. M. R. James (Oxford: Clarendon Press, 1924). Additional discussion of the dormition stories can be found in R. L. P. Milburn, *Early Christian Interpretations of History* (Harper & Brothers, 1954), pp. 161–192.
5. See Oscar Cullmann, in Schneemelcher, *New Testament Apocrypha,* 1:374.

6. "The Protoevangelium of James," 7, in *Apocryphal Gospels, Acts, and Revelations,* p. 5.

7. "Pseudo-Matthew," 6, in *Apocryphal Gospels, Acts, and Revelations,* p. 24.

8. *Ibid.*, 13, in *Apocryphal Gospels, Acts, and Revelations,* p. 32.

9. *Ibid.*, 19, in *Apocryphal Gospels, Acts, and Revelations,* p. 36.

10. "The Passing of Mary," in *Apocryphal Gospels, Acts, and Revelations,* p. 515.

11. *Ibid.*, p. 518.

12. *Ibid.*, p. 527.

13. "The Falling Asleep of Mary," in *Apocryphal Gospels, Acts, and Revelations,* p. 514.

14. "The Passing of Mary," in *Apocryphal Gospels, Acts, and Revelations,* p. 521.

15. See the analysis of the moon symbolism of Mary and the church by Hugo Rahner, *Greek Myths and Christian Mysteries,* trans. Brian Battershaw (London: Burns & Oates, 1963), pp. 154–176. Although much of this imagery is developed in later periods, the initial identification is certainly suggested here.

16. John Gough Clay, *The Virgin Mary and the Traditions of Painters* (London: J. T. Hayes, 1873), pp. 10–11.

17. Achilles Stubbe, *La Madone dans l'art,* Preface by Daniel-Rops (Brussels: Elsevier, 1958), pp. 19–20. Stubbe indicates that the essential aspects of Marian iconography were fixed by the fifth century, but the distinctions he notes between veneration and cultic worship become even more apparent in later centuries. Numerous artists have rendered scenes from Mary's own life without any reference to her relationship with Christ, e.g., her birth, her presentation at the Temple, her marriage, and her death.

18. Ruth Ellis Messenger, *The Praise of the Virgin in Early Latin Hymns,* The Papers of the Hymn Society, 3 (New York: Hymn Society, 1932), p. 7.

19. *Ibid.*, p. 5.

20. For a full discussion, see Charles William Neumann, *The Virgin Mary in the Works of Saint Ambrose* (Fribourg: University Press, 1962), pp. 35–38. See especially Book II of *De Virginibus* by Ambrose; Neumann calls the portrait of Mary which emerged from those pages "the most beautiful picture of the Virgin Mary that Ambrose or for that matter any Father painted" (p. 36).

21. *The Odes of Solomon,* ed. and trans. with notes by James Hamilton Charlesworth (Oxford: Clarendon Press, 1973), pp. 82–83. Note the contrast between this translation and that by J. Rendel Harris done in 1909. Unlike Harris, Charlesworth has placed "only manuscript readings . . . in the text" and relegated "all corrections and emendations . . . to the critical apparatus"

(p. 15). As a result, Charlesworth's translation is dynamic and archetypal, while the one by Harris can only be described as piously orthodox.

22. Gregory of Nyssa, "On Virginity," ch. 19, in *Gregory of Nyssa: Dogmatic Treatises, etc.*, trans. with prolegomena, notes, and indices by William Moore and Henry Austin Wilson, A Select Library of Nicene and Post-Nicene Fathers of the Christian Church, Second Series, Vol. 5 (Christian Literature Co., 1893), p. 365.

23. Tertullian is one of the few dissenters: "She who bare (really) bare; and although she was a virgin when she conceived, she was a wife when she brought forth her son" (Tertullian, "On the Flesh of Christ," ch. 23, trans. Dr. Holmes, in *The Ante-Nicene Fathers: Translations of the Writings of the Fathers down to* A.D. *325*, ed. Alexander Roberts and James Donaldson, Vol. 3: *Latin Christianity: Its Founder, Tertullian* [W. B. Eerdmans Publishing Co., 1957], p. 541).

24. The apocryphal stories indicate that even her relationship with the disciple John was characterized by separateness, e.g., they did not live in the same house.

25. Origen, "Commentary on John," 1, 6, trans. Allan Menzies, in *The Ante-Nicene Fathers,* X:300.

26. Aloys Grillmeier, *Christ in Christian Tradition,* trans. John Bowden, 2d rev. ed. (Oxford: Alden & Mowbray 1975–), pp. 451, 456.

27. Cyril of Alexandria, "Five Tomes Against Nestorius," I, 10, in *Five Tomes Against Nestorius: Scholia on the Incarnation: Christ Is One: Fragments Against Diodore of Tarsus, Theodore of Mopsuestia, the Synousiasts,* A Library of Fathers of the Holy Catholic Church, Vol. 46 (Oxford: J. Parker, 1881), p. 37.

28. Jean Daniélou, *A History of Early Christian Doctrine Before the Council of Nicaea* (London: Darton, Longman & Todd, 1964–; Westminster Press, 1973–), Vol. 2: *Gospel Message and Hellenistic Culture,* p. 198.

29. Although gnosticism rejected the Old Testament "in toto," the early church fathers did not and were anxious to show that there were foretastes of Christianity in the Jewish scriptures. Thus theologians such as Origen and Hippolytus used typology as a means to describe many of the women in the Old Testament as types of the church, e.g., Rebecca, Rachel, Susanna, Rahab, the Queen of Sheba, even Pharaoh's daughter. This practice was also extended to women of the New Testament and thus Mary, Mary Magdalene, and the Samaritan woman at the well are also considered types of the church. See the discussion in Daniélou, *A History of Early Christian Doctrine,* 2: 199–288.

30. Justin Martyr, "Dialogue with Trypho," ch. 100, in *Saint Justin Martyr,* trans. Thomas B. Falls, The Fathers of the Church: A New Translation, Vol. 6 (Christian Heritage, 1948), pp. 304–305.

31. Irenaeus, "Against Heresies," III, 21. 10, in *The Writings of Irenaeus,* trans. Rev. Alexander Roberts and Rev. W. H. Rambaut, Ante-Nicene Christian Library, Vol. 5 (Edinburgh: T. & T. Clark, 1869), I:358.

32. Irenaeus, "Against Heresies," III, 22.4, in *The Writings of Irenaeus,* I:362.

33. *Ibid.,* V. 19.1, in *The Writings of Irenaeus,* II:107; italics added.

34. See the description of the return of the repressed, Freud, "Moses and Monotheism," in *Psychological Works,* 23:127.

35. Henri de Lubac, *The Splendor of the Church,* trans. Michael Mason (Paulist Press, 1963), p. 215.

36. For instance, see Joseph Conrad Plumpe's excellent book *Mater Ecclesia: An Inquiry Into the Concept of the Church as Mother in Early Christianity* (Catholic University of America Press, 1943). This book provides a detailed analysis of the image of the church as mother and bride. Its one limitation is that it does not develop the theme of the church as Wisdom or Sophia. Cf. de Lubac, *The Splendor of the Church.* It should be noted, however, that Daniélou specifically rejects the idea of the church as Wisdom and calls that a Gnostic view. See Daniélou, *A History of Early Christian Doctrine,* 1:311–313.

37. The Shepherd of Hermas, Second Vision, 4.1, trans. Joseph M. F. Marigue, in *The Apostolic Fathers* (Christian Heritage, 1948), p. 242.

38. Clement of Alexandria, "The Miscellanies," 6.16, in *The Writings of Clement of Alexandria,* trans. Rev. William Wilson, Ante-Nicene Christian Library, Vol. 12 (Edinburgh: T. & T. Clark, 1869), II:391.

39. "The Homily Ascribed to Clement," ch. 14, ed. and trans. M. B. Riddle, in *The Ante-Nicene Fathers,* VII:513, 521. The author of this homily is generally regarded to be neither Clement of Alexandria nor Clement of Rome. Nor should the work be confused with the Ebionite Clementine homilies. See the discussion by Johannes Quasten, *Patrology* (Newman Press, 1951-), I:59–62.

40. Methodius, "The Banquet of the Ten Virgins; or, Concerning Chastity," Dis. 8.5, in *The Ante-Nicene Christian Library,* XIV:72; italics added.

41. Plumpe, *Mater Ecclesia,* p. 9.

42. *Ibid.,* p. 47.

43. These distinctions are somewhat arbitrary and are primarily used to emphasize the richness of the feminine imagery. Note, for instance, that the image of mother is often combined with the image of Wisdom. Cf. *The Odes of Solomon,* 33.

44. *The Odes of Solomon,* 33.5–13, trans. Charlesworth. For a full discussion of the understanding of the church as the "perfect virgin" in this passage, see p. 121. Cf. Plumpe, *Mater Ecclesia,* p. 26; Bernard, *The Odes of Solomon,* p. 118. Note the similarity between the "perfect virgin" here

and in The Shepherd of Hermas. A careful analysis of both these works which emerged about the same time would be very interesting because of their extensive use of feminine imagery.

45. Clement of Alexandria, *Christ the Educator,* trans. Simon Wood, The Fathers of the Church: A New Translation, Vol. 23 (Fathers of the Church, 1954), p. 40. In this same passage Clement elaborates on the church as virgin and mother and says that Christ is the milk the church gives her children.

46. Tertullian, "On Prayer," ch. 2, trans. S. Thelwall, in *The Ante-Nicene Fathers,* III:682. *"Ne mater quidem Ecclesia praeteritur. Si quidem in filio et patre mater recognoscitur, de qua constat et patris et filii nomen"* (Migne, *Patrologia Latina,* 1:1154). It should be noted that the last part of this statement is very strange and could almost be taken to mean that the concept of a divine Mother precedes that of Father and Son. I cannot believe that was Tertullian's intention; nevertheless, when one is dealing with the return of the repressed, one should not be surprised by "slips of the tongue" (or pen) which reveal ideas that vary widely from what is consciously acceptable.

47. Methodius, "The Banquet," Dis. 8.9, in *The Ante-Nicene Christian Library,* XIV:76. This last statement raises the issue of sacramental theology which appears to be another place where the repressed feminine divine appears. There is certainly evidence that the imagery associated with the sacraments is very feminine indeed, e.g., the baptismal font is the womb.

48. The Shepherd of Hermas, Ninth Parable, 13.8–9, in *The Apostolic Fathers,* p. 333.

49. See the discussion in Plumpe, *Mater Ecclesia,* pp. 78–83.

50. Cyprian, "On the Dress of Virgins," ch. 3, trans. Robert Ernest Wallis, in *The Writings of Cyprian,* Ante-Nicene Christian Library, Vol. 8 (Edinburgh: T. & T. Clark, 1868), I:336.

51. *Ibid.,* ch. 20, I:347.

52. The Song of Songs contains a multitude of dynamic feminine images which have long troubled theologians and scholars in both Judaism and Christianity. In the main the explicit sexuality of the poem and the independent and assertive qualities of the woman have been minimized by means of allegory. As this hermeneutical device has become less fashionable and acceptable some scholars have preferred to transfer this work from the domain of the sacred and to characterize it as secular or, at best, cultic poetry. Rather than allegory or secularization, this work may now require a straightforward interpretation as an unrepressed expression of the masculine and feminine dimensions of the divine in joyful and wholesome (holy) harmony. See analysis by Marvin Pope, *Song of Songs,* The Anchor Bible, Vol 7C (Doubleday & Co., 1977).

53. Origin, *The Song of Songs: Commentary and Homilies,* Second Homily, 3, trans. R. P. Lawson, Ancient Christian Writers, The Works of the

Fathers in Translation, No. 26 (Newman Press, 1957), p. 287.

54. See the discussion in Plumpe, *Mater Ecclesia,* pp. 74–76.

55. Philo, *Fuga* 52.

56. Wilken, *Aspects of Wisdom in Judaism and Early Christianity,* p. xvi.

57. Grillmeier, *Christ in Christian Tradition,* pp. 44–45.

58. *Ibid.*, p. 78.

59. I do not wish to imply that Sophiology constituted the entire basis of Christology or that it was the entire cause of the heresies and doctrinal disputes of the early church. However, I do believe Sophiology was an extremely important part of both.

60. The Shepherd of Hermas, Eighth Parable, III, 2, in *The Apostolic Fathers,* p. 310.

61. "The Pastor [Shepherd] of Hermas," Fifth Parable, 6, trans. F. Crombie, in *The Ante-Nicene Fathers,* II:35.

62. Grillmeier, *Christ in Christian Tradition,* p. 78.

63. *Ibid.*

64. Justin Martyr, "Dialogue with Trypho," ch. 62, in *Saint Justin Martyr,* p. 246.

65. *Ibid.*, ch. 100, p. 304.

66. Grillmeier, *Christ in Christian Tradition,* p. 103.

67. There is no question that Wisdom speculation always flourished at Alexandria, thus it is not surprising that Sophia is important in the Christologies that emerge from there. Cf. Wilken, *Aspects of Wisdom in Judaism and Early Christianity,* p. xviii.

68. Clement of Alexandria, "The Miscellanies," 6.7, in *The Writings of Clement,* II:337.

69. *Ibid.*, II:339. It is probable that here Clement is attempting to set up a form of Christian *gnōsis* to counteract the heretical Gnostic systems of Valentinius *et al.* which were then in vogue. It is true that Sophia plays a role in most Gnostic systems and that those systems utilized pairs of male/female aeons. It is again possible that Clement was sensitive to the androgyny inherent in gnosticism and that may account for his depiction of Christ in those terms. The role of Sophia and the feminine in gnosticism is an important issue. Further information on this topic can be gathered from Hans Jonas, *The Gnostic Religion,* and Elaine H. Pagels, *The Johannine Gospel in Gnostic Exegesis: Heracleon's Commentary on John* (Abingdon Press, 1973).

70. Clement of Alexandria, "Hymn to the Educator," in *Christ the Educator,* p. 277.

71. Quasten, *Patrology,* 2:22.

72. Origen, *De Principiis,* I. 2.4, trans. Frederick Crombie, in *The Ante-Nicene Fathers,* IV:247. See especially all of I. 2.

73. Origen, "Against Celsus," Book VIII, 13, in *The Ante-Nicene Fathers,* IV:644; italics added.

74. It should be noted that Origen was a complex thinker; and those opposed to Arianism, those who argued for the external generation of the Son by the Father, could also learn from his work. Cf. *De Principiis,* I. 2.4: "His [Christ's] generation is . . . eternal and everlasting" (in *The Ante-Nicene Fathers,* IV:247).

75. Quasten calls it "the greatest heresy of Christian antiquity." Furthermore, he says its birthplace was Alexandria, which was also the home of the "most famous theological school" of the same period. Thus Quasten observes, "The cradle of sacred science is the cradle of Arianism" (*Patrology,* 3:6).

76. Of course Arian Christianity continued to exist for several centuries after this date, and as one of the most stubborn and virulent heresies of the church it has also appeared in various guises since then. Even the Pneumatomachian controversy, which erupted after Constantinople, can be regarded as a continuation of the original Arian dispute, except now the Holy Spirit is regarded as a creature. The return of the repressed feminine in Pneumatology is another area that needs exploration even though it parallels the Christological developments rather closely.

77. Basil, "On the Holy Spirit," ch. XXX, trans. Blomfield Jackson, in A Select Library of Nicene and Post-Nicene Fathers of the Christian Church, Second Series, Vol. 8 (Christian Literature Co., 1895), pp. 48–50.

78. J. N. D. Kelly, *Early Christian Doctrines* (Harper & Brothers, 1959), p. 236.

Chapter 7. CONCLUSION

1. Harding, *Woman's Mysteries,* p. 241.

2. I am thinking here, for example, of Friedrich Nietzsche's interest in the "Dionysian" tendency in life as discussed in his book *The Birth of Tragedy.* See also Ludwig Feuerbach, *The Essence of Christianity,* trans. George Eliot (Harper & Brothers, Harper Torchbooks, 1957), pp. 70–73.

3. Jung, 11:461ff.

4. Jung, 11:171.

5. Eduard Schweizer *et al.,* "Spirit of God," in *Bible Key Words: From Gerhard Kittel's "Theologisches Wörterbuch zum Neuen Testament,"* Vol. 3, trans. and ed. Dorothea M. Barton, P. R. Ackroyd, and A. E. Harvey (Harper & Brothers, 1960), p. 6. Cf. Ringgren, *Word and Wisdom,* pp. 168ff.

Selected Bibliography

The following bibliography is divided into four sections that correspond to the four basic divisions of the book:

A. Psychology: Archetypes and Repression
B. The Hellenistic World: The Mystery Religions of Demeter and Isis
C. Sophia and Logos in Hellenistic Judaism and Early Christianity
D. Mariology, Ecclesiology, and Christology

Perhaps the greatest value of this bibliography is its integration of books that have always been regarded as part of the core of patristic study, such as the works of the fathers, with those that have been relegated to the boundary of that discipline, such as the Apocrypha. The bibliography also merges significant titles from the Hellenistic period regardless of religion. Thus pagan, Jewish, and Christian authors are bound together because they emerged from the same period and treated many of the same subjects.

For persons who wish to continue researching in this area, it can be expected that the future will bring an increasing number of titles concerning: (1) women and religion; (2) the Virgin Mary; (3) the role of Wisdom in Jewish and Christian theology; and (4) Hellenistic religions (see particularly the series published by the Brill Press, Études préliminaires aux religions orientales dans l'Empire Romain).

A. Psychology: Archetypes and Repression

Aldrich, Charles Roberts. *The Primitive Mind and Modern Civilization.* Introduction by Bronislaw Malinowski. Foreword by C. G. Jung. International Library of Psychology, Philosophy, and Scientific Method. London: Kegan Paul, Trench, Trubner & Co.; New York: Harcourt, Brace & Co., 1931.

Bakan, David. *The Duality of Human Existence: Isolation and Communion in Western Man.* Beacon Press, 1966.

———. *Sigmund Freud and the Jewish Mystical Tradition.* D. Van Nostrand Co., 1958.

Bettelheim, Bruno. *The Uses of Enchantment.* Vintage Books, 1977.

Brenner, Arthur B. "The Great Mother Goddess; Puberty Initiation Rites and the Covenant of Abraham." *Psychoanalytic Review* 37 (October 1950): 320–340.

Caldwell, William Vernon. *LSD Psychotherapy: An Exploration of Psychedelic and Psycholytic Therapy.* Grove Press, 1968.

Doniger, Simon. *The Nature of Man in Theological and Psychological Perspective.* Harper & Row, 1962.

Edinger, Edward F. *Ego and Archetype: Individuation and the Religious Function of the Psyche.* G. P. Putnam's Sons, 1972.

Eliade, Mircea. *Myths, Dreams, and Mysteries: The Encounter Between Contemporary Faiths and Archaic Realities.* Translated by Philip Mairet. The Library of Religion and Culture. Harper & Row, 1961.

Erikson, Erik H. *Young Man Luther: A Study in Psychoanalysis and History.* Austen Riggs Monograph, No. 4. W.W. Norton & Co., 1958.

Freud, Sigmund. *The Standard Edition of the Complete Psychological Works of Sigmund Freud.* Translated under the editorship of James Strachey in collaboration with Anna Freud, assisted by Alix Strachey and Alan Tyson. London: Hogarth Press, 1953–1974.

Fromm, Erich. *The Dogma of Christ and Other Essays on Religion, Psychology, and Culture.* Holt, Rinehart & Winston, 1963.

Goldenberg, Naomi R. "A Feminist Critique of Jung." *Signs* (Winter 1976): 443–449.

———. "Important Directions for a Feminist Critique of Religion in the Works of Sigmund Freud and Carl Jung." Unpublished Ph.D. dissertation, Yale University, 1976.

Grollman, Earl A. "Some Sights and Insights of History, Psychology and Psychoanalysis Concerning the Father-God and Mother-Goddess Concepts of Judaism and Christianity." *American Imago* 20 (Summer 1963): 187–209.

Harding, Mary Esther. *The "I" and the "Not-I": A Study in the Development of Consciousness.* Bollingen Foundation, 1965.

———. *Woman's Mysteries, Ancient and Modern: A Psychological Interpretation of the Feminine Principle as Portrayed in Myth, Story and Dreams.* G. P. Putnam's Sons, 1972.

Harkness, Georgia. *Women in Church and Society: A Historical and Theological Inquiry.* Abingdon Press, 1971.

Hostie, Raymond. *Religion and the Psychology of Jung.* Translated by G. R. Lamb. Sheed & Ward, 1957.

Jacobi, Jolande Szekacs. *The Psychology of C. G. Jung: An Introduction with*

Illustrations. Translated by Ralph Manheim. 7th ed. London: Routledge & Kegan Paul, 1968.
Jones, Ernest. *Essays in Applied Psycho-Analysis.* London: Hogarth Press, 1951.
Jung, Carl Gustav. *Collected Works.* Translated by R. F. C. Hull. Editors: Herbert Read and others. Princeton University Press, 1954–.
———. *Man and His Symbols.* Doubleday & Co., 1964.
———. *Psyche and Symbol: A Selection from the Writings of C. G. Jung.* Edited by Violet S. de Laszlo. Doubleday & Co., 1958.
Jung, Carl Gustav, and Kerenyi, C. *Essays on a Science of Mythology: The Myths of the Divine Child and the Divine Maiden.* Translated by R. F. C. Hull. Rev. ed. Harper & Row, 1963.
Jung, Carl Gustav, and Pauli, Wolfgang. *The Interpretation of Nature and the Psyche. Synchronicity: An Acausal Connecting Principle. The Influence of Archetypal Ideas on the Scientific Theories of Kepler.* Translated by R. F. C. Hull. Pantheon Books, 1955.
Moreno, Antonio. *Jung, Gods, and Modern Man.* University of Notre Dame Press, 1970.
Neumann, Erich. *Amor and Psyche: The Psychic Development of the Feminine: A Commentary on the Tale by Apuleius.* Translated by Ralph Manheim. Pantheon Books, 1956.
———. *The Great Mother: An Analysis of the Archetype.* Translated by Ralph Manheim. Pantheon Books, 1955.
———. "Narcissism, Normal Self-Formation and the Primary Relation to the Mother." *Spring* (1966).
———. *The Origins and History of Consciousness.* Foreword by C. G. Jung. Translated by R. F. C. Hull. Pantheon Books, 1954.
Reik, Theodor. *Dogma and Compulsion: Psychoanalytic Studies of Religion and Myths.* Translated by Bernard Miall. International Universities Press, 1951.
Rosenfeld, Eva M. "Dream and Vision: Some Remarks on Freud's Egyptian Bird Dream." *International Journal of Psycho-Analysis* 37 (1956): 97–105.
Rubenstein, Richard L. *My Brother Paul.* Harper & Row, 1972.
———. *The Religious Imagination: A Study in Psychoanalysis and Jewish Theology.* Bobbs-Merrill Co., 1968.
Ruether, Rosemary Radford, ed. *Religion and Sexism: Images of Woman in the Jewish and Christian Traditions.* Simon & Schuster, 1974.
Schär, Hans. *Religion and the Cure of Souls in Jung's Psychology.* Translated by R. F. C. Hull. Pantheon Books, 1950.
Schoenfeld, C. G. "God the Father—and Mother. Study and Extension of Freud's Conception of God as an Exalted Father." *American Imago* 19 (Fall 1962): 213–234.
Slater, Philip Elliot. *The Glory of Hera: Greek Mythology and the Greek Family.* Beacon Press, 1968.

Stendahl, Krister. *The Bible and the Role of Women: A Case Study in Hermeneutics.* Translated by Emilie T. Sander. Facet Books. Biblical Series, 15. Fortress Press, 1966.

Thrall, Margaret Eleanor. *The Ordination of Women to the Priesthood: A Study of Biblical Evidence.* Studies in Ministry and Worship. London: SCM Press, 1958.

Ulanov, Ann Belford. *The Feminine in Jungian Psychology and in Christian Theology.* Northwestern University Press, 1971.

White, Victor. *Soul and Psyche: An Enquiry Into the Relationship of Psychotherapy and Religion.* Edward Cadbury Lectures, 1958–1959. London: Harvill Press, 1960.

B. The Hellenistic World: The Mystery Religions of Demeter and Isis

Adkins, A. W. H. "Greek Religion." In *Historia Religionum: Handbook for the History of Religions,* Vol. 1, pp. 377–441. Edited by C. Jouco Bleeker and Geo. Widengren. Leiden: Brill, 1969.

The Ancient Egyptian Coffin Texts. Translated and edited by R. O. Faulkner. Modern Egyptology Series. Warminster, England: Aris & Phillips, 1973–.

The Ancient Egyptian Pyramid Texts. Translated by R. O. Faulkner. Oxford: Clarendon Press, 1969.

Angus, Samuel. *The Mystery-Religions and Christianity: A Study in the Religious Background of Early Christianity.* Charles Scribner's Sons, 1925.

Anthes, Rudolf. "Mythology in Ancient Egypt." In *Mythologies of the Ancient World,* pp. 15–92. Edited with an introduction by Samuel Noah Kramer. Quadrangle Books, 1968.

Apuleius Madaurensis. *The Apologia and Florida of Apuleius of Madaura.* Translated by H. E. Butler. Greenwood Press, 1970.

———. *The Golden Ass.* Translated by Jack Lindsay. Indiana University Greek and Latin Classics. Indiana University Press, 1967.

———. *The Golden Ass.* Translated by William Adlington. Edited with an introduction by Harry C. Schnur. Collier Books, 1962.

———. *The Isis-Book (Metamorphoses, Book XI).* Edited and translated by J. Gwyn Griffiths. Études préliminaires aux religions orientales dans l'Empire Romain, Vol. 39. Leiden: Brill, 1975.

Baltrušaitis, Jurgis. *La Quête d'Isis: Introduction à l'Égyptomanie.* Paris: O. Perrin, 1967.

Barthell, Edward E. *Gods and Goddesses of Ancient Greece.* University of Miami Press, 1971.

Bell, Harold Idris. *Cults and Creeds in Graeco-Roman Egypt.* Forwood Lectures, 1952. Liverpool: University Press, 1953.

———. "Graeco-Egyptian Religions." *Museum Helveticum* 10 (1953): 222–237.

Bergman, Jan. "I Overcome Fate, Fate Harkens to Me. Some Observations on Isis as a Goddess of Fate." In *Fatalistic Beliefs in Religion, Folklore and Literature.* Edited by Helmer Ringgren. Stockholm: Almqvist & Wiksell, 1967.

———. *Ich bin Isis. Studien zum memphitischen Hintergrund der griechischen Isisaretalogien.* Acta Universitatis Upsaliensis. Historia religionum, 3. Uppsala: Universitet; Stockholm: Almqvist & Wiksell, 1968.

Bleeker, Claas Jouco. *Egyptian Festivals: Enactments of Religious Renewal.* Studies in the History of Religions. Supplements to *Numen,* 13. Leiden: Brill, 1967.

———. "Guilt and Purification in Ancient Egypt." *Numen* 13 (August 1966): 81–87.

———. *Hathor and Thoth: Two Key Figures of the Ancient Egyptian Religion.* Studies in the History of Religions; Supplements to *Numen,* 26. Leiden: Brill, 1973.

———. "Isis as a Saviour Goddess." In *The Saviour God: Comparative Studies in the Concept of Salvation Presented to Edwin Oliver James,* pp. 1–16. Edited by S. G. F. Brandon. Manchester: Manchester University Press, 1963.

———. "The Religion of Ancient Egypt." In *Historia Religionum: Handbook for the History of Religions,* Vol. 1, pp. 40–114. Edited by C. Jouco Bleeker and Geo. Widengren. Leiden: Brill, 1969.

Bonner, Campbell. "Some Phases of Religious Feelings in Later Paganism." *Harvard Theological Review* 30 (July 1937): 119–140.

Brandon, Samuel George Frederick. "Life After Death: The After-Life in Ancient Egyptian Faith and Practice." *Expository Times* 76 (April 1965): 217–220.

———. "Saviour and Judge: Two Examples of Divine Ambivalence." In *Liber Amicorum: Studies in Honor of Professor Dr. C. J. Bleeker.* Studies in the History of Religions; Supplements to *Numen,* 17. Leiden: Brill, 1969.

Breasted, James Henry, ed. *Ancient Records of Egypt: Historical Documents from the Earliest Times to the Persian Conquest.* University of Chicago Press, 1906–1907.

Briffault, Robert. *The Mothers: A Study of the Origins of Sentiments and Institutions.* Macmillan Co., 1927.

Budge, Ernest Alfred Thompson Wallis. *The Gods of the Egyptians; or, Studies in Egyptian Mythology.* London: Methuen, 1904.

The Burden of Isis: Being the Laments of Isis and Nephthys. Translated with an introduction by James Teackle Dennis. The Wisdom of the East Series. E. P. Dutton & Co., 1910.

Burkert, Walter. *Griechische Religion der archaischen und klassischen Epoche.* Stuttgart: Verlag W. Kohlhammer, 1977.

Burrows, David; Lapides, Frederick R.; and Shawcross, John T., eds. *Myths and Motifs in Literature.* Free Press, 1973.

Campbell, Joseph. *The Hero with a Thousand Faces.* Pantheon Books, 1953.

———. *The Masks of God.* Viking Press, 1959.

Chailley, Jacques. *The Magic Flute, Masonic Opera: An Interpretation of the Libretto and the Music.* Translated by Herbert Weinstock. London: Victor Gollancz, 1972.

Charbonneaux, Jean; Martin, Roland; and Villard, François. *Hellenistic Art (330–50* B.C.). Translated by Peter Green. The Arts of Mankind, Vol. 18. George Braziller, 1973.

Clark, Robert Thomas Rundle. *Myth and Symbol in Ancient Egypt.* London: Thames and Hudson, 1960.

Cornford, Francis Macdonald. *Greek Religious Thought from Homer to the Age of Alexander.* The Library of Greek Thought. London: J. M. Dent; New York: E. P. Dutton & Co., 1923.

Cumont, Franz. *The Oriental Religions in Roman Paganism.* Introductory essay by Grant Showerman. Open Court Pub. Co., 1911.

Diehl, Katharine Smith. *Religions, Mythologies, Folklores: An Annotated Bibliography.* 2d ed. Scarecrow Press, 1962.

Dietrich, D. "Die Ausbreitung der alexandrinischen Mysteriengötter Isis, Osiris, Serapis und Horus in griechischrömischer Zeit." *Das Altertum* 14 (1968): 201–211.

Dodds, Eric Robertson. *The Greeks and the Irrational.* Sather Classical Lectures, Vol. 25. University of California Press, 1951.

———. *Pagan and Christian in an Age of Anxiety: Some Aspects of Religious Experience from Marcus Aurelius to Constantine.* The Wiles Lectures, 1963. W. W. Norton & Co., 1970.

Doresse, Jean. "Gnosticism." In *Historia Religionum: Handbook for the History of Religions,* Vol. 1, pp. 533–579. Edited by C. Jouco Bleeker and Geo. Widengren. Leiden: Brill, 1969.

———. *The Secret Books of the Egyptian Gnostics: An Introduction to the Gnostic Coptic Manuscripts Discovered at Chenoboskion.* Translated by Philip Mairet. Viking Press, 1960.

Dow, Sterling. "The Egyptian Cults in Athens." *Harvard Theological Review* 30 (October 1937): 183–232.

Dunand, Françoise. *Le Culte d'Isis dans le bassin oriental de la Méditerranée.* Études préliminaires aux religions orientales dans l'Empire Romain, Vol. 26. Leiden: Brill, 1973.

The Egyptian Book of the Dead: Documents in the Oriental Institute Mu-

seum at the University of Chicago. Edited by Thomas George Allen. University of Chicago Oriental Institute Publications, Vol. 82. University of Chicago Press, 1960.

Encyclopaedia of Religion and Ethics, 1912 ed. *S.v.* "Female Principle," by Edwin D. Starbuck.

Eranos Jahrbuch. Zurich: Rhein-Verlag, 1934–. Vol. 6: *Gestalt und Kult der Grossen Mutter,* edited by Olga Fröbe-Kapteyn, 1938.

Eranos-Jahrbuch. *Papers from the Eranos Yearbooks.* Pantheon Books, 1954–. Vol. 2: *The Mysteries* (1955).

Faulkner, R. O. "The Pregnancy of Isis." *The Journal of Egyptian Archeology* 54 (1968): 40–44.

Festugière, André Marie Jean. *Personal Religion Among the Greeks.* Sather Classical Lectures, Vol. 26, 1952. University of California Press, 1954.

Frankfort, Henri. *Ancient Egyptian Religion.* Harper & Row, 1961.

———. *Kingship and the Gods: A Study of Ancient Near Eastern Religion as the Integration of Society and Nature.* An Oriental Institute Essay. University of Chicago Press, 1948.

Fraser, P. M. "Two Studies on the Cult of Serapis in the Hellenistic World." *Opuscula Atheniensia* III (1960): 1–54.

Frazer, Sir James George. *The Golden Bough: A Study in Magic and Religion.* 3d ed. Macmillan Co., 1935.

Grandjean, Yves. *Une Nouvelle arétalogie d'Isis à Maronée.* Études préliminaires aux religions orientales dans l'Empire Romain, Vol. 49. Leiden: Brill, 1975.

Grant, Frederick C. "Greek Religion in the Hellenistic-Roman Age." *Anglican Theological Review* 34 (January 1952): 11–26.

———. *Hellenistic Religions: The Age of Syncretism.* The Library of Religion, Vol. 2. Liberal Arts Press, 1953.

Graves, Robert. *Greek Gods and Heroes.* Illustrated by Dimitris Davis. Doubleday & Co., 1960.

———. *The Greek Myths.* George Braziller, 1957.

Greene, William Chase. *Moira: Fate, Good, and Evil in Greek Thought.* Harper & Row, 1963.

Griffiths, John Gwyn. "Allegory in Greece and Egypt." *The Journal of Egyptian Archeology* 53 (1967): 79–102.

———. "Celestial Ladder and the Gate of Heaven in Egyptian Ritual." *Expository Times* 78 (November 1966): 54–55.

Guthrie, William Keith Chambers. *The Greeks and Their Gods.* Beacon Press, 1951.

Hamilton, Edith. *Mythology.* Illustrated by Steele Savage. Little, Brown & Co., 1942.

Harrison, Jane Ellen. *Prolegomena to the Study of Greek Religion.* 3d ed. Meridian Books, 1960.

Hatch, Edwin. *The Influence of Greek Ideas and Usages Upon the Christian*

Church. Edited by A. M. Fairbairn. 4th ed. London: Williams & Norgate, 1892.

Hesiodus. *Hesiod: The Homeric Hymns; and Homerica*. Translated by Hugh G. Evelyn-White. Loeb Classical Library. Greek Authors. London: William Heinemann; New York: Macmillan Co., 1914.

The Homeric Hymns. Translated by Charles Boer. Swallow Press, 1970.

Hus, Alain. *Greek and Roman Religion*. Translated by S. J. Tester. The Twentieth Century Encyclopedia of Catholicism, Vol. 142, Section 15: Non-Christian Beliefs. Hawthorn Books, 1962.

James, E. O. "The Female Principle." In *The Tree of Life*. Leiden: Brill, 1969.

Jonas, Hans. *The Gnostic Religion: The Message of the Alien God and the Beginnings of Christianity*. 2d ed., rev. Beacon Press, 1963.

Kaster, Joseph, ed. and tr. *Wings of the Falcon: Life and Thought of Ancient Egypt*. Holt, Rinehart & Winston, 1968.

Kerényi, Károly. *Eleusis: Archetypal Image of Mother and Daughter*. Translated by Ralph Manheim. Pantheon Books, 1967.

———. *The Gods of the Greeks*. Translated by Norman Cameron. London: Thames and Hudson, 1951.

———. *The Religion of the Greeks and Romans*. Translated by Christopher Holme. E. P. Dutton & Co., 1962.

Kirk, Geoffrey Stephen. *Myth: Its Meaning and Functions in Ancient and and Other Cultures*. Sather Classical Lectures, Vol. 40. University of California Press, 1970.

Kübler-Ross, Elisabeth. *On Death and Dying*. Macmillan Co., 1969.

Lange, Kurt, and Hirmer, Max. *Egypt: Architecture, Sculpture, Painting in Three Thousand Years*. With contributions by Eberhard Otto and Christiane Desroches-Noblecourt. Translated by R. H. Boothroyd. 4th ed., rev. and enl. Additional material in 4th German ed. translated by Judith Filson and Barbara Taylor. London: Phaidon Press, 1968.

Leclant, Jean. *Inventaire bibliographique des Isiaca (Ibid.). Répertoire analytique des travaux relatifs à la diffusion des cultes Isiaques, 1940–1969*. Études préliminaires aux religions orientales dan l'Empire Romain, Vol. 18. Leiden: Brill, 1972.

Legge, Francis. *Forerunners and Rivals of Christianity: Being Studies in Religious History from 330 B.C. to 330 A.D.* Cambridge: University Press, 1915.

Levy, Isidore. "La Légende d'Osiris et Isis chez Plutarque." *Latomus* 10 (1951): 147–162.

Loisy, Alfred Firmin. *Les Mystères païens et le mystère chrétien*. Paris: Émile Nourry, 1914.

Meautis, Georges. *Les Dieux de la Grèce et les mystères d'Eleusis*. Mythes et religions, 39. Paris: Presses Universitaires de France, 1959.

Morenz, Siegfried. *Egyptian Religion.* Translated by Ann E. Keep. Cornell University Press, 1973.

Morford, M. P. O., and Lenardon, Robert J. *Classical Mythology.* David McKay Co., 1971.

Mylonas, George Emmanuel. *Eleusis and the Eleusinian Mysteries.* Princeton University Press, 1961.

———. "Mystery Religions of Greece." In *Forgotten Religions (Including Some Living Primitive Religions),* pp. 169–191. Edited by Vergilius Ferm. Philosophical Library, 1950.

Mythological Papyri. Translated with an introduction by Alexandre Piankoff. Edited, with a chapter on the symbolism of the papyri, by N. Rambova. Pantheon Books, 1957.

Nilsson, Martin Persson. *The Dionysiac Mysteries of the Hellenistic and Roman Age.* Lund: Gleerup, 1957.

———. *Greek Popular Religion.* Lectures on the History of Religions, No. 1. Columbia University Press, 1940.

———. *A History of Greek Religion.* Translated by F. J. Fielden. 2d ed. Oxford: Clarendon Press, 1949.

Nock, Arthur Darby. *Conversion: The Old and the New in Religion from Alexander the Great to Augustine of Hippo.* Oxford: Clarendon Press, 1933.

Ochsenschlager, Edward L. "Cosmic Significance of the Plemochoe." *History of Religions* 9 (May 1970): 316–336.

Otto, Eberhard. *Egyptian Art and the Cults of Osiris and Amon.* Photographs by Max Hirmer. Translated from the German by Kate Bosse Griffiths. London: Thames and Hudson, 1968.

Otto, Walter Friedrich. *The Homeric Gods: The Spiritual Significance of Greek Religion.* Translated by Moses Hadas. Pantheon Books, 1954.

Pater, Walter Horatio. *Greek Studies: A Series of Essays.* Prepared for the press by Charles L. Shadwell. Macmillan Co., 1899.

Pépin, Jean. *Mythe et allégorie: Les Origines grecques et les contestations judéo-chrétiennes.* Paris: Éditions Montaigne, 1958.

Pestalozza, Uberto. *L'Éternel féminin dans la religion Méditerranéenne.* Translated with a preface by Marcel De Corte. Brussels: Latomus, 1965.

Pistis Sophia. Translated by George Harner. Introduction by F. Legge. London: SPCK; New York: Macmillan Co., 1924.

Plutarchus. *Plutarch's Moralia.* Vol. 5: *Isis and Osiris.* Translated by Frank Cole Babbitt. London: William Heinemann; Cambridge, Mass.: Harvard University Press, 1928–.

Pritchard, James B. *The Ancient Near East in Pictures Relating to the Old Testament.* Princeton University Press, 1954.

———, ed. *Ancient Near Eastern Texts Relating to the Old Testament.* 3d ed. Princeton University Press, 1969.
Real-Encyclopädie der classischen Altertumswissenschaft, 1916 ed. *S.v.* "Isis," by Günther Roeder.
Reitzenstein, Richard. *Die hellenistischen Mysterienreligionen, ihre Grundgedanken und Wirkungen.* Leipzig: Teubner, 1910.
Ringgren, Helmer, ed. *Fatalistic Beliefs in Religion, Folklore and Literature.* Scripta Instituti Donneriani Aboensis, Vol. 2. Stockholm: Almqvist & Wiksell, 1967.
Roeder, Günther. *Die ägyptische Religion in Texten und Bildern.* Die Bibliothek der alten Welt. Series: Der alte Orient. Zurich: Artemis Verlag, 1959–1961.
Rohde, Erwin. *Psyche: The Cult of Souls and Belief in Immortality Among the Greeks.* Translated from the 8th ed. by W. B. Hillis. Introduction to the Harper Torchbook ed. by W. K. C. Guthrie. Harper & Row, 1966.
Saffrey, H. D. "Origine en Grèce de la croyance en l'immortalité de l'âme." *Lumière et Vie* 4 (November 1955): 11–32.
Sanford, Eva Matthews. *The Mediterranean World in Ancient Times.* Ronald Press Co., 1938.
Schuon, Frithjof. *Gnosis, Divine Wisdom.* Translated by G. E. H. Palmer. London: John Murray, 1959.
Scott-Moncrieff, Philip David. "De Iside et Osiride." *Journal of Hellenistic Studies* 29 (1909): 79–90.
———. *Paganism and Christianity in Egypt.* Cambridge: University Press, 1913.
Showerman, Grant. *The Great Mother of the Gods.* Argonaut Books, 1969.
Simpson, William Kelly, ed. *The Literature of Ancient Egypt: An Anthology of Stories, Instructions, and Poetry.* Yale University Press, 1972.
Smith, Jonathan Z. "Native Cults in the Hellenistic Period." *History of Religions* 11 (November 1971): 236–249.
Spiegel, Joachim. *Die Götter von Abydos. Studien zum ägyptischen Synkretismus.* Göttinger Orientforschungen. Series 4, Ägypten; Vol. 1. Wiesbaden: Otto Harrassowitz, 1973.
Stiehl, Ruth. "Origin of the Cult of Sarapis." *History of Religions* 3 (Summer 1963): 2–33.
Trantam Tinh, V. *Isis Lactans. Corpus des monuments greco-romains d'Isis allaitant Harpocrate.* Études préliminaires aux religions orientales dans l'Empire Romain, Vol. 37. Leiden: Brill, 1973.
Vermaseren, M. J. "Hellenistic Religions." In *Historia Religionum: Handbook for the History of Religions,* Vol. 1, pp. 495–532. Edited by C. Jouco Bleeker and Geo. Widengren. Leiden: Brill, 1969.
Weblowsky, Raphael Jehudah Zwi, and Bleeker, C. Jouco. *Types of Redemption: Contributions to the Theme of the Study-Conference Held at Jerusa-*

lem 14th to 19th July 1968. Studies in the History of Religions. Supplements to *Numen,* 18. Leiden: Brill, 1970.

Willoughby, Harold Rideout. *Pagan Regeneration: A Study of Mystery Initiations in the Graeco-Roman World.* University of Chicago Press, 1929.

Wilson, John Albert. *The Burden of Egypt: An Interpretation of Ancient Egyptian Culture.* University of Chicago Press, 1951.

Witt, Reginald Eldred. "The Importance of Isis for the Fathers." In *Studia Patristica,* Vol. 8, Pt. 2, pp. 135–145. Edited by F. L. Cross. Berlin: Akademie-Verlag, 1966.

———. "Isis-Hellas." *Proceedings of the Cambridge Philological Society,* 192 (1966): 48–69.

———. *Isis in the Graeco-Roman World.* Aspects of Greek and Roman Life Series. Cornell University Press, 1971.

Wright, Frederick Adam. *Feminism in Greek Literature from Homer to Aristotle.* Kennikat Press, 1969.

Zandee, Jan. *Death as an Enemy According to Ancient Egyptian Conceptions.* Translated by W. F. Klasens. Studies in the History of Religions. Supplements to *Numen,* 5. Leiden: Brill, 1960.

———. "Gnostic Ideas on the Fall and Salvation." *Numen* 11 (January 1964): 13–74.

Zuntz, Günther. *Persephone: Three Essays on Religion and Thought in Graecia.* Oxford: Clarendon Press, 1971.

C. Sophia and Logos in Hellenistic Judaism and Early Christianity

Ahlström, Gösta Werner. *Aspects of Syncretism in Israelite Religion.* Translated by Eric J. Sharpe. Horae Soederblomianae, 5. Lund: Gleerup, 1963.

The Apocrypha and Pseudepigrapha of the Old Testament in English. Edited by R. H. Charles. Oxford: Clarendon Press, 1913.

The Apocrypha of the Old Testament. Edited by Bruce M. Metzger. Revised Standard Version. The Oxford Annotated Apocrypha. Oxford University Press, 1965.

Baer, Richard Arthur. *Philo's Use of the Categories Male and Female.* Arbeiten zur Literatur und Geschichte des hellenistischen Judentums, No. 3. Leiden: Brill, 1970.

Baird, William Robb, Jr. "Among the Mature: The Idea of Wisdom in I Corinthians II:6." *Interpretation* 13 (October 1959): 425–432.

Batey, Richard A. *New Testament Nuptial Imagery.* Leiden: Brill, 1971.

Brown, Raymond E., tr. *The Gospel According to John.* The Anchor Bible, Vol. 29. Doubleday & Co., 1966.

Bultmann, Rudolf. *The Gospel of John: A Commentary.* Translated by G. R. Beasley-Murray. General eds.: R. W. N. Hoare and J. K. Riches.

Oxford: Basil Blackwell; Philadelphia: Westminster Press, 1971.
———. *Primitive Christianity in Its Contemporary Setting.* Translated by R. H. Fuller. London: Thames and Hudson, 1956.
Conzelmann, Hans. *1 Corinthians: A Commentary on the First Epistle to the Corinthians.* Edited by George W. MacRae. Translated by James W. Leitch. Bibliography and references by James W. Dunkly. Hermeneia. Fortress Press, 1975.
Couroyer, B. "Idéal sapientiel en Égypte et en Israël (à propos du Psaume XXXIV, verset 13)." *Revue Biblique* 57 (April 1950): 174–179.
Dillon, Richard J. "Wisdom Tradition and Sacramental Retrospect in the Cana Account." *Catholic Biblical Quarterly* 24 (July 1962): 268–296.
Dodd, C. H. *The Interpretation of the Fourth Gospel.* Cambridge: University Press, 1953.
Eckstein-Diener, Berta [Helen Diner]. *Mothers and Amazons: The First Feminine History of Culture.* Edited and translated by John Philip Lundin. Introduction by Joseph Campbell. Julian Press, 1965.
Encyclopaedia Judaica, 1971 ed. *S.v.* "Wisdom; Wisdom Literature," by Robert B. Y. Scott.
Feuillet, André. "Jésus et la sagesse divine d'après les évangiles synoptiques; Le 'Logion Johannique' et l'Ancien Testament." *Revue Biblique* 62 (April 1955): 161–196.
Gaster, Theodor Herzl. *Myth, Legend, and Custom in the Old Testament: A Comparative Study with Chapters from Sir James G. Frazer's Folklore in the Old Testament.* Harper & Row, 1969.
Goodenough, Erwin Ramsdell. *By Light, Light: The Mystic Gospel of Hellenistic Judaism.* New Haven: Yale University Press; London: Humphrey Milford, Oxford University Press, 1935.
Habel, Norman C. "Symbolism of Wisdom in Proverbs 1–9." *Interpretation* 26 (April 1972): 131–157.
Hengel, Martin. *The Son of God: The Origin of Christology and the History of Jewish-Hellenistic Religion.* Fortress Press, 1976.
The Holy Bible; Containing the Old and New Testaments. Revised Standard Version. Abingdon-Cokesbury Press, 1952.
Johnson, Marshall D. "Reflections on a Wisdom Approach to Matthew's Christology." *Catholic Biblical Quarterly* 36 (January 1974): 44–64.
Klein, Viola. *The Feminine Character: History of an Ideology.* Foreword by Karl Mannheim. International Universities Press, 1949.
Knox, Wilfred Lawrence. *St. Paul and the Church of the Gentiles.* Cambridge: University Press, 1939.
Lang, Bernhard. *Frau Weisheit: Deutung einer biblischen Gestalt.* Düsseldorf: Patmos Verlag, 1975.
Lebram, Jürgen Christian. "Die Theologie der späten Chokma und häreti-

sches Judentum." *Zeitschrift für die Altentestamentliche Wissenschaft* 77 (1965): 202–211.

Levinas, Emmanuel. "Judaism and the Feminine Element." *Judaism* 18 (Winter 1969): 30–38.

Mack, Burton Lee. *Logos und Sophia: Untersuchungen zur Weisheitstheologie im hellenistischen Judentum.* Studien zur Umwelt des Neuen Testaments, Vol. 10. Göttingen: Vandenhoeck & Ruprecht, 1973.

MacRae, George Winsor. "Jewish Background of the Gnostic Sophia Myth." *Novum Testamentum* 12 (1970): 86–101.

Nock, Arthur Darby. *Early Gentile Christianity and Its Hellenistic Background.* Harper & Row, 1964.

Pagels, Elaine H. *The Johannine Gospel in Gnostic Exegesis: Heracleon's Commentary on John.* Society of Biblical Literature. Monograph series, No. 17. Abingdon Press, 1973.

Patai, Raphael. *The Hebrew Goddess.* KTAV Publishing House, 1967.

Philo Judaeus. *Philo.* Translated by F. H. Colson and G. H. Whitaker. Loeb Classical Library. Greek Authors. Harvard University Press, 1929–1962.

Rad, Gerhard von. *Wisdom in Israel.* Abingdon Press, 1972.

Ringgren, Helmer. *Word and Wisdom: Studies in the Hypostatization of Divine Qualities and Functions in the Ancient Near East.* Lund: H. Ohlssons boktr., 1947.

Robinson, James McConkey, and Koester, Helmut. *Trajectories Through Early Christianity.* Fortress Press, 1971.

Sanders, Jack T. *The New Testament Christological Hymns: Their Historical Religious Background.* Society for New Testament Studies, 15. Cambridge: University Press, 1971.

Schweizer, Eduard, *et al.* "Spirit of God." In *Bible Key Words: From Gerhard Kittel's "Theologisches Wörterbuch zum Neuen Testament,"* Vol. 3. Translated and edited by Dorothea M. Barton, P. R. Ackroyd, and A. E. Harvey. Harper & Brothers, 1960.

Scott, R. B. Y., tr. *Proverbs. Ecclesiastes.* The Anchor Bible, Vol. 18. Doubleday & Co., 1965.

Sugden, Edward Holdsworth. *Israel's Debt to Egypt.* London: Epworth Press, 1928.

Suggs, M. Jack. *Wisdom, Christology, and Law in Matthew's Gospel.* Harvard University Press, 1970.

Talbert, Charles H. "The Myth of a Descending-Ascending Redeemer Myth in Mediterranean Antiquity." *New Testament Studies* 22 (July 1976): 418–440.

Theological Dictionary of the New Testament, Vol. 4. Under "logos," by A. Debrunner *et al.*

Theological Dictionary of the New Testament, Vol. 7. Under "*sophia,*

sophos, sophizō," by Ulrich Wilckens and Georg Fohrer.
Throckmorton, Burton Hamilton, ed. *Gospel Parallels: A Synopsis of the First Three Gospels with Alternative Readings from the Manuscripts and Noncanonical Parallels.* 3d ed., rev. Toronto: Thomas Nelson & Sons, 1967.
Wedderburn, A. J. M. "Philo's Heavenly Man." *Novum Testamentum* 15 (October 1973): 301–326.
Whedbee, J. William. *Isaiah and Wisdom.* Abingdon Press, 1971.
Whybray, Roger Norman. *Wisdom in Proverbs: The Concept of Wisdom in Proverbs 1–9.* Studies in Biblical Theology, No. 45. London: SCM Press, 1965.
Wilken, Robert L., ed. *Aspects of Wisdom in Judaism and Early Christianity.* Studies in Judaism and Christianity in Antiquity, No. 1. University of Notre Dame Press, 1975.
Wolfson, Harry Austryn. *Philo: Foundations of Religious Philosophy in Judaism, Christianity, and Islam.* 1947. 4th printing, rev. Structure and Growth of Philosophic Systems from Plato to Spinoza, No. 2. Harvard University Press, 1962.

D. Mariology, Ecclesiology, and Christology

Allen, Edgar Leonard. "Mariology and Christology." *Congregational Quarterly* 35 (January 1957): 33–43.
Apocryphal Gospels, Acts, and Revelations. Translated by Alexander Walker. Ante-Nicene Christian Library, Vol. 16. Edinburgh: T. & T. Clark, 1873.
The Apocryphal New Testament. Translated by Montague Rhodes James. Oxford: Clarendon Press, 1924.
Ashe, Geoffrey. *The Virgin.* London: Routledge & Kegan Paul, 1976.
Athanasius, Saint. *Contra Gentes and De Incarnatione.* Edited and translated by Robert W. Thomson. Oxford: Clarendon Press, 1971.
———. *The Incarnation of the Word of God: Being the Treatise of St. Athanasius, De Incarnatione Verbi Dei.* Translated by a religious of C. S. M. V., S. Th. Introduction by C. S. Lewis. Macmillan Co., 1954.
———. *Letters Concerning the Holy Spirit.* Translated by C. R. B. Shapland. London: Epworth Press, 1951.
———. *Select Treatises of S. Athanasius, Archbishop of Alexandria, in Controversy with the Arians.* A Library of Fathers of the Holy Catholic Church, Vols. 8 and 19. Oxford: John Henry Parker, 1842.
Barnard, Leslie William. "Background of Early Egyptian Christianity. I. Graeco-Roman Egypt. II. The Jewish Diaspora." *Church Quarterly Review* 164 (July-September, October-December 1963): 300–310, 428–441.
———. "Origen's Christology and Eschatology." *Anglican Theological Review* 45 (July 1964): 314–319.

Barrois, Georges Augustin. "Rise of Marian Theology." *Theology Today* 12 (January 1956): 463–476.

Barth, Karl. *Church Dogmatics.* Edited by G. W. Bromiley and T. F. Torrance. Charles Scribner's Sons, 1936–1969.

Basilius, Saint. *The Treatise de Spiritu Sancto, The Nine Homilies of the Hexaemeron and the Letters of Saint Basil the Great.* Translated with notes by Blomfield Jackson. A Select Library of Nicene and Post-Nicene Fathers of the Christian Church. Second Series, Vol. 8. Christian Literature Co., 1895.

Benko, Stephen. *Protestants, Catholics, and Mary.* Judson Press, 1968.

Bode, Edward Lynn. *The First Easter Morning: The Gospel Accounts of the Women's Visit to the Tomb of Jesus.* Rome: Biblical Institute Press, 1970.

Bonhoeffer, Dietrich. *Letters and Papers from Prison.* Edited by Eberhard Bethge. Translated by Reginald H. Fuller. (Published originally as *Prisoner for God.*) Macmillan Co., 1962.

Bruns, J. Edgar. *God as Woman, Woman as God.* Paulist Press, 1973.

Caird, George Bradford. "New Wine in Old Wine-Skins. I. Wisdom." *Expository Times* 84 (March 1973): 164–168.

Campenhausen, Hans, Freiherr von. *The Virgin Birth in the Theology of the Ancient Church.* Translated by Frank Clarke. Studies in Historical Theology, No. 2. London: SCM Press, 1964.

Carol, Juniper B., ed. *Mariology.* Bruce Pub. Co., 1955–1961.

Chavasse, Claude. *The Bride of Christ: An Enquiry Into the Nuptial Element in Early Christianity.* London: Religious Book Club, 1939.

Christ, Felix. *Jesus Sophia: Die Sophia-Christologie bei den Synoptikern.* Abhandlungen zur Theologie des Alten und Neuen Testaments, Vol. 57. Zurich: Zwingli Verlag, 1970.

Chrysostomus, Joannes, Saint. *Baptismal Instructions.* Translated and annotated by Paul W. Harkins. Ancient Christian Writers; The Works of the Fathers in Translation, No. 31. Newman Press, 1963.

———. *Commentary on Saint John the Apostle and Evangelist; Homilies 1–88.* Translated by Sister Thomas Aquinas Goggin. The Fathers of the Church: A New Translation, Vols. 33 and 41. Fathers of the Church, 1957–1960.

———. *Commentary on the Epistle to the Galatians and Homilies on the Epistle to the Ephesians.* A Library of Fathers of the Holy Catholic Church, Vol. 6. Oxford: John Henry Parker, 1840.

———. *Homilies on the Gospel of Saint Matthew.* Translated by Sir George Prevost. Revised with notes by M. B. Riddle. A Select Library of the Nicene and Post-Nicene Fathers of the Christian Church. First Series, Vol. 10. Christian Literature Co., 1888.

Clay, John Gough. *The Virgin Mary and the Traditions of Painters.* London: J. T. Hayes, 1873.

Clemens, Titus Flavius, Alexandrinus. *Alexandrian Christianity: Selected*

Translations of Clement and Origen. Introductions and notes by John Ernest Leonard Oulton and Henry Chadwick. The Library of Christian Classics, Vol. 2. London: SCM Press; Philadelphia: Westminster Press, 1954.

———. *Christ the Educator.* Translated by Simon P. Wood. The Fathers of the Church: A New Translation, Vol. 23. Fathers of the Church, 1954.

———. *Clement of Alexandria.* Translated by G. W. Butterworth. Loeb Classical Library. Greek Authors. London: William Heinemann, 1919.

———. *Clement of Alexandria: Miscellanies Book VII.* The Greek text with introduction, translation, notes, dissertations, and indices by the late Fenton John Anthony Hort and Joseph B. Mayor. London: Macmillan Co., 1902.

———. *The Writings of Clement of Alexandria.* Translated by the Rev. William Wilson. Ante-Nicene Christian Library, Vols. 4 and 12. Edinburgh: T. & T. Clark, 1867–1869.

Cyprianus, Saint, Bp. of Carthage. "On the Dress of Virgins." Translated by Robert Ernest Wallis. In *The Writings of Cyprian.* Ante-Nicene Christian Library, Vol. 8. Edinburgh: T. & T. Clark, 1868.

———. "On the Dress of Virgins." In *The Ante-Nicene Fathers: Translations of the Writings of the Fathers down to* A.D. *325.* Edited by Alexander Roberts and James Donaldson. Vol. 5: *Hippolytus, Cyprian, Caius, Novatian, Appendix,* pp. 430–530. Wm. B. Eerdmans Publishing Co., 1957.

Cyrillus, Saint, Bp. of Jerusalem. *The Works of Saint Cyril of Jerusalem.* Translated by Leo P. McCauley and Anthony A. Stephenson. The Fathers of the Church: A New Translation, Vols. 61 and 64. Catholic University of America Press, 1969–1970.

Cyrillus, Saint, Patriarch of Alexandria. *Commentary on the Gospel According to Saint John.* Vol. 1 translated by P. E. Pusey; Vol. 2 by T. Randell, with a Preface by H. P. Liddon. London: Rivingtons, 1874–1885.

———. *Five Tomes Against Nestorius: Scholia on the Incarnation: Christ Is One: Fragments Against Diodore of Tarsus, Theodore of Mopsuestia, the Synousiasts.* A Library of Fathers of the Holy Catholic Church, Vol. 46. Oxford: J. Parker, 1881.

Daniélou, Jean. *A History of Early Christian Doctrine Before the Council of Nicaea.* 3 vols. London: Darton, Longman & Todd, 1964–; Westminster Press, 1973–.

Delius, Walter. *Geschichte der Marienverehrung.* Munich: E. Reinhardt, 1963.

De Satge, John. *Down to Earth: The New Protestant Vision of the Virgin Mary.* Consortium Books, 1976.

Emery, Pierre Yves. "Féminité de l'église et féminité dans l'église." *Études théologiques et religieuses* 40 (1965): 90–96.

Encyclopaedia of Religion and Ethics, 1912–1927. *S.v.* "Alexandrian Theology," by W. R. Inge; "Logos," by W. R. Inge.

Epiphanius, Saint, Bp. of Constantia in Cyprus. *Epiphanius de gemmis.* The old Georgian version and the fragments of the Armenian version by Robert P. Blake and the Coptic-Sahidic fragments by Henry de Vis. London: Christophers, 1934.

Feuillet, André. *Le Christ, sagesse de Dieu, d'après les épîtres Pauliniennes.* Preface by Y. M.-J. Congar. Paris: J. Gabalda et Cie., 1966.

———. "L'Heure de la femme et l'heure de la mère de Jésus." *Biblica* 47 (1966): 169–184, 361–380, 557–573.

Florentin-Smyth, Françoise. "Ce que la Bible ne dit pas de la femme." *Études théologiques et religieuses* 40 (1965): 76–89.

Frend, William Hugh Clifford. "Gnostic Origins of the Assumption Legend." *Modern Churchman* 43 (March 1953): 23–28.

Grabar, André. *Christian Iconography: A Study of Its Origins.* Translated by Terry Grabar. Princeton University Press, 1969.

———. *Le Premier art chrétien (200–395).* L'Univers des Formes, No. 9. Paris: Gallimard, 1966.

Graef, Hilda Charlotte. *Mary: A History of Doctrine and Devotion.* Sheed & Ward, 1964.

———. "The Theme of the Second Eve in Some Byzantine Sermons on the Assumption." In *Studia Patristica,* Vol. 9, pp. 224–230. Edited by F. L. Cross. Texte und Untersuchungen zur Geschichte der Altchristlichen Literature, Vol. 94. Berlin: Akademie-Verlag, 1966.

Gregorius, Saint, Bp. of Nyssa. *Gregory of Nyssa: Dogmatic Treatises, etc.* Translated with prolegomena, notes, and indices by William Moore and Henry Austin Wilson. A Select Library of Nicene and Post-Nicene Fathers of the Christian Church. Second Series, Vol. 5. Christian Literature Co., 1893.

Gregorius Nazianzenus, Saint, Patriarch of Constantinople. *Select Orations and Letters.* Translated by Charles Gordon Browne *et al.* A Select Library of Nicene and Post-Nicene Fathers of the Christian Church. Second Series, Vol. 7, Pt. 2. Christian Literature Co., 1894.

Grillmeier, Aloys. *Christ in Christian Tradition.* Translated by John Bowden. 2d rev. ed. Oxford: Alden & Mowbray, 1975–.

Hardy, Edward Rochie, ed. *Christology of the Later Fathers.* Edited by Edward Rochie Hardy in collaboration with Cyril C. Richardson. The Library of Christian Classics, Vol. 3. London: SCM Press; Philadelphia: Westminster Press, 1954.

Harnack, Adolf von. *History of Dogma.* Translated from the 3d German ed. by Neil Buchanan. Dover Publications, 1961.

Harris, James Rendel. *The Origin of the Prologue to St. John's Gospel.* Cambridge: University Press, 1917.

Hermas [Apostolic Father]. "The Pastor of Hermas." In *The Ante-Nicene Fathers: Translations of the Writings of the Fathers down to* A.D. *325.* Edited by Alexander Roberts and James Donaldson. Vol. 2:

Fathers of the Second Century, pp. 1–59. Wm. B. Eerdmans Publishing Co., 1956.

———. *The Shepherd of Hermas.* Translated by Joseph M. F. Marigue. In *The Apostolic Fathers.* Christian Heritage, Inc. 1948.

Hieronymus, Saint. *Saint Jerome, Dogmatic and Polemical Works.* Translated by John N. Hritzu. The Fathers of the Church: A New Translation, Vol. 53. Catholic University of America Press, 1965.

Hippolytus, Saint. *The Apostolic Tradition of Hippolytus.* Translated by Burton Scott Easton. Macmillan Co., 1934.

———. *Philosophumena; or, The Refutation of All Heresies.* Translated from the text of Cruice by F. Legge. Translations of Christian Literature. Series I: Greek Texts. London: SPCK, 1921.

Holmes, Urban Tigner, III. "The Feminine Priestly Symbol and the Meaning of God." *St. Luke's Journal of Theology* 17 (September 1974): 3–22.

Holte, Ragnar. "Logos Spermatikos: Christianity and Ancient Philosophy According to St. Justin's Apologies." *Studia Theologica* 12 (1958): 109–168.

"The Homily Ascribed to Clement." Edited and translated by M. B. Riddle. In *The Ante-Nicene Fathers: Translations of the Writings of the Fathers down to* A.D. *325.* Edited by Alexander Roberts and James Donaldson. Vol. 7: *Lactantius, Verantius, Asterius, Victorinus, Dionysius, Apostolic Teaching and Constitutions, Homily, and Liturgies*, pp. 509–523. Wm. B. Eerdmans Publishing Co., 1957.

Irenaeus, Saint, Bp. of Lyons. *St. Irenaeus, the Demonstration of the Apostolic Preaching.* Translated with introduction and notes by J. Armitage Robinson. Translations of Christian Literature. Series IV: Oriental Texts. London: SPCK, 1920.

———. *The Writings of Irenaeus.* Translated by Rev. Alexander Roberts and Rev. W. H. Rambaut. Ante-Nicene Christian Library, Vols. 5 and 9. Edinburgh: T. & T. Clark, 1868–1869.

Joannes, of Damascus, Saint. *St. John Damascene on Holy Images; Followed by Three Sermons on the Assumption.* Translated by Mary H. Allies. London: T. Baker, 1898.

Jugie, Martin. *La Mort et l'assomption de la Sainte Vierge. Étude historico-doctrinale.* Città del Vaticano, 1944.

Justinus Martyr, Saint. *Saint Justin Martyr.* Translated by Thomas B. Falls. The Fathers of the Church: A New Translation, Vol. 6. Christian Heritage, 1948.

Kelber, Wilhelm. *Die Logos Lehre von Heraklit bis Origenes.* Stuttgart: Urachhaus, 1958.

Kelly, John Norman Davidson. *Early Christian Doctrines.* Harper & Brothers, 1959.

Kretschmar, Georg. "The Councils of the Ancient Church." In *The Councils of the Church,* pp. 1–81. Edited by Hans Jochen Margull. Translated by Walter F. Bense. Fortress Press, 1966.

Lantero, Erminie Huntress. *Feminine Aspects of Divinity.* Pendle Hill, 1973.

Lubac, Henri de. *The Eternal Feminine: A Study on the Poem by Teilhard de Chardin Followed by Teilhard and the Problems of Today.* Translated by René Hague. Harper & Row, 1972.

———. *The Splendor of the Church.* Translated by Michael Mason. Paulist Press, 1963.

McArthur, Harvey K. "Son of Mary." *Novum Testamentum* 15 (1973): 35–58.

Messenger, Ruth Ellis. *The Praise of the Virgin in Early Latin Hymns.* The Papers of the Hymn Society, 3. Hymn Society, 1932.

Methodius, Saint, Bp. of Olympus. "The Banquet of the Ten Virgins; or, Concerning Chastity." In *Ante-Nicene Christian Library: Translations of the Writings of the Fathers down to* A.D. *325.* Edited by Alexander Roberts and James Donaldson. Vol. 14: *The Writings of Methodius,* pp. 1–119. Edinburgh: T. & T. Clark, 1869.

Michl, Johann. "Der Weibessame (Gen 3, 15) in spätjüdischer und frühchristlicher Auffassung." *Biblica* 33 (June-September 1952): 371–401, 476–505.

Miegge, Giovanni. *The Virgin Mary: The Roman Catholic Marian Doctrine.* Translated by Waldo Smith. Foreword by John A. Mackay. Westminster Press, 1955.

Milburn, R. L. P. *Early Christian Interpretations of History.* Harper & Brothers, 1954.

Müller, Aloys. *Ecclesia—Maria: Die Einheit Marias und der Kirche.* 2d rev. ed. Paradosis; Beiträge zur Geschichte der Altchristlichen Literatur und Theologie, 5. Freiburg: Universitätsverlag, 1955.

A Nestorian Collection of Christological Texts: Cambridge University Library ms. Oriental 1319. Edited and translated by Luise Abramowski and Alan E. Goodman. University of Cambridge Oriental Publications, No. 19. Cambridge: University Press, 1972.

Nestorius, Patriarch of Constantinople. *The Bazaar of Heracleides.* Edited and translated by G. R. Driver and Leonard Hodgson. Oxford: Clarendon Press, 1925.

Neumann, Charles William. *The Virgin Mary in the Works of Saint Ambrose.* Paradosis. Contributions to the History of Early Christian Literature and Theology, 17. Fribourg: University Press, 1962.

Neve, Juergen Ludwig, and Heick, Otto William. *A History of Christian Thought.* Fortress Press, 1965–1966.

New Catholic Encyclopedia, 1966 ed. *S.v.* "Mary, Blessed Virgin, I (in the

Bible)," by C. P. Ceroke; "Mary, Blessed Virgin, II (in Theology)," by J. B. Carol; "Mary, Blessed Virgin, Devotion to," by E. R. Carroll.
New Testament Apocrypha. Edited by Wilhem Schneemelcher. English translation by A. J. B. Higgins *et al.* Edited by R. McL. Wilson. Original German edition edited by Edgar Hennecke. 2 vols. Westminster Press, 1963, 1966.
Nicolas, Marie Joseph. *Marie, mère du sauveur.* Le Mystère chrétien, 9. Paris: Desclée et Cie., 1967.
Oberman, Heiko Augustinus. *The Virgin Mary in Evangelical Perspective.* Introduction by Thomas F. O'Meara. Fortress Press, 1971.
The Odes and Psalms of Solomon. Now first published from the Syriac version by J. Rendel Harris. Cambridge: University Press, 1909.
The Odes of Solomon. Edited and translated by J. H. Bernard. Texts and Studies; Contributions to Biblical and Patristic Literature, Vol. 8, No. 3. Nendeln/Liechtenstein: Kraus Reprint, 1967.
The Odes of Solomon. Edited and translated with notes by James Hamilton Charlesworth. Oxford: Clarendon Press, 1973.
O'Meara, Thomas F. *Mary in Protestant and Catholic Theology.* Sheed & Ward, 1966.
Origenes. *The Commentary of Origen on Saint John's Gospel.* Revised with a critical introduction and indices by A. E. Brooke. Cambridge: University Press, 1896.
———. *Contra Celsum.* Translated with an introduction and notes by Henry Chadwick. Cambridge: University Press, 1953.
———. *On First Principles: Being Koetschau's Text of the De Principiis.* Translated with an introduction and notes by G. W. Butterworth. Introduction to the Harper Torchbooks edition by Henry de Lubac. Harper & Row, Harper Torchbooks, 1966.
———. "Origen." Translated by the Rev. Frederick Crombie. In *The Ante-Nicene Fathers: Translations of the Writings of the Fathers down to* A.D. *325.* Edited by Alexander Roberts and James Donaldson. Vol. 4: *Tertullian, Part Fourth; Minucius Felix; Commodian; Origen, Parts First and Second.* Wm. B. Eerdmans Publishing Co., 1956.
———. *The Song of Songs: Commentary and Homilies.* Translated and annotated by R. P. Lawson. Ancient Christian Writers; The Works of the Fathers in Translation, No. 26. Newman Press, 1957.
Pagels, Elaine. "What Became of God the Mother? Conflicting Images of God in Early Christianity." *Signs* (Winter 1976): 293–303.
Palmer, Paul F. *Mary in the Documents of the Church.* With a word to the reader by Gerald G. Walsh. London: Burns & Oates, 1953.
Papal Documents on Mary. Compiled and arranged by William J. Doheny and Joseph P. Kelly. Bruce Pub. Co., 1954.
Parks, George Brunner. *The Greek and Latin Literatures.* Edited by George B. Parks and Ruth Z. Temple. The Literatures of the World in English

Translation: A Bibliography, Vol. 1. Frederick Ungar Publishing Co., 1968.

Pelikan, Jaroslav. *The Christian Tradition: A History of the Development of Doctrine.* University of Chicago Press, 1971–.

Plumley, J. Martin. "Early Christianity in Egypt." *Palestine Exploration Quarterly* 89 (January–June, 1957): 70–81.

Plumpe, Joseph Conrad. *Mater Ecclesia: An Inquiry Into the Concept of the Church as Mother in Early Christianity.* The Catholic University of America Studies in Christian Antiquity, No. 5. Catholic University of America Press, 1943.

Pope, Marvin H., tr. *Song of Songs.* The Anchor Bible, Vol. 7C. Doubleday & Co., 1977.

Quasten, Johannes. *Patrology.* Newman Press, 1950–.

Rahner, Hugo. *Greek Myths and Christian Mystery.* Foreword by E. O. James. Translated by Brian Battershaw. London: Burns & Oates, 1963.

———. *Our Lady and the Church.* Translated by Sebastian Bullough. Pantheon Books, 1961.

Ruether, Rosemary Radford. *Mary, the Feminine Face of the Church.* Westminster Press, 1977.

Saint Joseph Continuous Sunday Missal: A Simplified and Continuous Arrangement of the Mass for All Sundays and Feast Days with a Treasury of Prayers. Edited and compiled by Rev. Hugo Hoerer. Dialogue Mass Edition. Catholic Book Pub. Co., 1961.

Schlier, Heinrich. *Die Zeit der Kirche. Exegetische Aufsätze und Vorträge.* 2d ed. Freiburg: Herder, 1958.

Sellers, Robert Victor. *Two Ancient Christologies: A Study of the Christological Thought of the Schools of Alexandria and Antioch in the Early History of Christian Doctrine.* London: SPCK, 1940.

Semmelroth, Otto. *Mary, Archetype of the Church.* Translated by Maria von Eroes and John Devlin. Introduction by Jaroslav Pelikan. Sheed & Ward, 1963.

The Seven Ecumenical Councils of the Undivided Church: Their Canons and Dogmatic Decrees. Edited by Henry R. Percival. A Select Library of the Nicene and Post-Nicene Fathers of the Christian Church. Second Series, Vol. 14. Charles Scribner's Sons, 1900.

Shahan, Thomas Joseph. *The Blessed Virgin in the Catacombs.* John Murphy & Co., 1892.

Soulier, Henry. *La Doctrine du logos chez Philon d'Alexandria.* Turin: V. Bona, 1876.

Stubbe, Achilles. *La Madone dans l'art.* Preface by Daniel-Rops. Brussels: Elsevier, 1958.

Swete, Henry Barclay. *The Holy Spirit in the Ancient Church: A Study of Christian Teaching in the Age of the Fathers.* London: Macmillan Co., 1912.

Tertullianus, Quintus Septimus Florens. *Apology. De Spectaculis.* Translated by T. R. Glover. *Minucius Felix: [Octavius].* Translated by Gerald H. Rendall, based on the unfinished version by W. C. A. Kerr. Loeb Classical Library. Latin Authors. London: William Heinemann, 1931.

———. "On Prayer." Translated by S. Thelwall. In *The Ante-Nicene Fathers: Translations of the Writings of the Fathers down to* A.D. *325.* Edited by Alexander Roberts and James Donaldson. Vol. 3: *Latin Christianity: Its Founder, Tertullian,* pp. 681–691. Wm. B. Eerdmans Publishing Co., 1957.

———. "On the Flesh of Christ." Translated by Dr. Holmes. In *The Ante-Nicene Fathers: Translations of the Writings of the Fathers down to* A.D. *325.* Edited by Alexander Roberts and James Donaldson. Vol. 3: *Latin Christianity: Its Founder, Tertullian,* pp. 521–543. Wm. B. Eerdmans Publishing Co., 1957.

———. *De Oratione Liber. Tract on Prayer.* Translated by Ernest Evans. London: SPCK, 1953.

———. *Tertullian Concerning the Resurrection of the Flesh.* Translated by A. Souter. Translations of Christian Literature; Series II; Latin Texts. London: SPCK, 1922.

———. *Tertullian's Treatise on the Incarnation.* Edited and translated with an introduction and commentary by Ernest Evans. London: SPCK, 1956.

———. *The Writings of Quintus Septimus Florens Tertullianus.* Ante-Nicene Christian Library, Vols. 11, 15, 18. Edinburgh: T. & T. Clark, 1869–1870.

Vatican Council. 2d, 1962–1965. *The Documents of Vatican II.* Walter M. Abbott, general editor. Introduction by Lawrence Cardinal Shehan. Translations directed by Joseph Gallagher. Herder and Herder, 1966.

Walpole, Arthur Sumner. *Early Latin Hymns.* Cambridge: University Press, 1922.

Warner, Marina. *Alone of All Her Sex: The Myth and the Cult of the Virgin Mary.* Alfred A. Knopf, 1976.

Whale, John Seldon. *Victor and Victim: The Christian Doctrine of Redemption.* Cambridge: University Press, 1960.

Winslow, Donald F. "Christology and Exegesis in the Cappadocians." *Church History* 40 (December 1971): 389–396.

Wolfson, Harry Austryn. *The Philosophy of the Church Fathers.* Structure and Growth of Philosophic Systems from Plato to Spinoza, No. 3. Harvard University Press, 1956–.

Selected Bibliography for the Revised Edition

This addition to the bibliography contains books, written in English, which have been published since 1979. As anticipated, there has been a large outpouring of books on women and religion, Mariology and Christology, and, especially, in the field of Wisdom literature and biblical commentary. Because this brief list of titles cannot include everything, I would like to call attention to the following books which do contain important and comprehensive bibliographies: on women and religion—Ann Carr, *Transforming Grace* (1988); on the Virgin Mary and Hellentistic goddess figures—Stephen Benko, *The Virgin Goddess* (1993); and on Wisdom—Ronald Piper, *Wisdom in the Q-tradition* (1989). Many other books in the following list also contain bibliographic material which will benefit scholars.

Anderson, Sherry Ruth, and Patricia Hopkins. *The Feminine Face of God: The Unfolding of the Sacred in Women*. New York: Bantam Books, 1991.

Atkinson, Clarissa A., Buchanan, Constance H., and Margaret A. Miles, editors. *Immaculate and Powerful: The Female in Sacred Image and Social Reality*. Boston: Beacon Press, 1985.

Bankson, Marjory Zoet. *Braided Streams: Esther and a Woman's Way of Growing*. San Diego: LuraMedia, 1985.

_____. *Season of Friendship: Naomi and Ruth as a Pattern*. San Diego: LuraMedia, 1987.

____. *This Is My Body: Creativity, Clay and Change.* San Diego: LuraMedia, 1993

Berkey, Bobert, and Sarah A. Edwards, editors. *Christology in Dialogue.* Cleveland: The Pilgrim Press, 1993.

Begg, Ean. *The Cult of the Black Virgin.* London: Arkana, 1985.

Benko, Stephen. *The Virgin Goddess: Studies in the Pagan and Christian Roots of Mariology.* Leiden: E. J. Brill, 1993.

Boff, Leonardo. *The Maternal Face of God: The Feminine and Its Religious Expression.* New York: Harper and Row, 1987.

Bolen, Jean Shinoda. *Goddesses in Everywoman: A New Psychology of Women.* New York: Harper and Row, 1984.

Bowersock, G. W. *Hellenism in Late Antiquity.* Ann Arbor, Mich.: University of Michigan Press, 1990.

Brown, Raymond. *The Birth of the Messiah: A Commentary on the Infancy Narratives of Matthew and Luke.* New York: Doubleday, 1977.

____. *The Death of the Messiah: From Gethsemene to the Grave: A Commentary on the Passion Narratives in the Four Gospels.* New York: Doubleday, 1994.

Brown, Raymond, Donfried, K.P., Fitzmyer, J. A., and J. Reumann, editors. *Mary in the New Testament: A Collaborative Assessment by Protestant and Roman Catholic Scholars.* Philadelphia: Fortress Press, 1978.

Burnett, Fred. *The Testament of Jesus-Sophia: A Redaction-Critical Study of the Eschatological Discourse in Matthew.* Washington, D.C.: University Press of America, 1981.

Bynum, Caroline Walker. *Jesus as Mother: Studies in the Spirituality of the High Middle Ages.* Berkeley, Calif.: University of California Press, 1982.

Cady, Susan. *Wisdom's Feast: Sophia in Study and Celebration.* New York: Harper and Row, 1989.

Camp, Claudia. *Wisdom and the Feminine in the Book of Proverbs.* Sheffield, England: Almond Press, 1985.

Carr, Anne E. *Transforming Grace: Christian Tradition and Women's Experience.* San Francisco: Harper and Row, 1988.

Carroll, Michael P. *The Cult of the Virgin Mary: Psychological Origins.* Princeton, N.J.: Princeton University Press, 1986.

Chodorow, Nancy. *The Reproduction of Mothering: Psychoanalysis and the Sociology of Gender.* Berkeley, Calif.: University of California Press, 1978.

Clements, R. E. *Wisdom in Theology.* Grand Rapids: Mich.: W. B. Eerdmans, 1992.

Corrington, Gail Paterson. *Her Image of Salvation: Female Saviors and Formative Christianity*. Louisville: Westminster/John Knox Press, 1992.

Davidson, Robert M. A. *Wisdom and Worship*. London: SCM Press, 1990.

Day, Peggy L., editor. *Gender and Difference in Ancient Israel*. Minneapolis: Fortress Press, 1989.

Downing, Christine. *The Goddess: Mythological Images of the Feminine*. New York: Crossroad, 1981.

Dunn, James D. G. *Christology in the Making: An Inquiry into the Origins of the Doctrine of the Incarnation*. London: SCM Press, 1980.

Eaton, J. H. *The Contemplative Face of Old Testament Wisdom: in the Context of World Religions*. London: SCM Press, 1989.

Estes, Clarissa Pinkola. *Women Who Run with the Wolves: Myths and Stories of the Wild Woman Archetype*. New York: Ballantine Books, 1992.

Fitzmyer, Joseph A. *The Gospel According to Luke*. The Anchor Bible. New York: Doubleday, 1983.

Goldenberg, Naomi. *Changing of the Gods: Feminism and the End of Traditional Religions*. Boston: Beacon Press, 1979.

_____. *Resurrecting the Body: Feminists, Religion, and Psychoanalysis*. New York: Crossroad, 1993.

Good, Deidre J. *Reconstructing the Tradition of Sophia in Gnostic Literature*. Atlanta: Scholars Press, 1987.

Grant, Michael. *From Alexander to Cleopatra: The Hellenistic World*. New York: Scribners, 1982.

Halligan, Fredrica R., and John J. Shea. *The Fires of Desire: Erotic Energies and the Spiritual Quest*. New York: Crossroad, 1992.

Hanson, R. P. C. *The Search for the Christian Doctrine of God: The Arian Controversy 318-381*. London: T & T Clark, 1988.

Hengel, Martin. *Jews, Greeks, and Barbarians: Aspects of the Hellenization of Judaism in the Pre-Christian Period*. Philadelphia: Fortress, 1980.

Hoglund, Kennenth, editor. *The Listening Heart: Essays in Wisdom and the Psalms in Honor of Roland E. Murphy*. Sheffield, England: JSOT, 1987.

Johnson, Elizabeth A. *She Who Is: The Mystery of God in Feminist Theological Discourse*. New York: Crossroad, 1992.

King, Karen L., editor. *Images of the Feminine in Gnosticism*. Philadelphia: Studies in Antiquity and Christianity, Fortress, 1988.

Kraemer, Ross S. *Maenads, Martyrs, Matrons, Monastics: A Sourcebook on Women's Religions of the Greco-Roman World*. Philadelphia: Fortress, 1988.

Kung, Hans, and Jurgen Moltmann. *Mary in the Churches*. New York: Seabury Press, 1983.

Lang, Bernhard. *Wisdom and the Book of Proverbs: An Israelite Goddess Redefined*. New York: Pilgrim Press, 1986.

Lee Bernard. *Jesus and the Metaphors of God: The Christs of the New Testament*. New York: Paulist Press, 1993.

Loader, William Roh. *The Christology of the Fourth Gospel: Structure and Issues*. New York: Verlag P. Lang, 1989.

Maccoby, Hyman. *Paul and Hellenism*. London: SCM Press, 1991.

Macquarrie, John. *Mary for All Christians*. Grand Rapids, Mich.: Wm. B. Eerdmans, 1990.

Martin, Luther H. *Hellenistic Religions: An Introduction*. New York: Oxford University Press, 1987.

Mary, Woman of Nazareth: Biblical and Theological Perspectives. New York: Paulist Press, 1990.

Matthews, Caitlin. *Sophia: Goddess of Wisdom: The Divine Feminine from Black Goddess to World Soul*. San Francisco: Harper and Row, 1991.

McFague, Sallie. *Models of God: Theology for an Ecolgical, Nuclear Age*. Philadelphia: Fortress Press, 1987.

McKay, Heather A., and David S. A. Clines, editors. *Of Prophets' Visions and the Wisdom of the Sages: Essays in the Honour of R. Norman Whybray on His Seventieth Birthday*. London: JSOT Press, 1993.

Meier, John P. *The Mission of Christ and His Churches: Studies on Christology and Ecclesiology*. Wilmington, Del.: M. Glazier, 1990.

Mollenkott, Virginia Ramey. *The Divine Feminine: The Biblical Imagery of God as Female*. New York: Crossroad, 1983.

Moore, Thomas. *Care of the Soul: A Guide for Cultivating Depth and Sacredness in Everyday Life*. New York: Harper Collins, 1992.

Morton, Nelle. *The Journey Is Home*. Boston: Beacon Press, 1985.

Murphy, Roland E. *The Tree of Life: An Explanation of Biblical Wisdom Literature*. New York: The Anchor Bible Reference Library, Doubleday, 1990.

_____. *Wisdom Literature and Psalms*. Nashville: Abingdon Press, 1983.

Neusner, Jacob. *The Incarnation of God: The Character of Divinity in Formative Judaism*. Philadelphia: Fortress, 1988.

_____. *Symbol and Theology in Early Judaism*. Philadelphia: Fortress, 1991.

Newsom, Carol A., and Sharone H. Ringe. *The Woman's Bible Commentary*. Louisville: Westminster/John Knox Press, 1992.

Newsome, James D. *Greeks, Romans, Jews: Currents of Culture and Belief in the New Testament World.* Philadelphia: Trinity Press International, 1992.

O'Carroll, Michael. *Theotokos: A Theological Encyclopedia of the Blessed Virgin Mary.* Wilmington, Del.: M. Glazier, 1983.

Ochshorn, Judith. *The Female Experience and the Nature of the Divine.* Bloomington, Ind.: Indiana University Press, 1981.

Olson, Carl, editor. *The Book of the Goddess Past and Present: An Introduction to Her Religion.* New York: Crossroad, 1983.

Pagels, Elaine. *The Gnostic Gospels.* New York: Random House, 1979.

Pelikan, Jaroslav Jan. *Christianity and Classical Culture: The Metamorphosis of Natural Theology in the Christian Encounter with Hellenism.* New Haven, Conn.: Yale University Press, 1993.

Perdue, Leo G., Scott, Bernard Brandon, and William Johnson Wiseman, editors. *In Search of Wisdom: Essays in Memory of John J. Gammie.* Louisville: Westminster/John Knox, 1993.

Perkins, Pheme. *Gnosticism and the New Testament.* Philadelphia: Fortress Press, 1993.

Piper, Ronald A. *Wisdom in the Q-Traditon: The Aphoristic Teaching of Jesus.* Cambridge, England: Cambridge University Press, 1988.

Pogoloff, Stephen. *Logos and Sophia: The Rhetorical Situation of 1 Corinthians.* Atlanta: Scholars Press, 1992.

Preston, James T., editor. *Mother Worship: Theme and Variation.* Chapel Hill, N.C.: University of North Carolina Press, 1982.

Ruether, Rosemary Radford. *To Change the World: Christology and Cultural Criticism.* New York: Crossroad, 1981.

_____. *Sexism and God-Talk: Toward a Feminist Theology.* Boston: Beacon Press, 1983.

Sanders, Jack T. *Ben Sira and Demotic Wisdom.* Chico, Calif.: Scholars Press, 1983.

Schillebeeck, Edward. *Jesus: An Experiment in Christology.* New York: Seabury Press, 1979.

Schillebeeck, Edward, and Catherine Halkes. *Mary: Yesterday, Today, Tomorrow.* London: SCM Press, 1993.

Schneiders, Sandra. *Women and the Word: The Gender of God in the New Testament and the Spirituality of Women.* New York: Paulist Press, 1986.

Schussler-Fiorenza, Elisabeth. *But She Said: Feminist Practices of Biblical Interpretation.* Boston: Beacon Press, 1992.

_____. *In Memory of Her: A Feminist Theological Reconstruction of Christian Origins.* New York: Crossroad, 1983.

Scott, Martin. *Sophia and the Johannine Jesus*. Sheffield, England: JSOT Press, 1992.
Solmsen, Friedrich. *Isis Among the Greeks and Romans*. Cambridge, Mass.: Harvard University Press, 1979.
Stein, Murray, and Robert Moore, editors. *Jung's Challenge to Contemporary Religion*. Wilmette, Ill.: Chiron Publications, 1987.
Sturch, Richard. *The Word and the Christ: An Essay in Analytic Christology*. Oxford: Oxford University Press, 1991.
Trible, Phyllis. *God and the Rhetoric of Sexuality*. Philadelphia: Fortress, 1978.
_____. *Texts of Terror: Literary-Feminist Readings of Biblical Narratives*. Philadelphia: Fortress, 1984.
Wehr, Demaris. *Jung and Feminism: Liberating Archetypes*. Boston: Beacon Press, 1987.
Whitmont, Edward C. *Return of the Goddess*. New York: Crossroad, 1982.
Wilson-Kastner, Patricia. *Faith, Feminism and the Christ*. Philadelphia: Fortress, 1983.
Young-Eisendrath, Polly, and Florence Wiedemann. *Female Authority: Empowering Women Through Psychotheraphy*. New York: The Guilford Press, 1987.

Index